The Peacock Princess

The true-life story of an American woman and her daughters, trapped among decadent Iranian aristocracy in royal and revolutionary Iran

Sara Harris
and
Barbara Mosallai Bell

COOL HAND COMMUNICATIONS, INC.
BOCA RATON, FLORIDA

ISBN: 1-56790-006-2

COOL HAND COMMUNICATIONS, INC.
1098 N.W. Boca Raton Boulevard, Suite 1
Boca Raton, FL 33432

Library of Congress Cataloging in Publication Data

Harris, Sara.
    The peacock princess: the saga of an American woman held captive
by a brutal royal family in revolutionary Iran / Sara Harris and
Barbara Mosallai Bell.
        p.   cm.
    ISBN 1-56790-006-2 : $19.99
    1. Wife abuse--Iran. 2. Women--Iran--Biography. 3. Women--United
States--Biography. 4. Intermarriage--Iran. I. Bell , Barbara
Mosallai. II. Title.
HQ809.3.I7H37 1995
305.4'0955--dc20   95-14884
                                                                CIP

In memory of
Dr. Amir Abbas Hoveyda,

PRIME MINISTER OF IRAN FROM 1964–1977

A fierce fighter against corruption and injustice during the reign of Shah Mohammed Reza Pahlavi, he was a caring, warm friend. His open door to entrapped foreign wives of Iranian men, including co-author Barbara Mosallai Bell, saved many from suicide, or worse. On April 9, 1979 at 6:15 a.m., Dr. Hoveyda was killed by a firing squad after conviction by the Revolutionary Court of the Ayatollah Ruhollah Khomeini for "sowing corruption on earth".

For Our Children:

Judith Harris Selwyn
David B. Harris
Roxanne Mosallai Vu
Dawneh Mosallai Shapouri

Contents

Preface

This book is the lived-in-the-flesh memoir of an American woman, Barbara Bell—formerly Quajar Princess Barbara Mosallai of Iran—and her daughters Roxanne and Dawneh, set in Iranian society between the decadent, hedonistic and arrogant aristocrats surrounding the former Shah Mohammed Reza Pahlavi, and the Islamic fundamentalists, dedicated body and soul to the revolutionary regime of the Ayatollah Khomeini.

Beyond a memoir, this book tells the stories:

Of the lowly position Islamic women occupy, dictated more by tradition than by religion;

Of the violent sexuality, relentless eroticism and lethal ways of "love" between royal Iranian women and men;

Of Barbara's and Dawneh's own loves, lacerating and doomed from the start by the Moslem males' contempt for women, especially their inherent loathing for American women;

Of the love Iranian women feel for each other in a sisterhood so different from Western ideals because it's necessary for survival.

Barbara and her daughters told their true stories because they were eager to make Western women aware of the realities of living with traditionalist Islamic men.

"They need to know," Dawneh tells, "that Arab and Persian men believe that all Western women, especially American, are prostitutes who can be purchased for more or less money (*sic*). That attitude on their part goes way back. Although my father married my mother (his father having commanded him to bring home a beautiful, intelligent American wife), he called her 'American whore' from as long ago as I can remember."

Roxanne, who dearly loves her husband, Twon, yet has been unable to respond to him physically, hopes that through unfolding the story of her childhood, he will become aware of the experiences "that caused me, always, to shudder at even the thought of sex."

Barbara, however, had another passionate purpose for wanting this book published. She says, "The enslavement of women in Iran...perhaps the most shocking time of the seventeen years I spent there came when I discovered I was pregnant with Roxanne, and knew I could not bring up a child there. I was enabled, finally, through good luck and good friends in high places, to escape. But I cannot stop grieving for the fate of countless American and other women in Middle Eastern countries, who will never be freed from their bondage."

Thus their personal record and that of Iran's varying relations with America, as well as the religion, history and descriptions of the culture as it impacted these women, may help clarify some of the mystery behind a country that, in spite of a thousand headlines, is still mostly unknown to the West.

Sara Harris
August 28, 1994

BOOK ONE

———

Barbara

CHAPTER I

A College Romance

At nine o'clock in the morning of January 22, 1962, the door of Barbara's Advanced Psychology class at the University of Tehran suddenly swung open and a rabid, delirious band of paratroopers and other soldiers in the army of the Shah exploded into the room. Twenty of them, thirty, forty (who could correctly estimate their number?) screeched obscenities and came at the disoriented, stunned students from all sides, all angles. Ordering them to stand, then kicking them with their heavy boots. Striking their rifle butts against their heads and chests and spines until many cried and some collapsed with the pain.

Barbara's mind swarmed with the images of soldiers navigating between the lines of fallen students...The soldiers seemed to increase in number as time wore on and more students fell. When they were done with the men they surrounded the twenty-five women in this class of nearly one hundred, kicking and beating them. Barbara, trembling and drenched with sweat, was grabbed by a sergeant who began to whisper, breathing wet obscenities in her ear. His face was so close to hers she was overwhelmed, nauseated by the smell of his breath. She braced hard, calling on all her discipline to keep from breaking down, certain that her tormentor, relishing any weakness she showed, felt impelled to keep at her until she came completely apart.

She must have been right in her panicked logic because after minutes or hours (she'd lost track of time) of her sham coolness, he transferred his attention to a small girl with terrified, huge eyes staring out of her <u>chador</u> (the classic tent-like covering of female bodies and faces except for eyes and tip of the nose). He ripped off the chador and all of her clothes, threw her to the floor, and forced her to lie with her back up while he, laughing maniacally, stuck his rifle barrel into her rectum. The girl began crying; no, not crying, screaming—coming apart as Barbara had been afraid of doing, and did now, matching the girl scream for scream, cry for cry.

This bloodbath was the Shah's vengeance for the participation of some students in a one-day sympathy strike over scholarship cuts at a sister school, and occured not just in Barbara's classroom, but university-wide. It was the day when Barbara's passionate hatred for Mohammed Reza, long simmering inside her, came to absolute fruition. Thus it was that she, in her fifth year as a Tehran University student, came on a February day of winter darkness and icy blasts, to demonstrate, along with hundreds of other students and professors, against both the imprisonment of her fellow students and professors presumed to have led the strike, and the indefinite shutdown of her school that had been its result.

At the demonstration's head, as a shield, was the Ayatollah Teleghani, an associate of the Ayatollah Khomeini, whose name at the time meant little to Barbara.

Wearing a chador, as all the women did to avoid recognition, Barbara gathered with the rest outside Teleghani's small, modest house that contrasted so vividly with the Shah's palaces (and, for instance, her husband's family's seventy-two room mansion). Followed by his cortege of aides, Teleghani went to the head of the demonstrators. Strangely, once the Ayatollah took his place, and with no word from him, the formerly loud, feisty, eager-for-fracas students presented an image of silence and order and discipline. It seemed to Barbara, feeling herself a part of something very alien yet magical, that she and the hundreds of others marching in majestic, nearly simultaneous step, had submitted their wills to Teleghani's so utterly that he had only to think, not even speak, a command in order to have it obeyed.

At the University, where at least one hundred armed soldiers were massed at the high, green, steel-pike fence more fitted to a prison than a free institution of higher learning, Teleghani, a thin, frail man nearly sixty at the time, with a face that seemed fragile yet indomitable, addressed the soldiers:

"In the name of God, The Compassionate, the Most Merciful, I come before you to declare that you, following the commands of your reprobate Shah to keep this University closed at gun point, are at variance with the sacred precepts of Islam and the laws laid down by His Holiness, the Best of Mankind (the Prophet Mohammed); may the blessings of God rest upon Him and His Descendants."

His soft voice rose to become a shriek: "Do you, soldiers and servants of the Satan Shah, also call yourselves men of Islam? If you do, how can you have forgotten the words of His Holiness that 'At the end of time there will be tyrannical Amirs, vicious Viziers, treacherous judges, and lying jurists. And whoever will live to that time should not serve them in any way, shape or form.'

"Yet you are serving the SATAN SHAH, obeying his law, even though God's law is in conflict with it. Do you not know your Koran then, or is it that you don't care about it? Have you truly forgotten, or do you choose not to remember Allah's revelation to the Prophet? Learning is the obligation of every Muslim, male and female.'

"I declare to you that Mohammed Reza Pahlavi is the tyrannical Amir and you soldiers are his accursed policeman. And, although God is The Compassionate and The Most Merciful, He will show neither compassion nor mercy for those who stand against Him and His...These students you see before you are here out of their heart's deepest desire to obey God's commandment to learn. And the Shah, the DEMON SHAH, is preventing them. and so are you.

"Out of concern for your immortal souls as well as these students' rights, I ask you, each of you, to ask yourself, 'Whom will I serve, God or the devil?'"

He paused, and with a voice almost undone by emotion and conviction cried out, "If your answer is the latter, fire your guns. But if it is the former, THEN LAY YOUR GUNS DOWN."

Barbara felt herself and the whole crowd of students in whose midst she was standing breathe slowly, simultaneously. It was as though she and all those hundreds of other young men and women had become as one.

Suddenly a sob came from the soldiers' side that turned into uncontrollable weeping. It was from a major, their leader. He tried to speak, but could not pull himself together enough to bring out any words. He threw down his gun and went to kneel at the Ayatollah's feet, kissing his knee over and over until Teleghani lifted and embraced him. Standing beside the Ayatollah then, he said in a voice that trembled with his strong emotion: "I want to serve God, not the devil. I WANT TO SERVE GOD, GOD, GOD!"

Then a chant started among the soldiers. At first it was a few scattered soldiers laying down guns and chanting, "I WANT TO SERVE GOD, GOD, GOD!" Then others dropped their weapons, chanting; then it was total abdication, all of the hundreds of soldiers in a single voice, thundering, "I WANT TO SERVE GOD, GOD, GOD!"

The Ayatollah lifted his head and the soldiers became silent. "We, having begun as enemies, may now embrace one another as dear friends united in a single course—DOING GOD'S WORK AND WHIPPING THE DEVIL SHAH."

Pandemonium broke loose, everyone kissing and embracing, and everyone glowing.

In the midst of the celebration in the streets that grew ever louder and merrier as soldiers and students went on complementing and embracing one another, Barbara lost her friends and tried to merge into another group with whom she found herself. Suddenly, though, she felt her protective veil torn off and realized she was surrounded by people who flashed hatred and yelled insults at her.

"You scum! American carrion! Go home, Yankee! We don't need any Yankee garbage in our school! MARGH BAR AMERIKA! Death to America, and American shits in Iran! GO HOME, YANKEE SHIT AND CORRUPTION."

Barbara braced herself to keep from falling down. She couldn't breathe. She gasped for air, and with the gasp came a sob that caused her badgerers to smile, first triumphantly at one another, then mockingly at her.

"Cry, American carrion."

"Cry, Yankee garbage."

"Ah, the little Yankee daughter of dogs is afraid of us crude, cruel Persians."

"Poor little Yankee pup is crying even though she's got nothing to cry about YET."

"CRY, CRY, CRY, CRY!"

A tall girl walked over, cheered on by her companions. Coming close to Barbara, she took hold of her left arm, and twisted it back-ward so violently that Barbara screamed with pain. The girl pulled it back further, and twisted it time and again, letting it relax, and then jerking it again 'til the pain became sickening. Finally, she let the arm go, and stood looking at Barbara with such fury, contempt and hatred in her that Barbara thought, "She really wishes she could kill me instead of just hurting me...She'd like to see me dead, and so would all these others around me, my fellow students. Oh God."

This student enmity toward her as an American, particularly shown by the most chauvinistic ones, was, in its essence, nothing new to Barbara. She and every other American at Tehran University had experienced it to one degree or another. It had just never before been manifested so virulently as at this emotion-laden time.

"MARGH BAR AMERIKA! MARGH BAR AMERIKA! MARGH BAR AMERIKA! DEATH TO AMERICA!"

Other students entered the group surrounding Barbara. They spat in her face and screamed new imprecations, calling her a CIA spy. There was no telling what they might have done to her in their fury if Aysha, an important figure in The National Front Party, to which most of the demonstrators belonged, and Barbara's mentor and most beloved friend in Iran, had not finally found her and gone to stand beside her. Lifting her own veil, Aysha's words whipped Barbara's tormentors, who all knew her, and who were as deferential to her as they were disrespectful of Barbara. Shame, shame on the lot of them who claimed to be so fair and just and full of idealism. They might have believed that they were debasing Barbara, lessening her by their violence. Well, Aysha was here to tell them that by their cruelty toward Barbara, they only debased and lessened themselves.

Certainly she was an American, but that didn't automatically make her an enemy. Actually, she was a friend whose ideology was similar to theirs. They talked often about power and its abuse by the Shah and his toadies and by "imperialist America". Didn't it even occur to them that now they, themselves, were abusing the power they had over Barbara?

When Aysha was done speaking, a few of the students begged Barbara's pardon, and all of them cleared a path for her and Aysha.

Later, alone with Aysha, her insides shaking and every organ of her body paining but her voice emerging quite calm, Barbara said, "I want to share with you a strange thought I had while...It was that if I would be saved from death at the hands of this mob, a woman would be my salvation." Yet Barbara knew even as she was speaking the words that the thought was not so strange after all. Always, from the day of her arrival in Tehran, women had been her salvation in crises both great and small. First among them, of course, had been Aysha whom she'd met at her first dinner at Bahram's family's home...Later, in her life in Iran, through Aysha, Barbara would meet other women intrepid enough to pit themselves against the standard and assert their human equality and that of all women, in the face of Iranian patriarchy. But Aysha had been the only one Barbara had known during the months both before and after her marriage to Bahram who did this, and she'd looked to her as a standard bearer and a kind of example for her own coming life.

But Aysha, though doubtless the most significant feminine influence in Barbara's early (and later) life in Iran, was not the only one. There was also Farah, Bahram's charming American-educated niece. Three years older than Barbara, Farah had led her with patience and humor, through the many complex adjustments an American married to an Iranian had to make. And there was Barbara's gentle, tender grandmother-in-law, Khanoum-June, meaning Lady of My Heart, a name of respect and affection by which grandchildren often address their grandmothers. Harem-born and bred, Khanoum-June was always ready to bow down to men and considered her husband's slightest wish her command. Yet when the best interests of Barbara or any of her other daughters and granddaughters were at stake, she stood up to him, the family patriarch, and all of the men of the family.

And even the women to whom Barbara could not relate closely, Bahram's mother and maternal grandmother, for instance, even those women...Barbara learned something from them about Islamic women during her life in Iran. Being inheritors of the harem tradition, they knew that they had only one another to depend upon, that they had to sustain each other to survive. Therefore, when any woman was in need, even a <u>farangi</u> (foreign) woman like Barbara, they met her need with love, with acceptance, with selflessness.

So Barbara knew she could count on the Iranian women in her life, and during the seventeen years she lived in their country, they seldom, if ever, failed her.

Actually, Barbara had learned to count on women long ago when she'd been three or four years old and had begun to spend most of her time with her paternal grandmother. Dear, good, beautiful Grandma Srader, with her frizz of fashionable white curls, was considered outlandish in the lower-middle-class WASP neighborhood of Indianapolis where Barbara grew up, for the very reasons her granddaughter worshipped her. Long after her marriage to Grandpa Srader, a meat market proprietor, Grandma Srader had taught herself and Barbara to play the piano, and speak a little in Spanish and Italian, and soak in perfumed bathtubs, and revel in fairy tales.

Barbara's grandmother, unlike practically everyone else in the neighborhood, neither went to church nor voted Republican. Barbara's mother was the converse. Both a staunch Republican and a devout Methodist, she believed that anyone who did not vote as she did or share her message, as delivered to John Wesley, was headed for hell. She therefore strongly resented her mother-in-law's influence on her daughter, believing that it would result in Barbara's own eventual descent into hell. For Barbara not only followed her grandma's iniquitous ways but also added some of her own—she loved sophomoric figure-hugging clothes, Bill Haley and The Comets, and especially Elvis, and had been caught on the night of her sophomore prom ineptly French-kissing her equally inept escort.

"Barbara," her grandmother said of her, "my sunshine." Always she'd been praised in her grandmother's low, light voice as perfection, perfection itself. And she had profited so much by that unreasoning approval that her mother's disapproval, and to a lesser extent also her father's, hadn't hurt as much as it might have otherwise. Throughout her young life before leaving for college, she'd depended on her grandmother as her mainstay, her emotional support. She'd always been there while Barbara was growing up, to talk and listen and share with, to make plans with. She respected the person Barbara was, and the person she wanted to be. She never, in all their life together, treated her as her parents often did, like the bad little girl who refused to be good. She loved Barbara all the time, no matter when or why or how she, out of rebelliousness against her parents and environment, foundered and screwed up. And when, at ten years old, Barbara decided that she wanted to become a doctor, and her mother derided the idea, her grandmother began saving for her education. Then, when she graduated from high school where her ambition had been nourished and strengthened, and won the title "Palmolive's Prettiest Schoolgirl" and a four-year tuition scholarship, her grandmother added sufficient money to enable her to go not to the local college, but to the University of California in Los Angeles. She wanted to go there above any place because it was far away in miles and mood from Indianapolis (by now India-no-place to her), had a fine scholastic reputation, and was, in that time of general student conservatism, on the cutting edge of social consciousness.

For all these reasons, when Barbara announced she was going, her mother cried bitterly, in her bawdy, bubbling, fat-woman's voice, repeating over and over, "This college you have chosen, Barbara, goes against morals. It goes against the Bible and against Jesus and against God."

The University was, from the beginning, all that Barbara and her grandmother had hoped it would be, and she reveled in every minute of her life there, especially her social life. Her two closest friends were, as she perceived them, brilliant, charming, sophisticated people.

Betty Belkis, daughter of a New York civil rights attorney, was tall, nearly five-foot-ten, and had a big voice and a big laugh. She and her parents had been everywhere, sometimes on vacation, but more often on summer volunteer work projects in Mexico, Guatemala and Tanzania as well as in Appalachia and on the Navajo reservation. She was training to be a social worker and volunteered what spare time she had away from school and friends, to a school for handicapped children and a home for the aged. Betty liked men, she liked sex, and slept with those who pleased her with no thought of establishing a permanent relationship with them. She was funny and clever, and very direct and open about everything including her sex life, sometimes classifying her boyfriends, whether realistically or not, by the size of their penises, this one being "as small as a gherkin" and the other "as large as an eggplant".

Ann DeVries was a native Californian, the daughter of two Stanford University professors. She was beautiful and a bit of a genius, having learned the violin at seven, and mastered two languages at eleven. But because of driving parents who were never satisfied, Ann had no notion of her own value, and Betty and Barbara constantly tried to make her realize her worth. She loved animals; they'd been her friends through a lonely childhood, and she intended to become a veterinarian. Something about her touched Barbara as deeply as anything had ever touched her in her life.

Barbara, Betty and Ann, despite their different backgrounds, were all children of their time, the "beatnik" era, and so held a common philosophy of life. America, perpetrator of Hiroshima, was to them a country of violence and spiritual exhaustion, with the world being no better than America, having produced Mussolini, Hitler, and Dachau. As for the future, there wasn't any future since the coming of the atom bomb. Yet in spite, or perhaps because of, the atom bomb and the state of America and the world as they perceived it, they wished with everything in them to be important as individuals, to live their lives fully and to the hilt. Knowing everything, experiencing everything, leaving their mark so that when they died the world would both know and care that Betty Belkis and Ann DeVries and Barbara Srader had lived and worked to make it a better place.

This, then, was the Barbara Srader who would marry Bahram Sultan Mosallai, and go to live with him in his country.

Barbara bore a constant torch for Bahram, though she went unnoticed by him from the day that she first saw him sitting at a table in the cafeteria. She'd watch him surrounded by his countrymen and sometimes other students as well, and wonder to herself if ever there had been another living person who looked so sexy and unattainable, and kindled as much desire as did this legend of a man.

People said he was a baron in his country, and they said he was a prince and would someday be a king. And, although Barbara had never seen him with any women, his romantic escapades were supposed to be as colorful as his royal heritage. It was told that he'd bedded dozens of starlets and even some full-fledged stars.

Everything about Bahram—his blue-black hair coming down to a widow's peak, his eyes that were large and expressive and almost black, his physical grace, his look of power and privilege—touched Barbara's imagination. She ached to become a part of his charmed circle and spent days planning and calculating ways of attracting his attention, and nights anguishing over lost opportunities to do it and still retain her pride.

Then one day, having been encouraged by Betty and Ann, she went to where he sat at his table, and honestly told him how she felt. She knew, because she'd been told by many, that she had a magnetism that pulled people to her even more than her glorious blue-eyed, red-haired beauty and obvious good nature would have alone. She exerted it now, sending out waves of feeling that ordered Bahram to feel what she felt. And he responded as she willed. He looked into her eyes and locked them with his. And he took her face in both hands, examining it feature by feature for a long time, then told her, "You know what you look like to me, Barbara Srader? A small replica of one of those Greek goddesses, all golden."

Although Barbara, as a girl who both dabbled in the counterculture and had serious intent to change the world, mocked herself for it, her first date with Bahram made her feel like a combination Marilyn Monroe, Elizabeth Taylor and every glamorous woman she'd seen in movies. A long black Cadillac limousine pulled up to the door of her dormitory and a tall chauffeur, his cap sitting perfectly on top of his head, got out and opened the rear door. And Bahram, every inch the romantic Hollywood hero in his tux (such style, such elegance!) emerged.

Barbara and Bahram had dinner at the Bel Aire Hotel with its cloisters, patios, courtyards, gardens full of exquisite flowers and its exclusive restaurant about which Barbara had recently read: "...The cuisine is among the top three in the United States and the wine cellar ranks as one of the best in America." Bahram introduced her to the maitre d', who obviously knew him well; she became immensely excited when he said as he seated them, "There you are Miss Srader, Mr. Mosallai ... please don't hesitate to ask me for anything you may wish." It seemed unbelievable that she should be known by name by the maitre d' of the Bel Aire Hotel.

After dinner they drove to the Beverly Hills Hotel, sat near the blazing fire in the lobby, and talked. Barbara told Bahram about her life in Indianapolis, and he held her transfixed with his exotic tales about Iran and its people, especially its history of ancient, noble kings with their splendid harems of women who were musicians, dancers, poets, storytellers.

Bahram and Barbara were constantly together after that first date. He was a wonderful guide to Los Angeles, and he made the city seem a delightful toy for Barbara's entertainment. They sailed and swam, went to concerts, theaters, nightclubs, and to hear Barbara's beloved rock stars. Bahram threw hundred-dollar bills around as though they were just so many pieces of paper, and every maitre d' in town soon knew Barbara's name as well as his. And he sent daily bouquets of roses to her dorm.

But beyond all this that would have turned the head of any seventeen-year-old girl, and certainly one of Barbara's background, she fell in love with Bahram's softness, his gentleness, his sensitivity. He revered, truly revered nature—the mountains, the sea—exclaiming over sunrises, sunsets, trees, flowers, birds, bees, even ants. Thus, his presents to Barbara included Maeterlink's "The Bluebird", which he said was called "The Golden Dream" in Persian, as well as "The Life of the Bee", and "The Life of the Ant".

A poetry lover himself, he gave her many books of English, French, Italian, and especially Persian poets. He read to her from the "Rubaiyat", written more than a thousand years ago by Omar Khayyam, a man more admired in Persia as a mathematician and astronomer than a poet:

"A book of verses underneath the bough,
A jug of wine, a loaf of bread, and Thou
Beside me singing in the wilderness..."
And from the thirteenth century poet Haffiz:
"In wild Eternity's vast space
Where no beginning was wert Thou:
The Rays of all-pervading grace
Beneath Thy veil flamed on Thy brow.
Then Love and Nature sprang to birth
And Life and Beauty filled the earth."
And the final couplet:
"The world's possessions fade and flee
The only good is loving Thee."

Bahram graduated as a petroleum engineer on June 20, 1958, and he and Barbara spent that evening in the restaurant of the Beverly Hills Hotel. There, holding her face between his hands as he'd done at their first meeting, he said softly, "Marry me, Barbara, and let me take you to the mountains of the moon, my Persia."

Barbara was, of course, very happy at Bahram's proposal, yet found herself wondering whether it might not, after all, be a mistake to marry him. In accepting his Eastern world, wouldn't she be giving up her own Western one? It wasn't possible, was it, to live an Eastern and a Western life at the same time? And, really, what outside of the stuff of fairy tales and the stories with which he'd chosen to beguile her, did Barbara know about Bahram's world? Moreover, what reason did she have to believe that she, "a hick from India-no-place," would be accepted in his world? And suppose that world, and he with it, threw her out? Could she then return to her own world?

Bahram, when Barbara voiced her doubts to him, told her over and over until she was finally more or less convinced, that she didn't have to give up America, that he and she would divide their time between both countries. And that his family would love her as he, himself did, and that always, always, no matter what else happened, she'd have him to hold onto.

Bahram's grandfather, Baba Bozorg (Grandfather Big Man) had

sent his private plane, converted into a small flying palace—a living room, dining room, kitchen and three bedrooms and baths, all carpeted with the most exquisite Persian rugs—to fly Bahram and Barbara to Iran. They flew first to Indianapolis to spend a day and night with Barbara's family. The day passed uneventfully, even slowly, with Barbara, Bahram and Barbara's parents and grandparents making small talk with one another, and her mother saying to her in a tone of shock when they were alone for a moment, "Your children, Barbara, they are going, dear Lord, to be half-Persian!"

Then at six o'clock they were joined by Barbara's mother's brother and sister and their spouses and four daughters for dinner on the plane.

Both families arrived together and left the same way. They had always been tight, silent people, and were, under these circumstances, even tighter and more silent than usual; there was little table conversation. Barbara's uncles inveighed against drunks and addicts and girls with short skirts and boys with long hair, and Jews who were taking over the city, and "niggers" who cost good taxpayers like them money for welfare programs.

As for Barbara's aunts...There had always been tensions between her and them, and now every look they cast at her showed that they, like her mother, disapproved of this marriage and this husband. He might be wealthy beyond their comprehension, but money wasn't anything, was it, especially when compared to the good old American values? And he might be a member of royalty, but the royalty was only Persian, not British or even Swedish or Dutch.

And when she looked at her cousins' faces, she saw bitter resentment and virulence there; they detested her for having escaped the life they never would, as well as for Bahram's title and money and charm.

She couldn't wait for them all to go, and though they wished her and Bahram luck when they said good-bye, their cool tones showed they didn't mean it.

Barbara's parents left with the other relatives while her grandparents remained on the plane to spend the night with her and Bahram. And the whole mood changed when it was just the four of them; the happiest thing for Barbara was to realize the warm relationship between her grandparents, especially her grandmother, and Bahram. They shared champagne and caviar, talk and laughter like the best and oldest of friends. And sometime well after midnight Barbara's grandmother got down on the floor and began examining a Persian rug Bahram had said was a Tabriz "Garden of Flowers", and that was the most beautiful carpet Barbara had ever seen. It had, according to Bahram, been woven one knot at a time from angora and silk, and its marvelous colors had been taken directly from nature—roots, leaves, walnuts, rose petals.

"You know," Bahram smiled at Barbara's grandmother, "we Persians feel such admiration and love for our carpets that our poets have been inspired to write odes to them." He held his champagne glass up, moving it in accompaniment to this poem he quoted:

"...this carpet fair.
Its patterns were by angels wrought,
Those ardent hues from the blood of flowers came.
Of the garden of Paradise
'Tis token and counterpart."

"That's a lovely poem," Barbara's grandmother said, "and you, Bahram, are a lovely, lovely person."

Bahram grinned his pleasure and leaned to kiss her hand. "I thank you for the compliment, dear Grandmother, and only hope you'll feel the same way about me twenty years from now. As for my ode to the carpet, I only quote it so you'll know that this "Garden of Flowers" carpet is the most loving present your admiring new grandson can think to make you."

Barbara's grandmother whispered, "I couldn't...couldn't possibly...I can't thank you enough for the thought, Bahram, but how could I accept such an expensive gift?"

And she didn't begin to know how expensive it was. For as Bahram had told Barbara, a similar carpet had been auctioned at London's Sotheby Park Bernet for $200,000.

"Please, Grandmother," Bahram said softly, "please accept this gift with my affection and gratitude for all you've done to make Barbara the wonderful person she is."

And her grandmother did accept it then, and said to Bahram with tears in her eyes, "Dear Bahram, you know that I'd think any man who'd get our Barbara would be the luckiest man in the world. Now I can add that I believe her to be the luckiest woman in the world. And whatever sadness I feel to have her go so far away is lessened by the fact that you'll be by her side; I know that you'll give her all the happiness I've wished for her since the day of her birth."

CHAPTER II

Grandfather Big Man and Lady of My Heart

Barbara and Bahram flew first to Rome, then to Tehran. In those days before jets, the flight spanned twenty-seven hours; among the fuel stops that had to be made were those in Baghdad and Damascus, whose very names gave Barbara a thrill. All the same, by two o'clock when the plane finally dipped its wings and landed at Tehran's squat, old, ugly Mehrabad Airport, which offered no intimation of the impressive and opulent building of marble and glass that would replace it no more than six years later, Barbara was terribly nervous. "Be calm," she kept instructing herself, "Be calm." She began clenching and unclenching her hands. She swallowed. She could not breathe. She grabbed Bahram's hand and clung to it until it was time for him to disembark, as ceremony dictated, twenty minutes before she would.

As she looked out the airplane window she saw through the sun's glare an uncountable number of men, mainly in Western clothes, and women, some in black chadors that made them look funereal yet fascinating, and some wearing dark handkerchiefs covering all their hair and much of their faces, but not their bodies. Others, though, mainly the ones surrounding Bahram, were dressed in luxurious dresses and hats of black or brown or navy, colors the Persian fashion of the time decreed even for summer. In those days mass leave-takings and welcomes were the style (a person's importance could be judged by the number of people who came to greet him or say good-bye), and many dozens of family, friends and hangers-on had come to pay their respects, not only to Bahram and his American bride, but also to the whole Family Mosallai.

Barbara, excruciatingly hot in her stockings, garter belt, slip, formal black dress, and hat and gloves Bahram had chosen for the occasion, heard a band playing what sounded like a military tune as the stewardess, Fatima, signaled that the time had come for her to join Bahram. She thought, "Dear God, this cannot be for me," although she knew that it was.

She was escorted by Bahram through a mob of well-wishing friends and acquaintances who put bouquets of flowers in her arms, doused her with rose water, and tried to grab at her dress and hair. Finally they reached the compact group of people that was Bahram's family. There was his father, called Hajji Khadivar because he'd made the hajj (pilgrimage to Mecca) many times; Toobah, his mother; Mitrah, Toobah's mother; and Bahram's grandparents, Baba Bozorg and Khanoum-June, whom Barbara had heard so much about.

Baba Bozorg was a burly man with hairy ears, an extravagant pulpy nose, thick white-thatched hair and a voice that nearly shattered Barbara's eardrums as he welcomed her to his family. He wore an immense diamond ring on his index finger, and though he smiled benevolently when Barbara, as Bahram had instructed, bent to kiss his hand as a sign of filial respect, a certain expression on his face told her clearly that here was a man who held authority and expected to be obeyed, or else.

Khanoum-June appeared the exact opposite of her husband, as delicate and gentle as he was not. She wore a white chador that veiled her body, but not her beautiful classic face that looked as though it must have been sculpted. She was wonderfully warm to Barbara, holding her head in both exquisite hands, and kissing her face as though she were her daughter, to be careful and gentle with. This simple act caused some of the chill to leave Barbara's bones and some of the cement to slip off her shoulders.

The party separated into groups, and drove off in a series of blue Buicks. Persians often succumb to fads, and during Barbara's early years in Iran, blue Buicks, which in later years would be replaced by black and gray Cadillacs and Mercedes-Benzes, were the craze of the rich. Barbara and Bahram rode with Khanoum-June and Baba Bozorg, whose car, like everyone else's, had a bangle of blue beads hanging overhead and Persian carpeting in both front and back.

Tehran, as Barbara saw it during the hour and a half drive between the airport and Bahram's parents' mansion in the northern suburb of Shemiran where she would live, was a disappointment; it was nothing like the *Arabian Nights* city of her imagination. Its pervasive smell and taste, especially in the terrible heat, was one of dust, since it had, after all, grown out of the desert, and organic waste. Its water flowed in the street to supply the drinking and washing needs of a million people. Its poor neighborhoods were row upon row of huts built of the clay, sand and stone from the high Iranian desert. They had single doors and holes in the wall and ceilings to serve as windows and chimneys. Entire families ate, slept, made love and lived out the whole of their existence upon the dirt floors of these humble homes. The blooming gardens and exquisite mansions of the rich, like Barbara's new family, were protected from prying eyes and the wrath of the poor by ten-foot high walls of the same clay, sand and stone. The whole of the city presented a flat, bleak, grungy look.

But the wide-open street life was a wonderful contrast to the physical city. Barbara saw, on this first drive, turbaned bearded mullahs (the Islamic religious), and many chador-clad women appearing even more mysterious and strange than they had at the airport. There were itinerant barbers shaving faces and cutting hair on the streets, and fruit and candy sellers balancing their wares on their heads. Hawkers were peddling their kebobs (spicy soups), sweet pickled beets, and their ice and kerosene...all in what sounded like singing. Barbara saw horses draped in beads and necklaces, with henna stain (to bring good luck, Bahram told her) on their manes and faces, little white donkeys loaded with firewood and wearing turquoise necklaces (to ward off the evil eye), and fat-tailed Baluchi sheep led by their nomad masters just in from the desert.

And to Baba Bozorg's and Bahram's disgust and Barbara's delight, the Mosallai caravan of cars was stopped by a small camel caravan which had somehow made its way into the traffic lane from the far edge reserved for porters, horses, sheep and donkey carts, but not camels, since these had been banished from the city's streets by Reza Shah, Mohammed Reza's father, as long ago as 1923.

At that point Bahram ordered the chauffeur into the back seat while he took the driver's seat, to great applause from Baba Bozorg and Khanoum-June, who hadn't known he'd learned to drive in America. And Barbara, having gone to sit beside him, saw a different Bahram than she'd seen before, either in or out of a car. He and Baba Bozorg laughed hysterically as he nudged the camels with the car, arousing them to near panic before returning, finally, to their own lane. They continued laughing as Bahram ran red lights, wove in and out of traffic, and paid no mind to pedestrians whom he'd have run down if they hadn't somehow managed to escape him.

Later, Barbara would learn that Bahram's stunts in an automobile were not unique in Iran; she would learn that the mass of Persian drivers were more aggressive, self-centered and disdainful of other drivers than perhaps any others in the world. Passing others, as Bahram was doing now, with no motive except to show off their own agility. Tying up intersections so that neither they nor other drivers could move, rather than backing up a few feet, while cursing back at those who cursed at them.

As for pedestrians...During Barbara's time in Iran, and throughout all of Mohammed Reza's reign, drivers behaved as though pedestrians were a lower form of humankind, exhibiting a total unconcern for their life and limb. There were times Barbara went out into the streets and saw unbelievable scenes that excited her fear and indignation; people lying injured or dead on sidewalks a couple of feet from where they'd been hit, the cars that had hit them long gone, and passers-by looking briefly and walking on. The snuffed-out lives, so long as they were not their families' or friends', simply didn't matter; no one cared about them.

Barbara, of course, didn't know any of this on the day of her arrival, and so couldn't imagine why Bahram, whom she'd known as a careful enough driver in California, had turned so maniacal in Tehran. She was equally astonished by his reaction to another incident, when he stopped for a red light. She was distracted by a charging camel and, in leaning across Bahram, accidentally pressed her foot on the accelerator and caused the car to lurch forward and hit a taxi in front, knocking out the tail lights on one side. Barbara could not believe her eyes and ears when both Baba Bozorg and Bahram began yelling at and intimidating the taxi driver, behaving as though they believed that the fault was his, not hers. Baba Bozorg shook his fist at the driver, and Bahram would have reached into the taxi to grab his neck if Barbara hadn't stopped him by holding his arm and telling him that she, not the taxi driver, was to blame for the accident.

Bahram released himself from her, without any gentleness, and told her in a furious voice to "Shut your mouth, Barbara, okay?" Only then did she realize that Baba Bozorg's wrath had been transferred from the taxi driver to her. His eyes were hostile, and his lips folded inward making a gash across his chin as he yelled at her in Persian, during which one word, namus, stood out from the rest because he repeated it many times. Later, Bahram would explain that namus meant to offend one's family pride, which Barbara had done when she'd taken the side of the taxi-driver against "our own family." And when Barbara said she'd taken the side of truth, not the driver, he retorted that "truth is not the issue here, Barbara. In this dispute, as in any other, your place is beside our family. Right or wrong!" His words were precisely separated, cut apart, as if he were teaching English to a foreigner. "RIGHT OR WRONG!" he repeated.

This arrogant behavior toward the taxi-driver and toward her, coming from Baba Bozorg and especially Bahram—her gentle, tender, poetic Bahram—so appalled and frightened Barbara that her joy in the street life around her palled. She rode the rest of the way to Shemiran in a state of dejection that only lifted at her first sight of Bahram's parents' mansion. It was like nothing she'd ever seen or conceived of in her life before; it truly was a palace, but could not be called that since only the Shah's homes were designated palaces. The immense garden behind high walls was brilliant with blooming trees and flowers, and contained a giant pool bordered with aquamarine, orange and yellow mosaics. The huge building had many wings and was, as were many Persian homes, built to accommodate their tribal families. It was "home" not only to Barbara's parents-in-law, but also to their children and their children's children. Its enormous foyer was adorned with green panels of pure Persian silk and contained a cut-glass chandelier, dark green upholstered furniture and a display of priceless Chinese scrolls, rugs and porcelain.

Barbara was shown to her own suite of rooms by Bahram's mother and both his grandmothers. He had described Toobah, his mother and Mitrah, her mother, as great beauties, and they might well have been at one time. But by the time Barbara met them, when Toobah, who had been only thirteen when Bahram was born, was not yet out of her middle-thirties, and Mitrah was fourteen years older than that, they each weighed over two hundred pounds and had yellowed, coarse skin, a result of their incessant opium smoking. Barbara's bedroom was as exquisite as she might have assumed it would be from the look of the foyer; it held tapestries, rich rugs and satin sheets on a magnificent canopied bed she was almost afraid to lie down upon. When she did, though, she fell fast asleep and only wakened when she needed to go to the bathroom.

But she couldn't find any bathroom, although she walked up and down the long hallway and opened every door she passed. Finally, she discovered a small marble room with a hole cut into the floor's middle, and a porcelain base placed over it. It seemed a more likely toilet than any other place she'd seen, and she proceeded to use it as best she could. Her best, though, was not good enough. She was horrified to find she'd wet herself, and frantic to find a shower so she could clean up before she'd be seen by anyone. Suddenly, though, the door opened and Bahram entered.

Barbara said, "My God, Bahram, I've wet myself."

He shook his head and didn't say anything.

"Oh, Bahram, I'm sorry; this room isn't...it isn't the bathroom, is it?"

"This," he said as he pointed to the covered hole, "is an air vent into the kitchen, and a tube for communicating with the servants there."

Barbara said, "I don't know what to say, how to apologize..."

"The vent, as it happens, Barbara, is directly over the stove."

"You mean, oh my God, you mean that I...I..."

Slowly she began to smile, an idiot's grin of a smile, a wide and silly smile, as she pictured Betty telling her dorm-mates in her inimitable language that "the first thing Barbara did in that Persian palace she lives in was to not only piss over herself, but also over the royal dinner cooking on the stove."

"Barbara."

"What, Bahram?"

"YOU ARE LAUGHING," he hissed with disbelief. "Tell me please, what you find so funny."

"Nothing."

He frowned. "It isn't nothing, Barbara. I know you, and you don't ever laugh at nothing."

She looked up at him. "You know me." And she wondered to herself how it came to be that the same Bahram who'd vowed that, no matter what else happened, she'd always have him to hold onto, had chosen during these early terrifying hours in his home to totally separate himself from her.

"Barbara, condescending American lady," he spat, eyes ablaze, "I believe you're laughing because...you look down on us as Persians." His voice was as harsh as it had been when he'd yelled at her to shut her mouth while Baba Bozorg had yelled, "namus, namus" at her. The wall that had grown between them then was extended now, only this time she was responsible for having created it. How could her laughter not have been construed by him as condescension toward his country, his people and himself? And how would it not have provoked his fury at her?

"Bahram!" She reached for his arm. He pulled away and walked fast down the hallway.

Feeling miserable and on the verge of tears, she started walking to her suite when she heard a bright little voice behind her chirp in a beguiling Persian-New York accent, "I'll bet if you were offered three wishes like Aladdin was, your first one would be for a good long bath, Barbara, right?"

Barbara turned and looked into a young pretty face with a long narrow nose, full orange-red lips and the biggest, blackest eyes she'd ever seen.

"Yes," she said, "I surely do wish I could have a shower. Are you here to show me where to get one?"

"Bahram sent me here," the girl said, huge eyes a-twinkle, "to teach you all you need to know about living in a Persian household. Like where the toilet is, and how to use it so you'll never again..."

"Who are you?" Barbara interrupted.

"Farah. Your niece-to-be," the girl grinned.

"How old are you?"

"Twenty-one."

"Well, I'm eighteen."

Farah, realizing Barbara's surprise at meeting a new niece who was older than she was, smiled and said that one of the first things Barbara would have to learn about living in a Persian extended family, with its many-faceted relationships, was never to judge from a person's age what his relationship to her would be. Thus she, Farah, had a nephew named Loftallah whom Barbara had been meeting at dinner and who had a long black beard that had begun to gray, and a great aunt Sahyla, who was still in diapers.

By now they'd come to Barbara's room where a servant had unpacked her clothes. She got a dressing gown out of the closet and clean underwear out of a drawer, and asked Farah to take her to the shower.

Farah shrugged. "There isn't one in the house."

"Well, where's the bathtub, then?"

"Oh, there's no bathtub either."

Barbara said, "Oh, Farah, please, if this is some kind of a joke, I'm not quite up to it and..."

Farah touched her gently and told her that she was really not joking, that the elders regarded baths and showers in their houses as "Western nonsense." Now that she was living in the home, though, they might, out of courtesy to a farangi...

"My God, Farah, are you telling me that Persians don't bathe?"

Farah laughed and said that of course Persians bathed, but in a different manner from Westerners. They went to public baths where they could meet friends and exchange gossip; bathing in Persia was a form of socializing as well as a way of getting clean. And traditionally religious women like Toobah and Mitrah could not pray before they cleansed themselves at the public bath. "And that," Farah grinned, "is your first lesson in Persian tradition."

"Thanks for the lesson, Farah," Barbara said. "I imagine I'm going to need many more of them from you. But now, please tell me how I'm going to get a bath."

"If you want," Farah said, "I can have a servant bring basins of hot water here to your suite and..." Suddenly she grabbed Barbara's hand. "Listen, be brave, try to get over your Western modesty, at least for tonight, and give our public bath a chance. Then if you're offended by it, I promise you we'll find a way to keep you from ever having to go there again. But I'll bet you're going to feel like that American jingle, you know, 'You've tried the rest, now try the best.'"

There was such a sparkly humor in her eyes, and such electric currents of life zinging through her lithe young body, that Barbara couldn't have resisted anything she might ask of her. She said, "Well, if you're willing to take your chances with me, Farah...But if my Western modesty does spring up to hit us both in the face..."

Farah laughed and shook her crisp black curls. "My dear aunt, I firmly believe that before this night is done, you will be thrusting out your naked American chest along with the best of us Persian ladies." She illustrated by thrusting out her own remarkable breasts which were emphasized by her tight black sweater.

Barbara's first experience at the public bath, which was not really public since it was used only by Mosallai women and a few family friends, put her almost at once in the mood of a holiday. She and Farah, accompanied by their servants, Naila and Hosnay, who were carrying their clean clothes in suitcases, came into a large glittering room with a multi-colored dome ceiling. They were led up slippery steps to a mezzanine containing half a dozen rug-covered divans on which several naked women sat sipping tea and talking together as though at a conventional party. Across the room was another mezzanine, and the tableau of naked women repeated itself.

In the space between the mezzanines was a large pool with water jetting down upon it from someplace in the ceiling, and spilling down like a cascade into two lower yellow and orange tiled pools.

Naked women moved from pool to pool, smiling, laughing, playing games in the water. And they were so charmingly, delightfully unconcerned with their nudity that Barbara found her own embarrassment giving way, and she moved comfortably among them. Neither did she mind when a group surrounded her, pulled at her red hair and giggled at her, spurting water and asking, "Hoob? Hoob?" ("Is it good?") She giggled back and spurted water at them and told them through Farah that yes, it was very good.

Farah and Barbara had no sooner gotten home from the bath and into Barbara's room when Farah announced that the time had come to introduce her to the toilet. It was a small room much like the marble one she'd mistaken for it, and exuded a miasmic odor that nauseated her. Such a place in this elegant, exquisite house was unbelievable. The thought crossed Barbara's mind that Farah's bringing her here was a big joke she and Bahram had cooked up between them, a test of whether she was or was not an "ugly American." If she could not only take this toilet in stride, but also prove that its existence in no way mitigated her respect for Bahram's family or his country and its rich, ancient culture, they would have to believe in her sincere good will.

Farah squatted over the hole, straddling it. "How, dear aunt, is this for technique?"

"Looks fantastic to me."

"You want to try now?"

Barbara laughed and squatted, and looked up at her, this bright and bubbly new friend-niece, and thanked whatever fates there were for bringing her into her life.

Back in her room Barbara relaxed on the bed while Farah sat smoking and watching her in silence for what seemed a long time. Then she pulled a gold-wrapped package out of her purse and handed it to Barbara, smiling. She opened it to find three packets of toilet tissue. She looked at Farah. Her mind was boggled. She didn't know whether to cry or laugh at "the joke." It was, though, no joke; Farah told her that the elders, Hajji Khadivar and Baba Bozorg especially, eschewed the use of toilet tissue in the house, and that the family members who did use it were, of necessity, secretive about it.

"Farah," Barbara asked, "why should the elders reject the use of TOILET TISSUE?"

She shrugged. "Because they and all the faithful consider its use to be a careless, dirty, WESTERN habit. The Koran commands them to wash themselves after each toilet, and..."

"What do they wash themselves with?"

"Their hands."

"The same hands they eat with?"

"Well, actually, Barbara, they eat with their right hands and wash themselves with their left ones."

All of a sudden the humility with which Barbara wanted to approach Iran from the day she'd first thought of going there deserted her, and she found herself asking Farah in a tone she'd not have blamed anyone for labeling "ugly American", "And the Koran calls THAT a CLEAN habit?"

"Really, Barbara, I...I would think that you, about to marry a Persian, and having come here of your own will to live among us, would want to know the reason for the Koran's commandment before...condemning it." Suddenly all that bright and sunny laughter turned to hostility from Farah and guilt for Barbara when they gazed at each other across the barrier that now appeared to exist between them. For all her westernization, and many years spent in New York where she'd gone to high school and earned a degree in public relations from New York University, Farah was East. And Barbara, for all her fascination with Iran and desire to meld with it, was West. It was a lesson that she, if she expected to endure in Iran, would always have to remember. Farah and she could meet in peacefulness and love so long as they were aware of each other's peculiar sensibilities, or rather, so long as Barbara was aware of Farah's. She stammered out that she wouldn't knowingly have mocked at the Koran; even though Farah had told her toilet tissue was banned for religious reasons, she, in her ignorance, had connected what Farah said about washing after toileting, not with the Koran, "but rather with, you know, the primitive toilet facilities...Oh my God, Farah, there I go again. I'm so sorry, I..."

"Okay, okay, Auntie, listen. I myself have mocked the Koran a time or two, so I'm hardly in a position to hold your mistake against you. And now, come on and get ready for what may be the most important ordeal you'll face in this family, your first dinner in our midst. I can tell you that everyone's been waiting a long time to meet Bahram's farangi bride."

CHAPTER III

Paradise Lies At Mother's Feet

Barbara, on her drive from the airport with Baba Bozorg and Bahram, witnessed through them qualities so prevalent in the Persian character that they tend to dominate the views of foreigners about them...combativeness, contempt and utter lack of care and compassion for anyone outside the immediate circle of family and friends. Now, though, at her first dinner at the Shemiran mansion, she would experience what must be among the most beautiful of Persians' or any people's cultural patterns. Who, having once been accepted into the magic circle of Persians in Iran, or anywhere, can fail to be flattered by their compliments, overly-extravagant though you'd have to realize them to be? Or who wouldn't be enchanted by ta'roof (the complex code of etiquette for every situation), one element of which declares that "a guest is a gift from God" with all that this implies, while another says it is my obligation to offer you any possession of mine that you covet, or even admire. And, above all, who, having once basked in the generosity, the unbelievable-to-Westerners concern for one's well-being, the LOVINGNESS of Persians for family and friends that goes even beyond custom and etiquette, will fail to be moved, or ever forget them?

When Barbara and Farah entered the salon outside the family dining room, they found some thirty people, all relatives living in the Shemiran mansion, awaiting them. Everyone stood up and remained standing as Bahram introduced Barbara around and she kissed and was kissed by them. All were radiant, smiling, and their total attention was on Barbara. The women complimented her dress, her style, her good looks. And the men asked her such questions as whether her trip had been difficult, and whether she found the Tehran heat tolerable, literally hunging on her answers. Then someone asked the inevitable question of whether she preferred Iran or America (Iranians always, despite their overwhelming courtesy, ask such embarrassing questions as: "Which country do you like better, ours or yours?" or "Which of your children do you love best?" or, when speaking to children, "Whom do you love more, Father or Mother?") When Barbara gave the tactful answer, several of the women came to hang on her all at once, arms around her back in the Persian gesture of sisterhood.

Then Baba Bozorg entered the room, and everything changed. Those who were sitting sprang to their feet, and everyone first bowed deeply, then stood at rigid attention with palms against their chests to indicate humility. Baba Bozorg was, without question, the most important person in the room, and everyone was required to show they knew his exalted place and their lowly one by comparison. Only after he took his seat on a throne-like chair in the center of the salon did others dare seat themselves.

Baba Bozorg then summoned people—grandchildren as well as sons and daughters, some of them fifty years of age—to take their turns beside him while he questioned them, as though they were children, about their activities of the week and other matters. His head thrown back, his bellow volcanic, the room shook with his out-cries and pronouncements when their answers did not please him. And though Barbara could scarcely believe it, he spat on the floor to show his anger at this or that child, or in-law, or grandchild. Eyes fierce with malice, he stormed at them 'til he broke them down and then ordered them away from his presence in order to make way for others. Upon leaving, half-crouching with respect, they bowed out and away in order not to show him their unmannerly rears.

At the four-hour dinner, though, during which Barbara, Bahram beside her, occupied the seat of honor to the right of Baba Bozorg, she saw a whole other man who charmed her. Bahram had told her that his grandfather, like himself, and indeed all Persians of every caste and class, knew and loved poetry. Now Baba Bozorg proved it by sonorous recitation of long stanzas from the epic poem "Shanama" by the poet Firdausi, from whose works Bahram had often read to Barbara while they were in California. And for Barbara's sake, he told wonderful stories about the heroes of ancient Persia—such as Cyrus the Great, the world's first emperor, more than 2,500 years dead. He treated all the peoples he conquered with benevolence and dignity, honoring their gods as he did his own. And there was Darius, Cyrus's successor who created a sovereignty where farmers raised food, workmen made clothes and furniture, and artists and artisans created Persepolis.

"But the world, my daughter," Baba Bozorg proclaimed, "did not respect this most splendid civilization in the whole of its history, but instead pillaged and humbled it. First came the early Turkish and Mongol invaders, and then," his voice rose, "then...Ah, it's a long, terrible story that continued into our own century, when the Russians and British extorted such crushing compromises as makes the blood boil. But I don't wish to cause you sadness on your first night among us, I want you to be happy, and so..." He beamed, and acted out, with use of feet and hands and face, some of what Barbara would come to know as his favorite jokes. They featured ingenious fellows (like himself) who always "put hats on the heads" of others (fooled or outsmarted them), and especially on the heads of policemen, for whom Baba Bozorg had, as did many upper-class Persians in the Shah's time, a kind of good-natured contempt.

In the future, Barbara would be faced far more often by the tyrant Baba Bozorg than by the poetry-quoting, amiable one she met at her first dinner. She didn't know it at the time, however, and so quite fell in love with him and, in fact, with the whole of Bahram's warm, friendly family. Then on the way out of the dining room, when Baba Bozorg dismissed the company at two o'clock in the morning, two incidents occurred that changed her mood of well-being. First she noticed that the servants had cleared away all of the dinner dishes except hers, and when she asked Bahram the reason for it, he explained that her dishes had been set aside because she was not a Moslem, and was therefore unclean. No one could eat again from her plates until they had been washed three times in separate water.

This revealed, as Barbara perceived it then, that her new family's compliments, smiles, warmth and affection toward her were false. That, really, there was no place for her in their circle; they didn't accept her as one of them. And what about Bahram? There hadn't been even a hint of an apology in his explanation. It was as though he believed what had happened was perfectly normal and natural...and right. And since during the past year he and she had been eating the same meals out of the same dishes, and done much else together, why weren't HIS plates considered defiled?

As Barbara was thinking this way, Aysha—the same Aysha who less than six years later would save her from the Tehran University mob—came to say good-bye. Bahram's cousin, Aysha was in her middle or late thirties, exceptionally tall for a Persian woman, perhaps five feet eight, and very slim and athletic in a tailored skirt and blouse. With her shiny black hair floating loose, she looked like a dark Katherine Hepburn and stood out from the other women, who were hot-house flowers—exotic dolls with high-piled hairdos, eyes outlined with kohl, and iridescent bright red or orange lips.

Aysha's warm brown eyes smiled at Barbara as she told her that she'd enjoyed meeting her. She added, "I want to offer, Barbara, to be your guide to Tehran—well, one of them anyway. Because..."

Before she could finish her sentence, Bahram, mouth tight, took Barbara by the elbow so firmly it hurt and said, "You'll have to excuse us now, Aysha."

After Aysha had gone, Barbara protested Bahram's behavior, saying, "I liked her so much even at first sight, and you..."

Now the wall came yet again between Bahram and Barbara, as he commanded that he didn't want her to have anything to do with Aysha.

"Listen, Bahram, I am the one to decide whether or not I have anything to do with her. My friends, the people I'll want to be my friends, are my business."

"As my wife, Barbara, you have a position to maintain, and a responsibility to me. Your friends must be upstanding and respectable, and since you can't know for yourself which people whom you'll meet in Iran are wrong and which are right, you'll have to accept my judgment."

"Are you telling me, Bahram, that YOU'LL be choosing my friends, that my feelings...?" She stopped, almost in tears.

"It's exactly what I'm telling you."

"Oh no, Bahram" she said, "oh no."

"Oh yes, Barbara," he said in a low, grim voice, and added, "Let me tell you something about Aysha. She's...can't you see for yourself how evil she is? She is obscene!"

Barbara stared at him. "What are you talking about?"

"I'm talking about the fact that she's thirty-seven years old, and spends her whole life at the University of Tehran teaching and learning...still learning although she's already got her Ph.D..."

"My God, you sound as though you think there's something terrible...what is wrong with that, Bahram?"

"What's wrong with it is, that there were many men who wanted to marry her...I mean, she didn't have to remain a spinster, she chose to. And the reason she did... That woman you want for a friend is a LESBIAN, Barbara."

Barbara said she didn't know why Bahram labeled Aysha that way, and that Mohammed, Bahram's secretary and gentleman-in-waiting who was constantly with him, "looks much more typically gay, whatever that means, than Aysha does. Yet you don't object to having him in our lives. In fact, you..."

Bahram said, "The reason that I don't object to having Mohammed in our lives, and do object to having Aysha...My country, Barbara, makes a distinction between men and women, and what is permitted to the one is certainly not permitted to the other."

And as Barbara would learn from painful personal experience, what was permitted to men and not women was, quite simply, everything. She would learn that according to the Shariah, (religious law by which family relations are governed) men could have four simultaneous wives and as many zighes (mistresses) as they could afford. Moreover, men could divorce their wives at will by going before a mullah on three separate occasions a month apart and declaring, "I repudiate you, I repudiate you, I repudiate you," while women were not entitled to divorce for any reason. Divorced women's children over three years old belonged to their fathers who could, if they wished, prevent the mothers from ever seeing them, and if the fathers died, the children went, by law, not to the mothers, but to the father's male relatives. And the Shahriah also stated that married women could neither take a job nor travel out of the country without their husbands' explicit permission.

Barbara would learn that to have been born a woman in Iran was a very bitter thing, and that to have come there as a grown woman out of another culture was even more bitter.

On her second morning in Iran, Barbara met Toobah, Mitrah and Bahram, by arrangement, in the family salon. Bahram, smoking a cigarette and toying with a string of prayer beads Barbara had never seen him wear before, sat between Toobah and Mitrah, who both beamed lovingly at him. And, although he'd always looked at least as much Western as Persian to her, his features seemed suddenly to have changed so he looked all Persian; more Persian, in fact, than any of his relatives she'd met yesterday, except for Baba Bozorg. When she came into the room, he didn't get up to greet her, but instead pointed her to a seat across the room from where he, his mother and his grandmother were seated, with a gesture that could have belonged to Baba Bozorg. She felt then as though their thread of communion that had begun to snap during the ride home from the airport was now completely broken.

"My mother and my grandmother," Bahram said in a strangely formal tone, "have many matters of import to discuss with you, and would have preferred to do it out of my presence. But since it is necessary for me to interpret you to them..."

"And them to me," Barbara interrupted.

"Yes, of course."

Then ensued a conversation between Barbara and Toobah, with Mitrah nodding vigorously to all that was said, and Bahram translating—a conversation at which Barbara could not tell whether to laugh or cry.

Toobah said first that Barbara's and Bahram's wedding would take place in three months. When Barbara asked why it could not be sooner, Toobah said that there were many preparations; for instance, the sewing of her six gowns for the three days and nights of the wedding. Barbara had not known the wedding would last for three days and nights; Bahram had never thought to tell her. She made no mention of Bahram's oversight, however. She did say that she didn't mean to be impertinent, but it seemed to her, farangi that she was, that even six gowns ought not to take three whole months to make.

Toobah said that it was not only the making of the gowns that would delay the marriage, but other, more important things. For instance, Barbara needed to learn to speak Persian. She answered that there was nothing she wanted more than to speak Bahram's language, but wondered whether she could learn enough in three months to warrant holding up the wedding for that reason.

Toobah said that she could at least learn how to say "please" and "thank you" and other words of courtesy. Besides, she said—and Bahram translated exactly, as though the words made sense—Barbara also had to be tutored in English. She gulped at that, and cried out at Bahram, "What makes her think, what makes you think that I need to be taught...I mean, MY OWN LANGUAGE, Bahram, no, you and she have got to be fooling. That's it, isn't it? It's your and her little joke, and..."

But it turned out that they were not fooling, that what they really wanted was for Barbara to learn to speak with a British accent that could be used on occasion, because the family had many dealings with Britons who would be charmed by a daughter-in-law who could speak as they did. Before Barbara could react to the pretentious and ridiculous nature of this which, if it was not meant as a joke, seemed pure insanity to her, Toobah said that she also needed to be taught how to walk before her wedding, and that she knew an ideal teacher.

Barbara looked first at Toobah, then Bahram, before asking in a voice that she labored to keep under control, "Can you please tell me what...what is wrong with the way I walk, Bahram?"

Bahram let the question go unanswered as he smiled and nodded at his mother, who continued talking with much waving of arms and stamping of feet. When she was done, finally, Bahram smiled at Barbara and said, "And Sweetheart, she also wants you to go on a diet before the wedding."

"A diet? Me? I mean really, Bahram, how much less than a hundred and fourteen pounds would you, she, both of you want me to weigh?" Again she looked at Toobah, all two-hundred-plus pounds of her, and remembered the picture she'd tried to get out of her mind of her future mother-in-law at dinner: shoveling down food, gurgling, sloshing and spitting fruit pits and watermelon seeds without regard for where they would land. It seemed unbelievable that she should feel that Barbara needed to lose weight. She said to Bahram, "Honestly, I don't know whether to laugh or to cry. I don't know whether you and your mother are joking or have gone crazy. Or whether I have. Gone crazy, I mean. Really, this whole business would be hilarious if it weren't so, so..." And feeling both vulnerable and terribly nervous, she heard herself against her own will laughing hysterically as she repeated over and over, "Hilarious, hilarious."

And Toobah laughed with her as she made her final incredible demand: Barbara would need, first, to have all her teeth capped, and then to have her wisdom teeth pulled to give her the fashionable, lean, royal look of Grace Kelly, whom most of the wealthy young Persian women who strove for Western sophistication modeled themselves upon at that time.

Barbara argued that her dentist in California had told her that her straight white teeth were in perfect condition, and that people said she had a pretty smile. Toobah countered that her smile was not as pretty as Liz Taylor's or Doris Day's.

Now Barbara, angry as she was with Bahram, grinned at Toobah and told her in a loud voice that, oh certainly, certainly, she'd be happy to have her wisdom teeth pulled and the others capped. "I mean, there isn't any place I'd rather spend my time than in a dentist's office."

Toobah grinned with her, pulled a diamond bracelet off her arm, went to where Barbara sat and put it on her arm. Then she and Mitrah kissed her and Bahram, and went out.

"Paradise lies at mother's feet," the Prophet Mohammed proclaimed long ago. And Islamic mothers, therefore, regardless of caste or class, are of a type. Though always behaving with restraint and self-effacement in their husbands' presence, they rule their sons with pacts of steel. And when there are differences between men's wives and their mothers, it is a rare man who will side with a wife against a mother. No matter how right wives may be, or how wrong mothers, men will stand with their mothers. And of course, there are special problems when mothers-in-law are, as many were in Barbara's day and are again in Khomeini's Iran, child-brides and child mothers.

Barbara took off Toobah's bracelet and returned it to Bahram. "If this bracelet is supposed to be a reward for...I don't want to be cloned, Bahram, and I can't understand how you can be a part of such a ridiculous...You really do want me to have my wisdom teeth pulled and my good white teeth capped, and..."

Bahram interrupted, saying, "Of course I do, since it will give my mother pleasure in my wife..."

"And where'll I get my pleasure, Bahram? In her dentist's office?"

The argument continued for an hour, two hours, after which Barbara, in a state of exhaustion, screamed out, "IT'S A MATTER OF MY DIGNITY, BAHRAM."

"And what about my mother's dignity, damn it?" Bahram walked away a bit, hands in pockets, then turned and said in a voice he tried to make reasonable, "Listen, Barbara, it isn't going to kill you...I ask you, how do you think that you or your dignity are going to be hurt by bringing happiness to a woman who's had all too little of it since she married my father at twelve years old? A baby. And then, when she had me at thirteen...I was the only one who lightened her life in any way, and yet she was the one, she and my grandmother, to insist I go to school abroad from the time I was nine years old. That's the kind of generous person, noble woman she is, Barbara; you'll realize that when you know her better. You'll understand why she means as much as she does to me, and why there's nothing I wouldn't do...She's so sweet and lovely and pitiful..."

Hearing Bahram, Barbara felt, on the one hand, an almost limitless sympathy for Toobah, not as a person but as a twelve-year-old child overwhelmed by the burdens of marriage while others her age were just giving up their dolls. On the other hand, though, she was hurt and terribly frightened by something in Bahram's tone when he spoke about his mother. It seemed to her that he was speaking about a lover, not a mother, and the small difference in their ages encouraged the morbid perception. And hardly knowing what she was saying, she screamed out, "What is this mother to you, anyway, Bahram, a mother or..."

Bahram leaped forward and pointed a finger in Barbara's face. "If you dare say what I think is on your mind, I'll...Goddamn it, Barbara, you're showing your American contempt again...You dare attack MY MOTHER, American big-shot?"

Barbara was ashamed of her thoughts now that Bahram knew them, but also, she felt hurt at the name he had called her. She despised with her whole being those whom she herself had labeled "ugly American," and that she should have given Bahram any reason to perceive her that way was unbearable. And this, coupled with her need to have him close, influenced her to submit to Toobah's demands much as they went against her grain; she hoped, by her accession, to at least win Bahram's gratitude. And it seemed she'd accomplished her purpose. He sat beside her and held her close. He stroked her hair. He took her face between his hands and kissed her eyelids, kissed her mouth. Then he took her hand and kissed it, and they sat holding each other's hands for a long time while he told her that he appreciated her kindness to his mother more than he could say, and that he loved her very much, and that they would have a wonderful life when they married. So Barbara believed in him again, and everything that had closed tight in her when Bahram had become so frighteningly different opened up again, and she felt light, triumphant and full of hope for the future.

CHAPTER IV

The Manufactured Eunuchs

But the future, it seemed, could not begin 'till the three-month wait Toobah had imposed was done and Barbara and Bahram's marriage took place. Meanwhile, Barbara lived a life of such monotony, such sameness of days and nights as threatened to break her. Her day began about eight, when she would call for her maid, Naila, to bring a basin of hot water. After washing and dressing, she went down to breakfast in the dining room where she would find some of the thirty assorted relatives who lived in the house. Bahram would be sitting by his father or grandfather, and also by Mohammed, his secretary and gentleman-in-waiting; he with a perfect oval face, dominated by enormous eyes, seemed to be more an exotic doll than a contemporary man. The sight of him gave Barbara an eerie feeling.

Often, there were guests in addition to the family members. Relatives and friends dropped in at all hours, and Barbara, along with the rest of the family, was required to welcome them with traditional politeness and hospitality. They had, first of all, to rise and remain standing 'till the visitors were seated. This could be a long process since Baba Bozorg or Hajji Khadivar would offer visitors seats of honor near the head of the table that they, with varying expressions of humility or self-negation ("I am unworthy to be your slave" or "I am the dust beneath your feet") would decline in favor of seats at the lower table occupied by unmarried girls.

These girls had the responsibility of urging the guests to partake of the sweets, nuts and fruits that were placed beside their plates at breakfast or at any meal to which they invited themselves. Once the visit was over, all would rise to their feet and one of the girls, palm on chest, would accompany the guest or guests to the front door.

It would be many years before Barbara, from her American vantage point, would come to realize that Persian hospitality, insincere and even comical as it might seem to her, was genuine. The universal saying among rich and poor alike, of "a guest is a gift from God," was always meant from the heart.

Many of the guests, some of the men of the family and almost all of the women, lingered over breakfast 'till the servants came to clear off for lunch. Barbara, though, went to her suite for her fittings and lessons. Her teachers were an elderly English woman who soon despaired of her ever learning British English, but nevertheless continued valiantly to try to teach her, and a young French "walking teacher" who piled books on her head, then held them with both hands as they walked back and forth together.

Barbara found both them and their lessons comical, as did Farah, who sometimes joined her for the fun of it. Barbara did, though, take her Persian lessons seriously. Her teacher, Cyrus, was a short, wiry rodent-faced man who must seldom have bathed. Barbara smelled him before she saw him, and was in a constant state of nausea while with him. But she loved the sound of the beautiful, liquid language that is truly, as Persians boast it is, the language of poetry. And Cyrus was so inspiring a teacher that, after three years of study with him, she would speak like a native. After only a couple of months she would know colors, numbers, foods, many of the complex phrases of courtesy and even some poetry.

Barbara's fittings and lessons were over by two o'clock, when she joined the women of the family and guests, of whom there were usually more than had been at breakfast, for lunch. Everyone ate elaborately of salads, soups, chelo-kebab (the wonderful Iranian rice dish like no other in the world) and lamb, beef, or camel meat; and for dessert, baklava, or halvah, or ice cream, or all three. Barbara, though, was served fruit in deference to her diet, and Farah voluntarily kept her company.

After lunch, people retired for a nap until five, when more visitors drifted in for tea and cakes, often remaining 'till ten when dinner was served. The young girls, though, were driven to beauty shops—of which there were an uncountable number in Tehran— two, three, or even four times a week; these were the only places outside of their homes where they could meet their friends and exchange gossip.

And Barbara, nervous and tense, was driven to the office of Dr. Minai, considered to be one of Iran's foremost dentists. He made jokes while he worked on Barbara and clucked sympathetically whenever he hurt her. And, although she behaved affably enough, she was in a fury all the time she was in his office, not so much at him, or even Toobah and Bahram, as at herself for being there.

Next to her sessions with Dr. Minai, perhaps the most irritating part of Barbara's day was the time after she left his office and was received in Toobah's suite by Toobah, Mitrah and one or another English-speaking cousin who would translate for them. Ostensibly, she was there for instruction in the ways of ta'roof, but really, all that Toobah wanted to talk about was the matter of her merieh (dowry). Even though she was American and had no family to negotiate for her, she would receive merieh exactly as if she'd been a Persian girl from a good family. As the Koran commanded, she, as Bahram's bride, would receive from his family six separate presents. First would be a ring (some families gave inexpensive stones but the Mosallais gave only diamonds of the best quality), then a mirror, a copy of the Koran, two candlesticks and a shawl; and finally, a cash payment for her and Bahram's immediate use of seven hundred thousand tomans (ten thousand dollars). A promissory note of three million five hundred thousand tomans (fifty thousand dollars) would be drawn in case Bahram divorced her.

Barbara was overwhelmed by the generosity and embarrassed by the whole idea of merieh; she would have been happier without it. Toobah, though, laughed when she heard this because she was certain that Barbara, as any Persian girl would have done, was only pretending. Ta'roof, after all, required her to make a ritual refusal that she knew beforehand would neither be accepted nor believed.

Toobah usually dismissed Barbara around seven o'clock, allowing her three hours to spend by herself or with Farah before the daily dinner, which was much the same as lunch, except that there were even more visitors. Ten, twenty, even thirty guests was not an unusual number. Most of them, who weren't speaking Persian, carried on their conversations in French, a language Barbara didn't speak. Her communication at table during her early weeks was, therefore, nil or practically so.

Although she longed with everything in her to explore the bazaars, the food markets, the bakeries, the chaikhanes tea houses, the rug factories and the mosques of Tehran, she was compelled, like a prisoner, to remain in the house. As an unmarried girl she was unable, except if she would be accompanied by Bahram or another male relative or by a married woman or an engaged couple, to go anywhere. Within the house she was treated as a child, just as all the girls of the family were 'till they married. She had to rise when older people—not only guests for whom everyone rose, but also family members—entered the room, and stay standing till they told her to sit. And she could not speak to older people unless they spoke to her first.

Her prime, her only pleasure during the dreary months before her wedding were the days she spent with Khanoum-June in her and Baba Bozorg's home in Shiraz. After Barbara's first week in Iran she and Farah flew to Shiraz in Baba Bozorg's plane every Thursday afternoon, and remained there over Friday, the Moslem Sabbath.

Shiraz, like Isfahan, is in its reverent traditionalism one of the most glorious cities of the world, at one and the same time delicate and overpowering. Its massive entrance arch is exquisitely tiled in blue and named "Allahu Akbar" (God is Great) for the expression of wonder with which visitors greet their first sight of the blooming, beautiful city. Orange trees and stately cypress line the wide boulevard leading down from the entranceway into the town of fragrant baghs (gardens), with terraces and streams and berry beds and waving poplars and many-roomed pavilions tiled in patterns of the flowers growing so lushly around them. And there are the Masjid-i-no (the New Mosque) and the Masjid-i-Ateq (the Ancient Mosque) with soaring minarets laid in vivid mosaic.

And visitors also witness in awe the tombs of two of the most beloved men in all of Persian history, not kings or statesmen or military men, but the 13th century poets Saadi and Hafez. Both their graves are places of annual pilgrimage for Persians of every caste and class.

It is a custom for many who pay homage to Hafez under his kiosk in its elegant garden to use the occasion to appeal for his help in resolving their personal problems. A book of his in hand, they ask, "Hafez, is it well for me to take the test for university this year?" or "Hafez, is this the man my daughter should marry?" Then they open the book at random and find the answer. All their lives they have done this with the poet who has been household prophet to them and their ancestors, and have told one another when trouble threatened, "May God help you, may God keep you, may God give you Hafez."

As Shiraz was the most enchanting place Barbara had ever been in her life, so Khanoum-June was the most enchanting person she'd ever met. Bahram, Aysha, Farah, Mitrah, Toobah and Hajji Khadivar, and even Baba Bozorg, were members of her family, albeit her Persian one. Khanoum-June, though, was Aladdin and His Lamp and the Rubaiyat and Sheherezade, and all the dreams and fantasies she'd had about Persia from childhood on, rolled into one. And her pavilion, or rather Baba Bozorg's, one of the few that had not yet been taken over by the Shah for his use or as a government building, struck Barbara as a fit setting for the Arabian Nights. It had been built in 1857 by Baba Bozorg's grandfather, Prince Ali, one of the Quajar dynasty overthrown by Reza Shah in 1923. Ali's uncle, Mohammed Shah, the first Quajar, had overthrown Shah Karin Khan Zand in 1779. Karin Khan had gone down in history as the most just, benevolent, humane ruler Iran ever had. For all his "humaneness", though, Karin Khan, while in power, ordered Mohammed's testicles cut off even though he, himself, was married to Mohammed's sister at the time. And some historians believe this to be the reason why Mohammed Shah became far and away the cruelest of the Quajar Shahs, and indeed of all the Shahs in history. Among an uncountable number of his atrocities against the people was having the eyes gouged out of twenty thousand people in Kerman who, out of loyalty to the Zands, had refused to bow to him. He was assassinated in 1797, and was succeeded by his nephew, Baba Bozorg's great grandfather, Fath Ali Shah. It was during Fath Ali's reign that Britain and Russia first began carving up Iran, but history portrays him as the Shah who fathered two thousand princes and princesses and gave rise to the saying that "all over Iran there are camels, lice and Quajar royals."

The pavilion, built around an immense courtyard and exquisite with flowers of many varieties but especially roses, and shaded by plants and ancient cypress trees, contained three giant pools: a clover-shaped one in front, a heart-shaped one in back and an octagonal one at the entrance-way, all stocked with many sizes and varieties of goldfish. The clover-shaped pool, tiled in aquamarine, yellow and orange mosaics, had steps leading to a balcony surrounding one of three main salons on the second floor. Its walls were hung with the Baluchi tribes' "Tree of Life" carpets that are a heritage of the primitive shamanism of Northern Asia, and with the Quashquai tribes' star and diamond motif. The floor was carpeted with a Baluchistan rug of blue, dark brown and camel colors that came from the use of natural camel hair. There was no furniture except for a single, continuous sofa, perhaps twelve inches from the floor, softly padded and covered with Persian silk. Outside the salon was a small reception room where people took off their shoes, since no shoes were worn in Khanoum-June's Persian rooms. To the right of the reception room was another, smaller salon, which to Barbara's astonishment and discomfiture that lasted through all her years in Iran, was openly referred to as "the opium room." It was fitted with braziers containing charcoal and tongs so smokers might hold the glowing coals close enough to their pipes to make the opium sizzle and smoke. There was also a low table on which sat a varied collection of Baba Bozorg's pipes, egg-shaped porcelain bowls at the end of stems made from mesquite or cherry wood. Such opium rooms were quite usual during the reign of both Pahlavi Shahs, and all the shahs before them, since they were to the upper-class smokers what the dens were to the lower-class ones; in 1955 when Mohammed Reza made an ineffectual attempt at control, there numbered almost two million.

At the left of the reception room was the "women's salon", hung mainly with the elaborate paintings crafted during the Quajars' reign of kings, queens, princesses and dancing girls. This adjoined the former andarum (harem) where Khanoum-June had lived from 1905 to 1945 (when it was turned into suites for married family members). She lived with her daughters, her granddaughters, other female relatives, her sons till they were five years old and female servants. It had been built, though, to house Baba Bozorg's grandfather, and later his father's four wives and zighes, and their daughters and young sons.

Across the court and up another flight of stairs, in the guest house of twenty bedrooms that had once sheltered Baba Bozorg's father's and grandfather's many zighes, were two dining rooms. One, the "Western dining room", was furnished in the ordinary Western manner. The main dining room, like the main salon, held a continuous low sofa and no other furniture. Khanoum-June's most festive dinners were served much as they must have been in Baba Bozorg's grandfather's day when embroidered cloths were placed on the carpet, and on them a kind of buffet containing a vast variety of foods from which servants filled the guests' plates.

Underneath the dining rooms and bedrooms were the kitchen and quarters for the cooks and kitchen servants. Quarters for the other servants were under the main salon, where there was also a reception room for entertaining the servants of important guests. In Baba Bozorg's father's and grandfather's time, these people came with their coaches and horses, always requiring a driver and, for dignity's sake, at least two servants behind.

Barbara couldn't get her fill of exploring Khanoum-June's pavilion and was intrigued and happy during all her holidays there, though her happiest times were those when Aysha was present. From the beginning, Aysha was one of the people Barbara most admired in Iran, or anywhere, and whose memory she reveres today for her brilliance and warmth and, especially, her courage.

And whenever the word "courage" occurred to her in connection with Aysha, Barbara found herself thinking also about Khanoum-June. For when Baba Bozorg, despising Aysha for her ability to live on her own, her independence and her reputed lesbianism, did as Bahram had done to Barbara and ordered Khanoum-June to close her door against Aysha, Khanoum-June refused. "To reject my granddaughter is to reject her mother, my daughter and to reject a part of myself," she declared. "And if my home cannot be hers and her mother's, then it is no home to me either."

In the end, Baba Bozorg, who prided himself on never compromising with anyone, did with Khanoum-June. Aysha could visit her whenever she liked, but she was never to be any place where he could meet her.

Barbara and Aysha talked often about whether Barbara, under her circumstances, would ever be able to adjust to the Iranian life of oppression where men commanded and women obeyed. It was Barbara's feeling that if Aysha, who had been born to this life of oppression, could have risen above it to become her own person—well, maybe she would be able to do the same.

"But of course," Aysha said, "you pay a price for being your own person instead of a man's toy even in your country, Barbara, and certainly in mine. Men, and too often also women, call you arrogant, they call you prostitute and whore, they say you're a lesbian and therefore crazy, and lock you up in insane asylums that are the same as jails in Iran.

"God, God, the number of my colleagues, women in my own department, who've just disappeared to...Nobody, not their families or closest friends, know where. Savak (the newly formed secret service) fingers them as, I don't know what; Tudeh members, whores, lesbians—perish the thought—anything! And next thing, they're gone, disappeared.

"Are they dead? Have they been so tortured in prison or the insane asylum that they wish they could die? Have they been unable to hold up under the torture and turned traitor to everything they once stood for? Will they someday, though hating and despising themselves, lead Savak to finger their best friends?"

Barbara was terrified for Aysha, and wondered each time they met whether she, would survive the battlefield of the life she had chosen. And Barbara waited for her from Thursday to Thursday, worried that she might not appear because of having been taken by Savak.

For different reasons, Barbara took as much joy in her time with Khanoum-June as with Aysha. She loved to sit for hours in the small gold and white salon off Khanoum-June's bedroom and listen, while Farah translated, to spell-binding stories of her early and later life.

Khanoum-June was born and brought up untill age fourteen in Meshed, in Khorasan, in a mansion that was even grander and more opulent than the one she lived in when Barbara knew her. Her father, like Baba Bozorg and his father before him, owned opium and sugar-beet farms and many more villages and fiefdoms than Baba Bozorg's father did. He was also distinguished for his aristocratic lineage from Kings Shahpur I and II, and for his life's passions, transmitted down through the generations of Sassanian kings since perhaps 200 AD: dancing, poetry, painting and music. For this reason he saw to it that the andarum, where Khanoum-June, her mother, the mother's two co-wives and their daughters, as well as five aunts and assorted cousins lived (his zighes were housed away from the main palace), was staffed with female teachers of music, poetry, art and dancing, although not reading or writing. There were also female maids, from cooks to beauticians to house-servants and personal body servants.

Last, but hardly least, there were the twin eunuchs, some ten years older than Khanoum-June, whom her mother, co-wives and aunts had christened Fifi and Fufu; they were the only male non-family members before whom the women went unveiled.

Khanoum-June told Barbara that she had never been happier in her life than during those early years in the andarum. There had been such love and caring there among the women for one another. There had been such peace there, such harmony among the wives, who never would have humiliated or harmed one another. And there was such safety for the children, who felt as though they belonged to all the women.

"Didn't the wives ever carp at one another and fight?" Barbara asked.

Khanoum-June nodded and smiled. "Mostly, though, the fights were over before they began."

"What if they didn't get over quickly?"

"Then the women would call my father in, and he would decide who was right and say what was to be done."

"But suppose the women didn't like your father's decision?"

No, Khanoum-June said, it could never have happened that the women would disapprove any verdict her father rendered or refuse to abide by it.

"How," Barbara asked, "did you spend your days and nights in the andarum?"

"Dancing, singing, playing music. We also engaged in more serious pursuits; we memorized poetry, memorized the Koran." Looking up at Barbara, her eyes full of humor, she said, "If I told you that I know all of the Koran and all of the Rubaiyat by heart, would you believe me, Barbara-junam?"

Barbara-junam meant Barbara, darling of my soul, and she melted whenever Khanoum-June called her that. "Khanoum-June," she said, "I can't imagine anything you could tell me I would not believe."

Farah, taking Khanoum-June's hand and holding it for a moment against her cheek, turned to Barbara and said, "She's being modest when she tells you all she knows by heart are the *Koran* and the *Rubaiyat*. Believe me, she can quote you most of our Persian classics, maybe all of them, stanzas long."

"Dear Khanoum-June," Barbara asked, "how could you have memorized all those important and difficult works when you were not able to read them?"

"Oh," she said, "Fifi and Fufu read them to me over and over until I knew them by heart. They were so good, so patient. They'd read to me for as long as I could listen, taking turns. First Fifi, then Fufu, then Fifi again."

"Khanoum-June," Barbara asked, "how old were Fifi and Fufu when they first came to live with your family?"

"Five."

"How did they learn to read? Who educated them?"

"Oh, they went to school. My father educated them."

"Khanoum-June," Barbara said, hoping the love in her tone of voice would overcome the note of censure toward Khanoum-June's father that was also bound to be there, "why would your father educate eunuchs who were not his, rather than his own daughters?"

Khanoum-June sat silent a while, then said, "He educated them for his daughters'—for our—sake. They could teach us, as Fifi and

Fufu did me, and transmit to us everything that they learned."

Barbara asked, "But, why didn't your father...?", and was silenced by Farah's hand pressing on her shoulder.

Khanoum-June left the andarum when she was fourteen to marry Baba Bozorg, to whom she'd been engaged when she was two years old and he was thirteen. She told Barbara about her exhausting, terrifying three-week journey from Meshed to Baba Bozorg's home in Shiraz, where the marriage was to take place. She, her mother, her tai (wet nurse) and her sisters rode in curtained carriages, and her father, brothers and Fifi and Fufu, who were part of her father's wedding present to her, rode in open ones. The servants rode on camels and pack mules, on which were also piled the presents her family brought to Baba Bozorg's family. At night they camped on the desert. Khanoum-June, in her new dignity as a soon-to-be wife, tried not to show her panic when she heard the wolves and wildcats, that maimed or even killed some of the animals and servant guards on many of the nights during their journey, growling all around her.

Khanoum-June told Barbara all about her trip but nothing about her arrival in Shiraz, or her first meeting with Baba Bozorg, or her wedding. And Barbara saw her sitting with her head in her hands, such an unusual position for her, and knew she was thinking about all those matters.

Barbara wanted very much to ask her about her wedding and the early years in Baba Bozorg's home, but asked instead about Fifi and Fufu. Were they considered servants or were they closer than that? Were they, by chance, thought of as equals?

They were not equals, Khanoum-June explained, and yet they were much more than servants. They were "luxuries, like expensive paintings,"; high fashion for Khanoum-June's mother and her co-residents in the harem and later, for Khanoum-June herself in Baba Bozorg's mansion.

"Excuse me, Khanoum-June, but were Fifi and Fufu mere displays in the andarum, and in your own home, or...?" Barbara heard her voice tinged with sharpness and tried to modify her words once they were out. "What I mean is, did they perform any important functions for you and the ladies of the andarum, do anything that the other servants did not, since as you say, they were more than servants?"

Khanoum-June, with her lovely, gentle smile, explained that since Fifi and Fufu could move freely in both the men's and women's quarters, they acted as go-betweens for her father, mother and all the other ladies of the andarum. They took messages from the wives and other ladies to her father, and from him to them. And they wrote the ladies' letters for them, as they still write Khanoum-June's today, and were even allowed to attend the little girls of the andarum as they later attended Khanoum-June's daughters and granddaughters whenever they went visiting. "My mother believed, as I also do, that the children could be trusted with them as with no other servants; they were both wiser and more highly principled than all other people of their station."

"Why did your mother...why do you believe that, Khanoum-June?"

"Because, Barbara-junam, they were not troubled, as ordinary humans are, by passions of the heart, and so could make better use of their heads. Also, having no one of their own to love, they loved us, especially the children, beyond anything else. We could always count on their loyalty as we could not on any other servants'."

Barbara asked whether eunuchs were very prevalent in Persia when she was growing up, and Khanoum-June answered that every family that could afford a eunuch had one.

"Well, there couldn't have been enough of them born to go around, right?"

No, there were not, Khanoum-June said easily, and so the majority were manufactured. Her own Fifi and Fufu were manufactured eunuchs, and neither ever gave anyone in the andarum, or later, Khanoum-June in her home, a day of trouble. There were those who said that manufactured eunuchs were angry at the families whom they served. But Khanoum-June did not find this to be the case with Fifi and Fufu. And anyhow, why should they or any manufactured eunuch bear grudges? They should, rather, be grateful for having been made into the kinds of men-women wealthy families like Khanoum-June's would want to take in and provide for all their lives.

Barbara could hardly believe that those callous words had come from generous, gentle, loving Khanoum-June. She'd understood, almost from the time of her arrival in Iran, that people of Bahram's class had no caring for poor people and thought of them (when they troubled to think of them at all) with a kind of condescending contempt. But to believe, as Khanoum-June obviously did, that poor men should be grateful to the wealthy, for whose amusement and pleasure they underwent castration, was altogether beyond her comprehension. It went so much against her grain that she could hardly contain herself from speaking her feelings out.

But she did contain herself. And after a few moments Khanoum-June asked her if she wished to meet Fifi and Fufu, and added, smiling mischievously but lovingly, "That will be something to write to your American friends about, will it not?"

Fifi and Fufu came soon after Khanoum-June rang for them. They were sweet-faced, plump-bodied men in their late seventies who wore black ballooned trousers, bright yellow shirts and black satin skull caps over their bald heads. They bowed gracefully, and bent and kissed first Khanoum-June's hands, then Farah's, and finally Barbara's. Then, responding to direction from Khanoum-June, they began talking to Barbara about their lives in sing-song, high-pitched voices.

They were five years old, they said, when their father, a kind, loving man but one overwhelmed by his poverty, called them to him and said:

"Lights of my eyes, I have decided to take you to Behdjat, the midwife, so she may excise your genitals and make eunuchs of you. Then you will never need, as I've done all my life, to go cold or hungry or unclothed."

Fifi and Fufu remembered all the details of their operations, and talked about them freely and without embarrassment. Their father and elder brother brought them to Behdjat, the midwife's hut, on a soft gray morning ("that the sun did not shine was a good omen") and left them there alone. First, Behdjat explored them with long fingernails, then dunked them into freezing cold water in order to "dull the pain before she'd cut us."

"Did the water dull the pain?" Barbara asked.

Fifi grinned and shook his head. "The pain was bad, terrible."

Fufu said, "Some boys died during the operation, but we survived it."

"BALI, yes, we survived because it was Allah's will," Fifi said.

Fufu, eyes soft and melting, added, "Allah has been kind to have granted our father the wisdom to have us turned into what we are. We returned to our village when we were twenty-one, and saw the men with whom we'd played as boys. And our hearts bled for their poverty, their ignorance. More than one of them told us, 'You two are very lucky. How I wish my father had thought to do for me what yours did for you; how I wish I were living as a eunuch today, instead of what I am.'"

CHAPTER V

The Garden of Love

When Khanoum-June dismissed Fifi and Fufu and retired for a nap, Barbara and Farah sat smoking and talking about Baba Bozorg, who intrigued Barbara even more than he frightened her. Again, as always, Barbara asked Farah about the children of his two other wives aside from Khanoum-June. Once again Farah responded with the family gossip. After Barbara had permitted her fantasies about Baba Bozorg to run riot (she enjoyed visualizing him as in possession of uncountable numbers of zighes and children) irrepressible Farah, a ringleader of the unmarried girls, suggested they go to Baba Bozorg's "Garden of Love" where the men of the family were always welcome, but the women could not come without special invitation. Barbara was frightened, yet unable to resist the temptation of getting behind the high walls of the place that Bahram had declared during their courtship to be "a horizon full of wonders, my Barbara."

The "Garden of Love" turned out to be even more spectacular than Bahram had described it. The garden was made up of rows and hedges of camellias, azaleas, gardenias, orchids and roses. And the "cottage" located in the center of the "Garden of Love" was a Moorish castle with minarets rising against the skyline.

At first the servants, aware of Baba Bozorg's regulations about female family members, had not wished to admit Farah and Barbara, since Baba Bozorg was not present and they had no way of knowing whether he had invited them. In response, Farah lifted her eyebrows in the fashion that always intimidated people of their station when practiced by those of hers. She declared that they had Baba Bozorg's granddaughter's word (and did they presume to doubt *that*?) that Farah and his granddaughter-to-be from half the world away were here on his invitation, and were, in fact, going to await his presence. The servants apologized profusely, saying "chasm, chasm" (your least wish is as dear to us as our eyes), and admitted them with low bows.

Baba Bozorg's "cottage" had twenty bedrooms, two dining rooms and three salons. The main salon contained a pink silk divan that had an apple tree growing from its center. The apples were red rubies, and the stems were made of gold.

When Barbara and Farah had explored all of the "cottage" except Baba Bozorg's bedroom suite, Barbara's fears reasserted themselves and she could hardly wait to get away. But Farah, reminding her that Baba Bozorg was neither there nor expected by the servants, insisted she see Baba Bozorg's bedroom. His bed, she said, consisted of Persian rugs piled table-high. Barbara's curiosity overcame her anxiety, and she followed Farah up the stairs and down the hallway, with its red carpeting embossed with black lions, into Baba Bozorg's bedroom where, to their surprise, fat, ugly Baba Bozorg was on his belly bucking and bucking over some slight figure.

He wheeled and cascaded off the bed when the door opened, and Barbara was sickened to see that his girl was a child, maybe nine or ten years old.

"Buro! (out!)" he yelled. "Daughters of burned fathers, you camel-headed girls, you'll get yours for this. Buro! Buro! Buro!"

Finally back in the car, Barbara whispered, "She was a child, Farah, a baby. And he..."

"Yes, Barbara," Farah said, "Baba Bozorg has a penchant for children, for babies. I ought to know if anyone does." And she laughed bitterly as she told Barbara her own experience with her great-great-grandfather during the summer of her fifth birthday. Her father had divorced Soraya, her mother, by going before the mullah in the prescribed fashion. Soraya had some money; Mohammed's family had paid a decent, even impressive merieh when they'd married. But the money wouldn't last forever, and Soraya, although talented in dancing and music, was unequipped to get a job; she hadn't been educated for work. And she had no home; the mansion belonged to Mohammed, as did Farah, her three sisters and two brothers.

Farah was in the room while Soraya pleaded with Mohammed to let her see her children, if not every day, then once a week, once a month. He told her he would not permit her to have anything to do with them; he didn't want her influencing them in any way. After he'd finished talking, there came such a scream from Soraya as Farah had never heard in her life before. And Farah, terrified, nevertheless ran into Soraya's arms and hugged her and clung to her. Soraya, on her knees, bundled her close while they cried together.

Little as Farah was, she realized and wouldn't ever forget the contempt of Mohammed's expression as he looked at her mother and her.

"Listen," Soraya told Mohammed, "you just planted this baby and all of our children. I fed them in my body, with my body. You can't separate me from them."

Mohammed walked slowly out with no word to Soraya. And two menservants came in, removed Farah from Soraya's arms, and carried her, screaming, out of the mansion and onto the street.

Soraya went to her father, Bahram's sister's husband Shahpur, and begged him to try and get her children back from Mohammed, and let them all come and live with him. But Shahpur was angry; he hadn't wanted Soraya to marry Mohammed. He'd given in because she'd cried and screamed she was in love, and threatened to kill herself if she couldn't have Mohammed. Well, now she was reaping the results of her disobedience. He'd warned her about Mohammed, and told her she could not count on any help from him if the divorce happened, as he'd known it would.

She went next to Hajji Khadivar, her father. He wanted nothing to do with her, either. She'd disobeyed him as well as her father when she'd married against his will.

So, she went finally to Baba Bozorg, kneeled to him and begged as she had her father and grandfather. Baba Bozorg would have turned her away, but Khanoum-June begged him too, in Allah's name; she quoted Mohammed the Prohet at him: "Shall I tell you the greatest of virtues? It is taking in your daughter or sister after her husband has repudiated her."

So Baba Bozorg, albeit ungraciously, offered Soraya a home and agreed to negotiate with Mohammed for her daughters; there was no sense even asking for the sons.

Mohammed, out of deference to Baba Bozorg, agreed to release the daughters to him, not to Soraya. And Farah, her mother and sisters went to live in the Shiraz andarum with Khanoum-June.

One day, perhaps a month or so after their coming to Shiraz, Baba Bozorg came to the andarum to get Farah all by herself, and take her to the Garden of Love. She was dazzled; she'd never seen such a place. And she hadn't ever known Baba Bozorg to be as gentle and kindly as he was that day. He picked flowers with her, and after she'd tired of picking, took her onto his lap and held her and rocked her and sang to her 'til she went half-way to sleep. Then she felt his hands creeping, creeping near that most mysterious, most dangerous place on her. She was terrified, and yet she was also pleased: Baba Bozorg loves me.

After a while, when she came somewhat more awake, Baba Bozorg put her off his lap and lay her on her back on the marble bench. He himself sat on the side of the bench.

He kept calling Farah "darling of my heart" and "light of my eyes", and asking if she wanted to make him happy. And when she said she did, he opened his pants and leaned over her.

"Come on now, Farah, treasure of your grandfather's heart, take it. That's a good girl, Baba Bozorg's good, good girl; come on, come on, don't stop."

Farah's jaws hurt, her mouth felt sore, she couldn't breathe as Baba Bozorg pulled her head tighter in and hung on to her long hair with his fists.

Back in the andarum, Soraya realized there was something wrong with Farah and asked her what the matter was. Eyes filled with tears, Farah explained in the best way she could. She didn't want to be dirty or bad; all she meant to do was just to please Baba Bozorg, as her mother had always said she must do.

Farah saw Soraya's hands folded in her lap. They were blue-white. She didn't say anything for a long time, just looked at her hands in her lap, never at Farah. Then suddenly: "Daughter of a burned father," she hissed out, "don't you dare ever tell such a lie again about your great-great-grandfather, who took us in when my father and grandfather would not raise a finger to help us; and if HE should ever throw us out...Farah, listen to me...You must not repeat this lie to Khanoum-June or anybody, because if you do..." She collapsed, crying.

Farah, needing privacy, as most people would after stepping back into such a past, sat for long minutes absorbed in her own thoughts. After awhile, though, she put her head on Barbara's shoulder and muttered into her ear that for most of her life since she was five years old, she'd hated Soraya almost more than she hated Baba Bozorg. SHE WAS HER MOTHER. SHE SHOULD HAVE PROTECTED HER, SAVED HER.

Farah's voice was low as she told Barbara that finally, on the day of her nineteenth birthday, she and Soraya talked about this that had stood between them for so long. And Soraya told her then how she'd been like a beast caught in a trap, and had felt her scream of terror and fury at Baba Bozorg start from her gut as she listened to Farah; her anger, though, of necessity, had to be controlled. Not for her own sake, because she didn't really care if she lived or died at the time, but rather for Farah's and her sisters' sake. She knew she had to bend if they, who Baba Bozorg considered his chattel because he supported them, were to survive in his home. And, by bending, she was able to help Farah and her sisters by using her merieh money, which would otherwise have gone for her and their support during their growing years, to educate them.

"You know, Barbara," Farah said quietly, "my mother hasn't got a dime left of all of that merieh money. My sisters and I have these fancy foreign educations, and she is totally dependent on the largesse of Hajji Khadivar and Baba Bozorg. And she says that she's happy 'because your daughter, my darling, will never have to live through what mine did.'"

There were no tears in Farah's eyes, but her color was leaden. How did a mother get a love so strong, she asked, and how do you pay such love back?

"There is one thing she's asking of me, Barbara, and it makes me feel...But of course I'm going to do it."

"What is it?"

Farah crossed her arms over her chest and sat back, leg thrown up across her other knee. "I'm going to have my hymen recon-structed."

"You're...what did you say, Farah?"

"I said I'm going to have my hymen..."

"I heard what you said, Farah. I just don't know what you mean by it."

"I mean that I'm going to have a plastic surgeon perform an operation that will enable me to pass for a virgin on my wedding night."

"But why should you need to pass for a virgin...I mean, Mehrdad knows you're not a virgin."

Mehrdad, who worshipped the ground Farah walked on, was her fiancé, and had been her lover during the last two years she'd lived in New York.

Barbara said, "Knowing Mehrdad, I can't believe he'd ask such a ridiculous thing of you."

"Mehrdad's not asking it, Barbara. I already told you my mother is the one who's asking."

"But why?"

"Because when...if...Hajji Khadivar and respectable, good, moral Muslim Baba Bozorg realize I'm not a virgin, they'll want to see me properly punished for my 'crime'. And since there'd be little they could do to me, they'd do it to my mother instead. I can see them throwing her out into the streets with public pomp and ceremony. 'This adulterous woman. We disown her, as well as her wanton har-lot daughter; she is none of ours from now on. Let her starve in the streets, let her die there.'"

Barbara, feeling sick for Farah, managed to ask, "How are Baba Bozorg and Hajji Khadivar going to know you're not a virgin? Who's going to tell them? You? Mehrdad? How are they going to know what'll happen in your and Mehrdad's bedroom?"

"THEY'RE going to know, Barbara, believe me. Other fathers and grandfathers might not know. BUT HAJJI KHADIVAR AND BABA BOZORG WILL KNOW."

"But HOW, Farah?"

She changed the subject. "Listen, Barbara, how come your

American social conscience hasn't led you to ask me how expensive this operation is going to be, and what happens to poor women who find themselves in such a position?"

Barbara said, "Farah, come on, answer my question. How're Hajji Khadivar and Baba Bozorg going to know...?"

Farah said, "Well, talking about being expensive...the operation, though simple, is very expensive. And, talking about what poor women do, Barbara..."

"Farah, how are Hajji Khadivar and Baba Bozorg..."

"Poor women who can't afford plastic surgeons have all kinds of other tricks. They'll arrange their marriage dates to coincide with their menstrual periods, or..."

"Farah, will you please answer..."

"They'll insert pouches of chicken blood in their vaginas, and..."

"Farah, how..."

Farah put her hands on Barbara's arms very tightly. "Do me a favor, Barbara, and don't ask me any questions. All I'll tell you now is that you'll know what I'm talking about on your wedding night."

"But, Farah..."

"I said do me a favor, Barbara, okay?"

"Okay, Farah," Barbara said, though cold with dread over this unknown thing that awaited her as well as Farah.

There is an old Persian proverb, "Drown him even if I drown too," that is quoted as often as, say, "May God give you Hafez" or "A guest is a gift from God." It signifies the Iranian readiness to engage and revel in revenge. Baba Bozorg's ancestors' vengeance on the 20,000 people of Kerman who wouldn't bow to him was different only in extent, not in essence from, say, that of the huge numbers of peasants constantly brought before the law for killing or maiming one another's animals (and sometimes also relatives) in retaliation for real or fancied insults.

Of course, not all Iranian vengeance is violent, but is often exceptionally subtle. Such was the case among Mohammed Reza's courtiers, who made a fine art of knocking one another out of favor with the monarch in revenge for having the same done to them.

And sometimes vengeance is exacted in a mood of "typical

Persian playfulness and humor." Thus, Toobah had related at one of the earliest dinners Barbara attended, the story, received with guffaws of amusement, of how she'd punished a former friend she'd discovered had talked behind her back. Since the friend, a hypochondriac, loved chocolate cookies, Toobah placed a batch, to which she'd herself added chocolate laxative, beside her place. And when the friend, having gorged herself on the cookies, called to complain of her stomach upset, Toobah declared that the "stomach upset was most likely dysentery and fatal." And when the doctor disproved her diagnosis, Toobah said that everyone knew that doctor to be a charlatan and a fraud. And when a specialist to whom her doctor had sent the friend found her fine, Toobah said, "Are you, at your advanced age, unaware of the fact that all doctors scratch one another's behinds, and that your so-called specialist would see you die before he'd place his colleague in a bad light?"

It took many weeks before the friend finally realized Toobah's role, and quit depending on her medical advice. "But first she challenged me, said that she believed I meant her harm. And I," she laughed uproariously, "told her that of course I meant her harm, since she had tried to harm my reputation."

Baba Bozorg had his own story along the line of Toobah's that Barbara had heard many times even in the short while she'd been in Iran, and that was always received by whatever company he told it in with rousing "bravos".

"Now this uncle, who dared to mock me when I was a young child," Baba Bozorg began, "loved brandy as much as Toobah's fool loved chocolate cookies. And he always had a stock of brandy in his room. Every day he'd drink half a bottle, and I...I would pee in the bottles once they were open. It meant that my uncle would have his brandy straight on the first day and peed-in on the second. And I went on with my peeing and he with his drinking 'til I was eighteen and he was thirty. Then on his marriage day I said to him in the guests' presence, 'My dear uncle, I have a story to tell you about a certain camel-headed man of your and my acquaintance, that begins ten years ago...'"

Barbara knew, therefore, that Baba Bozorg was bound to avenge himself on her and Farah, and only wondered what form the retribution would take. And when, at seven o'clock, she and Farah were ready to depart for Tehran and were informed that the plane was already gone to bring the Tehran family to Shiraz for dinner, she knew that the dinner would signify their downfall.

All through dinner, however, while Barbara held her breath waiting for the fireworks, Baba Bozorg was his most intriguing, fascinating self, much as he'd been at her first dinner with him, reciting poetry and telling jokes. Then as quickly as the snapping of a light he changed. He frowned and stared malignantly at everyone, although for no longer at Barbara and Farah than at anyone else. Finally, though, his jabbing eyes fastened on Khanoum-June, and he exacted his vengeance on Barbara and Farah by taking his fury out on her instead of them, knowing that would be most hurtful to them. He shouted that she was as responsible for their "criminal acts" as though she'd committed them herself. If she were not "an old fool in charge of young fools" (all the unmarried girls of the family who visited in the andarum), she'd have kept them under proper surveillance and taught them the principles of decent behavior. The most important one was that he, Baba Bozorg, was to this whole extended family what the Shah was to the country. And, as Mohammed Reza had the right to kill or imprison those who challenged his rule, so Baba Bozorg had the right to "flog unto the point of death" family members, KHANOUM-JUNE INCLUDED, who were insubordinate to him.

For long minutes Baba Bozorg belabored Khanoum-June, as Barbara knew from his tone and expression even though she did not understand his words. And finally he screamed at her, "Buro, buro, camel-headed woman, and TAKE YOUR DONKEYS' DAUGHTERS WITH YOU so I don't have to look at any of your faces on this night."

And Khanoum-June, with every eye in the room glued upon her, bowed to Baba Bozorg and, with dignity, guided Barbara and Farah out of the room.

Barbara and Farah sat through the night in Khanoum-June's sitting room while SHE comforted THEM for what Baba Bozorg had put her through on their account. She stroked their hair and cheeks as she told them that neither they nor she needed to fear that Baba Bozorg would carry though on his threats against them. His wrath had expended itself in his public humiliation of them all. And she wanted them to know that she, like Baba Bozorg, blamed herself more than them for their "bad-girl" behavior. She had not sufficiently emphasized to Barbara or to Farah, who admittedly was more Western than Iranian in her outlook, that they could not survive in Baba Bozorg's world unless they would give him total obeisance. Oh, she knew how difficult that was for them, and also for her other granddaughters—like Aysha, who had so much knowledge that MEN came to learn from her, or Maryam the doctor, or Fahti the lawyer, or Sherezade the biochemist—to understand or tolerate. And she lamented the plight of these brilliant women she loved, because nobody in their colleges and graduate schools had ever taught them the lesson her mother and her mother's co-wives had taught her from babyhood; namely, that they had to accept the inevitable, that they had no power to change. Men controlled the world, and women had no choice except to yield to that control gracefully and graciously instead of fighting against it, because what good does it do to fight when you know there's no way you can win? Better to accept what you cannot change, and know that with acceptance comes a certain serenity.

CHAPTER VI

The Ceremony of the Bloodied Handkerchief

On October 3, 1958, Barbara's wedding day, or rather the first of the three days that her wedding celebration would last, she woke before dawn and sat at the window listening to the sound of the pool running into the garden, and dreaming of how it would be once she and Bahram came together for the first time as a man and wife.

"Darling," he would say in the tender tone that had sometimes brought tears to her eyes during their days in California, "darling Barbara." And he would hold her close in that way that had always caused the wild joy to surge in her, only this time her need for him wouldn't have to be denied. And afterward, they would lie touching hands and reciting poetry (how surprised Bahram would be to discover how many of his favorite poems she'd memorized), and confiding all their thoughts to one another.

But Barbara also felt great fear in the midst of her joy. She could not forget Farah's statement that Barbara would discover on her wedding night why she, Farah, had to have her hymen reconstructed before her marriage. Or Khanoum-June's declaration that Persian men expected their women to bow and scrape to them. Of course she'd heard the sentiment many times in America, but never expressed with Khanoum-June's fatalistic acceptance, her "serenity."

Barbara's conflicting thoughts and feelings were interrupted when, at ten o'clock, her door swung suddenly open to admit Khanoum-June, Toobah, Mitrah, Bahram's eleven-year-old sister Farideh, Farah, Soraya and all of the women and girls of the immediate family who lived in Khanoum-June's and Toobah's houses. They were all wearing chadors, and they dressed Barbara in one. Then they lifted her onto a kind of mattress of quilted blue, green and turquoise silk. And, sometimes singing, sometimes ululating, they carried her to the bath-house. There she was met by other family members and friends. Then Mitrah, holding onto her right arm, and Toobah grabbing her left, delivered her to her <u>klotflat</u> (scrubber) for the pre-wedding bath. The klotflat massaged Barbara under hot water and scrubbed her with a rough glove and an abrasive volcanic stone that sloughed off the dead skin she was not even aware she had. She used a special cleansing mud for Barbara's feet, and shampooed her hair with slimy-looking green sadre that nevertheless left it marvelously shiny.

Now, oiled and perfumed, Barbara joined the women in the hot pool. They pulled her into their midst and laughed while teasing her about the terrors of the nuptial bed. "...You're a little girl, and it is said that Bahram has a dick like a donkey. You're going to scream bloody murder when you see his pole and when he sticks it into you..."

When Barbara was carried back to her suite some four hours after she'd been carried out, she was met by Monsieur Henri de Paris and two of his staff, who dressed her hair and made her up to the tune of fourteen thousand rials (two hundred American dollars). And when Monsieur Henri was done with her, her seamstress, Sheherezade, sewed her into her beaded and pearled white satin gown and put over it her kelly-green cape with a seven-meter train.

At six o'clock there was a knock at the door, and Barbara opened it to see Bahram's three little nieces who were to be her trainbearers, accompanied by their maids, and six honor guards who were to escort her to the main ballroom where this night's festivities would be held. They flanked her two in front, two in back and one on either side.

The garden and the road leading toward it were ablaze with colored lights and Japanese lanterns, and the ballroom was decorated with great baskets of lilies and had sunbursts of roses around the Persian and Western-style orchestras. The hundreds of lavishly dressed and bejeweled guests (more than a thousand would be accommodated during the three nights) rose from their seats on Barbara's entrance and applauded her.

As she walked to the gold and red velvet covered chairs on

which Bahram, his parents and grandparents sat at the far end of the room, all the guests blew kisses at her.

Soon after Barbara took her place beside Bahram, Khanoum-June, sitting on her other side, rose from her chair to stand behind Barbara's. She caressed her forehead with her cool fingers while she placed a veil over her head. Then the mullah, looking like a patriarch of old in his beard and black turban, came and sat on a sofa across from Bahram and Barbara, and delivered a discourse to which Barbara listened solemnly as though the words made sense.

After the mullah left, Bahram told Barbara that they were one-third married, and the party began in earnest. Servants moved among the guests with champagne, cocktails and lavish bottles of arrak, as well as imported liquors of every variety. And belly dancers, clowns and singers moved about everywhere, entertaining the guests.

Finally Sheherezade, a premier dancer, appeared. Her long black hair flowed out behind her and the sequins on her red satin dress flashed as she leaped and gyrated, then wiggled and shook her body in front of Hajji Khadivar, trying to entice him to dance with her. When he would not, she began a hypnotic gyration in front of Baba Bozorg that Barbara had to admit was thrilling. She felt a little sick, though, at the look on Baba Bozorg's face as he watched Sheherezade; he sat looking into her eyes, swaying back and forth to the sound of the cymbals and fiddles and drums. And when the music exploded and the dance ended, and Sheherezade stood before him holding her hands out for a money offering, he dropped a full purse at her feet. Then he joined her where she stood, and moved against her 'til she screamed in a simulation of wild orgasm.

Barbara, fuming at the display, could not take her eyes off Khanoum-June watching them with her magnificent face in repose, without expression. And as she turned to Barbara and read her feelings in her eyes, she smiled and reached for her hand. Barbara's heart filled with the greatest admiration for Khanoum-June. Where, she asked herself, does she get such strength as enables her not only to rise above her public humiliation, but also to offer me consolation over what she is going through?

At eleven o'clock, gongs summoned the party into the garden, where tables had been set up for the wedding feast. There was wild duck with pomegranates, lamb with prunes seasoned with cinnamon, ground beef with spinach and orange juice, camel meat with onion and egg on skewers, hot <u>dolmehs</u>, cabbage leaves wrapped around meat, cold dolmehs and grape leaves wrapped around currants. And baklava and halvah and <u>paludeh</u>, an ice cream made of fruits and melted snow that came from the mountaintops. At midnight, the lights dimmed and forty-eight male servants marched out in single file, carrying a dozen whole roasted lambs suspended from long horizontal poles. Each lamb head sprouted a slender, long, sparkling candle.

Dinner continued 'til four o'clock in the morning and dancing until noon, when Barbara fell into bed, exhausted. Her second wedding day was much the same as the first, except that this time her gown was green satin and her train was white. And the guests were younger than those on the first night, and the mood was gayer.

The third and final day, though, to which only the family had been invited, was something for which neither Barbara's zealous three-month preparation nor conversations with Farah had equipped her. Wearing a white gown with a hoop and bejeweled ruffles, and a long veil, she was escorted to a room off the main ballroom where the women awaited her while Bahram and the men were congregated in the ballroom. An exquisite piece of Persian silk with gold thread woven into its design was spread in the center of the room, and Barbara sat in its middle with a mirror and tall candelabra behind her, and a copy of the Koran beside her.

After minutes that seemed like hours, she looked in the mirror to see Bahram in a red velvet jacket kneeling behind her as the mullah asked her whether she was being forced into the marriage. When she answered <u>nockhair</u> (no), he asked her whether she would take Bahram to be her husband. Eyes downcast, she did not answer. He asked her again and she, continuing to play shy, made no reply. The third time he asked, though, she lifted her head, smiled, and said a soft "Yes". At that the women squealed and everyone clapped. Then Khanoum-June, standing behind Barbara, crushed two cubes of sugar between her fingers, allowing a stream of crystals to fall on her head; this signified she would always be sweet to her husband. Tradition follows the rolling of the sugar with the closing of the mouth of the mother-in-law by a relative of the bride who sews into the air with needle and thread. But since Barbara had no relatives there, the sewing did not occur.

Now Bahram and Barbara, clasping hands, ran upstairs to the bridal suite Toobah had prepared for them. They were followed, to Barbara's shock, by a throng of shoving, shrieking people who remained outside their door after they'd closed it.

Barbara rushed into Bahram's arms, kissing his head, his face, his neck. He did not kiss her back, but instead tore off her dress, pulled down her panties, and pushed her onto the bed. Without undressing himself, he forced himself into her.

She heard a scream, hers; it was more a ripping sound than a scream, and it mixed maniacally with the tumult from outside. For an instant she had a crazy sensation that she was imagining this rape, for that was what it was; the entire thing had been a nightmare, and in a minute she would wake up. But no, there Bahram was, looking at her smilingly but with no expression of regret for what he'd done. He wiped up her blood with his handkerchief, then sprang off the bed and opened the door to the sight of a hundred people watching Barbara cowering there. Grinning, he handed the handkerchief to Toobah, who waved it while the crowd cheered and kept looking in at Barbara. She wanted to scream at them to go away, but she couldn't talk. She felt so little and so alone and so dumb to have followed this stranger called Bahram to this hostile land. Why had Bahram first raped her, then put her on exhibit like an animal or a freak in a show? Why had they, her other family, even including Khanoum-June, gotten together to inflict this nightmare on her? She covered her head with the sheet, making a tent to hide herself; she saw Farah's face there, heard her say, "Now, the mystery's solved, isn't it, Barbara? Now you know WHY I've got to have my hymen reconstructed." And Barbara saw Khanoum-June's and Mitrah's and Toobah's faces under her tent.

And she saw Bahram's face and said to herself..."I wonder if I'll ever want to make love to him again. I wonder if I'll ever forget, in a moment of sex, how he first raped, then humiliated me on my wedding night."

And she admitted to herself that loving and needing Bahram as she did, she might, in that moment of sex, forget everything but him. And she despised herself for that. She felt like she'd died and been born again in the last hour. She'd died a warm, caring, idealistic girl filled with joy at the thought of Bahram and her being together as man and wife, as two human beings loving and sharing everything, and was reborn a slut.

When she finally emerged from under the sheet, she realized that the people outside were gone and Bahram and she were alone. He rose from the bed, combed his hair, straightened his clothes and smiled.

"You and I showed them a thing or two, Barbara."

"Showed who?"

"The wedding guests."

"What'd we show them?"

"We showed them that I could go to America and find a virgin bride there." As much as anything, it was the cast of his voice Barbara couldn't bear...all rowdy, and breaking into a kind of adolescent snicker.

"So that is what all this is about," she said. "You had to show those people out there you'd landed an American virgin. My God, Bahram, you didn't MAKE LOVE to me tonight, you RAPED me, because all you cared about was getting blood on your handkerchief. Those people out there, and SHOWING THEM, are more important to you than I am, aren't they?"

Bahram did not answer her accusation of the raping; it was as though he hadn't heard it as he said, "It's not a question of importance to ME, although that handkerchief did demonstrate my virility, and I won't pretend that isn't of some moment to me. But the real reason for the handkerchief lies in my tradition; my religion demands my bride to prove she's a virgin to my family and friends."

In 1958, and indeed throughout Mohammed Reza's later reign, the families of even the most sophisticated urban bridegrooms often insisted on medical inspections, and the operation Farah planned to have was not unusual. But the "dost-mal-e-jofaf" (the ceremony of the bloodied handkerchief) which Barbara experienced was certainly not the practice of the majority of Tehran's young. The wealthy young mocked it as a tribal custom, or worse, a primitive carry-over from the 19th century. Some tyrannical heads of families like Baba Bozorg, though, *were* 19th, not 20th century men. They paid homage to their 19th century customs and insisted their children and grandchildren abide by them. And as rebellious as a Bahram or Farah might be in their hearts, when they married they didn't dare to defy Baba Bozorg openly. The best they could hope was that the dost-mal-e-jofaf would be witnessed only by family members, and that their friends whose parents and grandparents were more Western-oriented would not discover their submission.

Bahram, though, would not tell Barbara that Baba Bozorg and Hajji Khadivar were responsible for her humiliation; he preferred to blame it on "my religion and tradition."

Barbara said, aghast, "Are you telling me then that your tradition required you to humiliate your bride as you did me, that your religion..."

Bahram said that they would discuss the philosophy and traditions of his religion at some future time, because all he wanted to talk about now was the wonderful surprise that he'd arranged for Barbara. The best part of their wedding was still to come. Mohammed Reza himself would welcome Barbara at a party he was giving her and Bahram at the Golestan Palace.

CHAPTER VII

The Shah's Party

The Golestan Palace, the Palace of Roses given by Mohammed Reza to the country as a museum in 1971, is unlike any other palace in the world. Salons, reception halls, a throne room are made only of glittery, shiny mirrors, all molded by hand into cubes, triangles, flowers and all kinds of incredible shapes. It is easy, in such a place, to imagine the characters out of your books of fairy tales carrying on their enchanted lives. Princesses being kissed awake by handsome prices, wicked queens poisoning their pretty stepdaughters, kings turning into lions and lions into kings.

And Barbara thought that Shah Mohammed Reza Pahlavi and his Shahbanou Soraya were the perfect rulers for such an incredible place. Soraya was like a fairy tale queen, twenty-five, with a figure like a ballerina; her face was a perfect oval, and her green eyes dominated her face. She wore a red taffeta gown, and her black hair, gleaming with blue lights, was pulled back in a tight chignon and topped by a magnificent diamond tiara.

Mohammed Reza was thirty-seven years old, five-foot-eight, lean and straight with heavy, black graying hair and eyebrows, a strong jaw, and a fine Persian nose. But the cut and fit of his medal-laden, full-dress purple uniform, when Barbara inspected it while on the receiving line, startled her. The tight blouse emphasized the curve of Mohammed Reza's chest and the strength of his back. And his pants came up tight against his crotch and around his buttocks, giving an impression of bold eroticism rather than dignity and majesty. Barbara wondered how Mohammed Reza dared indulge in such an effect. Today she believes that he was able to dare such because he had been imbued with the belief that, no matter how he dressed or what he did, his royalty would have been apparent to anyone who viewed him. He felt he was, quite simply, SUPERIOR TO ALL OTHER PEOPLE OF THE EARTH.

Bending to kiss Mohammed Reza's hand with its incredible

diamond, infinitely more massive than even the one worn by Baba Bozorg, Barbara said, "I can't thank you enough, Your Majesty, for giving Bahram and me this party."

He smiled, his teeth as white as snow, but his eyes were not warm, and neither was his voice as he said, "I hate to disillusion you so early in your time with us, Barbara, but I must tell you anyhow, that this party's to honor our guests from Denmark and Egypt, not you and your husband. As for his having told you it was in your and his honor...Bahram Mosallai, being Persian, doesn't regard sticking to the truth as any kind of virtue."

But Soraya, defined by many as capricious, childlike and arrogant, was so warm and friendly that she forever endeared herself to Barbara. She left her place on the reception line and led Barbara into a quiet corner. There they sat alone and Soraya asked Barbara questions about her life in America, and told her about her own life. Her family name was Esfandiari; the name signified a sub-tribe of the fierce Bahktiaris of Isfahan whose masses were poor nomads, but whose leaders, tribal princes and princesses were among Iran's "beautiful people". They were wealthy, foreign-educated, multi-lingual (Soraya herself spoke fluent French, Russian, German and English), more international than Iranian.

Soraya's grandfather dominated the region in southwest Iran where oil was first found; her father studied and played in London, Rome and Paris. He met her Russian-born German mother in Germany, married her and lived in Berlin, Zurich, Lausanne and London with her and their only child until Soraya was seven, when they returned to Isfahan. They left again when Soraya was fifteen.

She was twenty and in school in London when she was introduced to Mohammed Reza by his sister Shams. He had, two years earlier, divorced the Egyptian Princess Fawzia. Soraya married the Shah a year after they met.

Soraya did not dismiss Barbara until after half an hour of conversation, and said she was sure that they'd be seeing more of each other. Barbara, though, never saw Soraya again, and the last she heard about her was in November of 1958 when the Shah, his voice breaking, told the nation on TV that "I come before you tonight brokenhearted. I am divorcing my wife, the love of my life, because the high interests of this nation require an heir, and she has been unable to conceive." Those who loved Soraya, including Barbara, believed that Princess Ashraf, Mohammed's twin, had given Soraya drugs to make her sterile because she was jealous of her brother's great love for her.

After Soraya dismissed her, Barbara was approached by a tall, distinguished-looking man in white gloves and a charcoal-gray uniform. In British English, he told her that His Majesty's Minister of Court, to whom he was "a humble assistant," requested in his Imperial Majesty's own name the honor of her presence in the Royal Theater for a private showing of her country's film, *The Merry Widow*.

. The theater was in total darkness, though the film had not yet begun. Barbara swooned with delight as she entered with her elegant escort, who seated her with a pomp and ceremony usually accorded to the Empress herself. He even wiped her velvet chair many times with his white-gloved hand before permitting her, finally, to sit. She had just begun to relax in her seat, though, when she felt something crawling down her bare back. At the same time she heard women's voices shrieking and screaming in panic.

Lights came on then to reveal an audience of about sixty, equally divided between men and women. Most of the women were standing, as was Barbara, and shaking spiders and frogs off themselves. Mohammed Reza was there also and was in a mischievous humor. He laughed hilariously at what was obviously one of his jokes. He was flanked by his Court Minister's assistant and three other tall, handsome men, also done up in gray uniforms. They may have been the ones who planted the spiders and frogs. All the company joined the Shah in his merriment, the men giving out with "good-old-boy" raucous laughter. It reminded Barbara of the good-old-boys' attitudes she saw in Indianapolis at the Saturday night parties of her mother's brother and brother-in-law.

Barbara hunted everywhere for Aysha and Farah, who were also at the party that night. When she saw them, she yelled at them for failing to warn her about the humiliation she'd undergone earlier.

"The ceremony of...Aysha, what kind of religion is Islam to impose such a ceremony? SOME CEREMONY! GOD! And speaking of God, will you tell me what kind of cruel God this Allah is, and who exactly is his prophet Mohammed, to give Bahram and his family the right to TURN ME INTO A PUBLIC SHOW?" Barbara wept.

Aysha wiped her tears with a handkerchief, and told her that Islam was Islam, Allah was Allah, and Bahram and his family were Bahram and his family. Barbara was making a mistake when she lumped them together. The custom of dost-mal-e-jofaf was not, nor ever had been, a part of Islam. Mohammed never claimed that Allah decreed that brides be put through public humiliation. "I promise you that Mohammed, if he were alive today, would rise up in righteous wrath at such a 'ceremony'," Aysha declared.

"But Bahram told me that the dost-mal, whatever, is a definite part of his religion and tradition."

Yes, Aysha replied, Bahram was right when he told Barbara that dost-mal-e-jofaf was part of his tradition, but he was lying when he claimed it was also part of his religion. The Koran, as Mohammed spoke it in the 7th century, was compassionate toward and respectful of women. It was the historic Baba Bozorgs and Hajji Khadivars who perverted the Koran to suit their patriarchal purposes. "Anyone who knows how women in Arabia were treated at the time Allah revealed Himself to Mohammed," Aysha stated, "will have to know also that the Prophet came as a savior, not enslaver of women."

CHAPTER VIII

The Tribal Family

The first thing that Bahram said to Barbara the day after her marriage and the Shah's party was, "It is my desire, Barbara, that you become a Muslim."

She stared at him for several stunned moments, then said, "Why, Bahram?"

"For the reason that it will please Baba Bozorg and my mother."

"But what about my mother? How do you think it will make her feel to know that I've given up Christianity? And, aside from her, I myself feel that..."

"First of all," Bahram interrupted, "what you mother doesn't know won't hurt her. And as for you, we both know, don't we, Barbara, that you're not such a passionate Christian? And anyway...Listen, nobody's asking you to give up Christianity in your heart, or to accept Islam as a true believer. All I want you to do for my mother's sake is to proclaim yourself a Muslim, and go to mosque on Fridays. That's not asking too much, is it?"

Barbara answered that there were plenty of things she would lie about, but that "when it comes to religion, that's one thing I can't bring myself to be anything but honest about."

"There you go again, Miss Holier-Than-Thou, Smart-Ass American," Bahram rasped out, no longer nonchalant.

This time Barbara, full of bitterness over last night's rape, met his anger with her own, screaming out that if being honest about a matter as important as religion made her a 'Miss Holier-Than-Thou, Smart-Ass American', she was proud to be it.

Contemptuously Bahram hissed, almost in a whisper, "You and your fucking American honesty. You!"

Barbara didn't know at the time that one overwhelming difference between her and Bahram, or rather his culture and hers, was her "fucking American honesty." How could she, a product of a Puritanical background, ever have understood him who had been

brought up from babyhood to believe that dishonesty and its vari-
ants—duplicity, guile, pretense—were not only acceptable, but also
desirable? That any trickery is permissible so long as it isn't discovered? How could she have hoped to penetrate a civilization whose
generations-old proverbs caution people to "conceal thy gold, thy
destination and thy creed?", and whose poet Saadi wrote as long ago
as 1300 that "well-meaning falsehoods are better than truths." And
whose people support, even honors taquiyah, the art of dissem-
blance? There is a reason for this; the early Sunni Muslims who
dominated what is now Iraq would not permit the Iranian Shiites to
make pilgrimages there, and therefore they had to profess themselves Sunnis if they wished to honor their God. But the mass of
Persians do not know the history, and so take the instruction at face
value, using it to justify their own acts.

From the day of Barbara's arrival in Iran, Bahram and she
clashed over their cultural differences. She had expected to have a
home of her own, shared only with her husband and children. He
could not comprehend her misery at living in a tribal family. She
resented his constant allegiance to his mother; he was angered at this
resentment. She was humiliated by his shameless groveling to Baba
Bozorg; he was furious because she did not grovel. She wanted to
spend all her time with him; he grudgingly gave her an hour or two
before escaping to his male friends. Barbara believed that she and
Bahram would live together as equals. Bahram had been bred
according to the Islamic proverb that "a woman should question her
husband three times a day. What to think, what to say and what to
do", and so found her demands for equality intolerable. After all, he
was the son of Hajji Khadivar, and Hajji Khadivar had married
Toobah when she was only twelve so he could "mold her as a father
does a child."

Bahram thought he could do the same with Barbara. When he
discovered those first few months that he could not, he was filled
with fury. That fury was even expressed when they were making
love.

One night, two and a half months into the marriage, Barbara
was wakened by Bahram at five o'clock in the morning. He was a lit-

tle bit drunk, a little bit sick after a night on the town; she could smell perspiration and vomit on him.

She heard him taking off his clothes and hurling them aside; heard his breath resembling an animal's dry panting. He got into bed, lay down beside her and said, "Well, are you ready?" And then suddenly he was on her, he was in her, he was like a pole. She panicked. "Let me go! Please let me go. Please." She cried out in agony, and only stopped when she realized her cries of pain were only titillating Bahram, making him harsher and more ferocious.

She lay deathly still then, submitting to him with resignation while thinking to herself, "GOD, GOD, IT SHOULDN'T BE LIKE THIS," and struggling to find a way to make him feel, or at least understand, some of what she was feeling.

"Bahram," she said, after he was at last done with her, "you've got to tell me why you need to diminish and degrade me all the time. If I were Persian instead of American..."

"Diminish? Degrade? I don't know what you're talking about."

"I'm talking about every time we make love, have sex I mean, I'm left feeling humiliated, dirty. I thought our marriage was going to be so perfect; you seemed to care so much about my happiness when we were in America, and now when we make love...have sex, I mean...it's like 'zip zam, thank you ma'am.' Only, all I get is the zip zam, not even any thank you, ma'am."

"Thank you for what, ma'am? You happen to be my wife."

"I'm not...You say 'wife' like you mean 'slave', Bahram. Doesn't my satisfaction, my pleasure...?"

"Look Barbara, it's late and I'm exhausted, so stop nagging, okay?"

"Okay," she said, "I'll stop nagging, because if you've had it with me, then I have had it with you, too. I want you, from now on, to stay the hell away from me...Oh, my God, let's not be like this, Bahram, please let's try to make it together."

She reached into the drawer of her nighttable and took out a copy of a Japanese sex manual she had, placing it in his hands. "Do me a favor, Bahram, do us both a favor, and read..."

Bahram threw the book down hard as he rasped out that he did not need any guidance from either her or her "foreign sexperts."

For the next few weeks Barbara, disgusted at even the thought of being touched by Bahram, pretended to be asleep when he came to her. And he, either because he was too drunk or didn't actually care, never made much of an effort to waken her.

Then she discovered she was pregnant, and for a few days afterward felt like dying. She didn't want a baby conceived as this one had to have been, on the ugly night of her marriage. The only satisfaction she had when she heard the news was in assuring herself that now she could give Bahram a little taste of his own medicine. She'd be in a position to taunt him, say to him, "You married me because you wanted sons. And now a child is going to be born to us. And since I'm leaving you, you'll never see that child, never even know if it's the son you've longed for."

But then something happened in Barbara, and she thought that, for the child's sake, she really ought to attempt to make the marriage work. Also, her feelings for Bahram were not totally dead. There were so many happy recollections of their time in California.

And what, she asked herself, had changed Bahram so much? Would he have been different if they'd remained in America, away from the influence of his parents and grandparents? She thought he might have been, and fantasized about their returning to America and beginning a new life there. Yet she knew this couldn't be.

Then she wondered whether her reaction to Bahram's world and the people he held most precious, her maligning them as she had, had not been one cause of his terrible response to her. She wondered whether their miserable sexual relationship was not also partly her fault. Hadn't she been arrogant and selfish also? Carping, complaining, calling Bahram a rotten lover to his face. Had she been any more sensitive to his needs than he had been to hers? Had she ever once troubled to ask him what she could do to please him?

With these thoughts in mind, she ignored his drunken condition the next time he came to her, and threw her arms around him, intending to tell him about the baby. No, before she'd do that she would admit to her share of the blame for what was wrong between them.

"I love you, Bahram," she whispered, "and I want to make you happy. Just tell me how, my darling."

"If you want to make me happy, hot for you," he retorted, the ugly adolescent sound in his voice again, "roll over then."

"What do you mean,'roll over'?"

"I mean roll over and give me your ass. I want to fuck you in the ass, have anal sex as your manuals would put it. And if you'd consulted Persian sexperts instead of foreign ones, you'd know that Persian men relish ass-fucking above anything else."

Bahram was neither misinterpreting nor exaggerating some Persian men's preference for anal sex. Since Persian men married late, they had to find sexual outlets other than those available to their peers in more permissive societies. Prostitutes offered some relief, and the men sometimes entered into homosexual liaisons. And some women of respectability would engage in oral or anal sex, since their virginity would still remain intact.

Barbara did not, at the time, realize the reasons behind Bahram's demand for anal sex, but really, that was not important. Her roommates and she had talked a good deal about sex, and had concluded that anything that pleased two people in love was all right...It wasn't the idea of anal sex that hurt Barbara, it was the nasty, vulgar way that Bahram had demanded it. Barbara began to cry and asked him, still again, whether he would "diminish and debase a Persian wife as you do me."

Bahram answered that he would not need to diminish and debase a Persian wife because she would have been raised to know that her function, in return for the home, children and security that her husband gave her, was to satisfy him sexually, and in every way. And she would never dare demand that he satisfy her. "So turn over, Barbara, and give me your fucking ass."

Barbara heard this with an ache in her stomach and brain as well as her heart. She leaned back in the bed and closed her eyes, going into a quiet, darkened place in her mind. There she saw America, her grandmother and her school friends in California. Then, to her surprise, she heard herself as though she were hearing another woman in agony, a strange woman she loved but did not know personally, assaulting Bahram with words through breaths of choking air. "You sick, crazy son-of-a-bitch...PERVERT. I'm not...Oh, my God, but you're sick. Don't come near me, don't ever come near me again, or I'll..."

She was interrupted by a stream of stomach-turning obscenities from Bahram, an avalanche of filth that shocked her into immobility. And Bahram jumped astride her, still cursing, beating her, hurting her. Holding down her shoulders, he bit at her lips and pummeled and struck her everywhere, finally rousing her to punch back, bite back, and rake his shoulders with her nails.

When she came to herself again, Barbara realized that Bahram had enjoyed her fury and relished her attack on him. She could tell it because he had a superior look on his face, a smirk of self-satisfaction, as he got up off the bed and told her as he left the room that he'd always be available when she felt ready for another "such stimulating encounter." She obviously "got off" by beating and being beaten, didn't she? Actually, so did he.

Bahram's words, the smirk on his face, as well as everything else that had taken place revealed, finally, that he had such utter hatred and contempt for Barbara that no compromise between them was possible any more, that she could not survive in his home and presence for another day. And now that she was pregnant there was even more reason for her to leave. She felt she must confront Bahram immediately, force him to give her money so she could leave him.

She looked for him in the suite he'd occupied before their marriage and still kept, and in Toobah's quarters where he spent so much more time than he did in Barbara's. She searched in Mitrah's suite and, feeling faint, in the room assigned to Mohammed, saying to herself over and over again, "Oh God, God, I hope I don't find what I'm afraid I will. Because if I do, it will signify Bahram's ultimate diminishment, his ultimate debasement of me as his wife." She went to Mohammed's room prepared to bang the door down if she had to. Instead, it was unlocked. And there were Bahram and Mohammed having sex. Barbara had the feeling that Bahram had wanted, had willed her to find them.

She looked at him grinning at her from the bed, and at

Mohammed beside him, who appeared even paler than usual. He wrapped his arms around himself, and Barbara could see that he had tears in his eyes as he looked from Bahram to her and back to Bahram again. It was a look of slavish devotion, whenever his eyes caught Bahram's, a dog's look at its master.

Incredibly, she found herself desperately sorry for Mohammed, as sorry as she was for herself; both of them were Bahram's victims. She stood at the door, head held deliberately high, and said in the coolest voice she could muster, "Bahram, I just came here to tell you that I'm leaving you tonight. Right now. What I see in this room...I'm not surprised at it; I had to know that you and Mohammed were lovers; I couldn't bear to admit it to myself but, really, I knew it all the time." She turned to Mohammed and said, "I want you to know, for whatever it may be worth to you, that I'm leaving Bahram for many reasons, and what I've seen here is only one among many."

Then she told Bahram over her shoulder as she walked out the door fast, "You may also be interested to know that I'm carrying your baby, maybe the son you want so much."

Back in the suite she brought out trunks and suitcases and was throwing things into them when Bahram came in. He tried to put his arms around her, and she sprang away from him. "YOU DIS-GUST ME. You make me sick to my stomach. You..."

"Barbara, please let me explain, Mohammed doesn't mean any-thing to me. He's just a...nothing, a..."

She said in a soft tone that conveyed her venom more effectively than a scream could do, "If he's such a nothing to you, Bahram, then how come you'll risk being publicly humiliated...Let's suppose that, instead of leaving as I intend, I chose to stay and fight, to tell people what you are...To tell the Shah what you are...I could embar-rass you so much that you'd never again be able to hold up your head in Iran."

Bahram smiled slightly and said, "But Barbara, I wouldn't be the least embarrassed if you told anyone, or everyone, including Mohammed Reza, that you'd found me fucking Mohammed in the ass. Listen, plenty of men in Iran fuck their menservants. The only disgrace for me would be if you'd found him fucking me. The fucker's a man, the way we see it in Iran; the fuckee's a shit."

Inconceivably, he had such a look of pride that Barbara was almost, but not quite, frozen into silence.

"My God," she finally screeched out, "your 'fuckee', your 'shit' Mohammed, is really in love with you. Don't you even give a damn that he cares for you the way he does?"

"Barbara, listen, I don't want to talk about Mohammed...You and I are the ones who count, especially now that we'll have...Oh, I'm so happy about our son."

"Why, Bahram?"

"Why what?"

"Why are you so happy about our...son, if my baby turns out to be a son?"

"Every Iranian wants sons, Barbara."

"Yes, but why are you so anxious for my son?"

"Because I love you."

Barbara knew by now that if Bahram had loved her once, he did not anymore, and that his eagerness for her son was motivated by something other than love.

As indeed it was.

During Barbara's years in Iran, the Shah and his advisers courted America as vigorously as they ever would in the coming years. They bought American military supplies, hired American advisors for civilian and governmental programs, solicited American governmental and business investments, and granted America 40% of the shares of the world's consortium for exploitation of Iranian oil.

These were also the years when American-style music, dance and slang became, even more intensely than before, the manias of the upper and middle classes. And to have an American wife, and especially a half-American son, was considered to be a passport to success.

"My child is my child, Bahram," Barbara screamed out, "and I'm going back to America where I'm going to become a person again; I'm going to go back to school and become a doctor after my child is born. I know my grandparents will help us."

"You might as well know sooner as later, Barbara," Bahram waved the cigar he was smoking, "that you are being carried away when you talk about going back to America; you are indulging in a fantasy."

"What the hell are you talking about?"

"I'm talking about...I do not intend to give my permission for you to leave Iran."

"Permission? Permission? I AM NOT YOUR PROPERTY, BAHRAM."

"Ah, but you ARE my property, according to the laws of Iran; therefore, you can't travel to America or any other place without my permission in writing."

"That's the craziest thing I ever...I have an American passport."

Bahram folded his arms, smiling sardonically. "When you married me, Barbara, you became an Iranian citizen; the fact that you have an American passport is, therefore, irrelevant."

"I never gave up my American citizenship."

"You gave up your citizenship, Barbara, on the day that you married me."

"I don't believe a word you are saying," Barbara screamed.

Bahram gazed at her coolly and said, "Ask Farah if you don't believe me, ask your precious Aysha. Or, better yet, ask the people at your Embassy."

At the Embassy, Barbara was escorted into the office of Edward Springer, the American consul, whom she had often met at parties. He greeted her warmly, and asked about Bahram and Hajji Khadivar and Baba Bozorg.

She said, "Edward, I can't tell you much about the men of my family, including my husband, since I don't see them very often. Besides...forgive me for saying I'm not here to socialize, but...look, I'm pregnant and I want to, I MUST leave Bahram, go back to America, and he tells me I can't...I mean he says that I can't go anyplace out of the country without his written permission, and..."

"My dear, I'm so sorry to have to tell you..." He let the sentence hang and said, "Please, may I fix you a drink?"

"No. Are you telling me, that Bahram is telling the truth, and that I have no choice but to remain here as his slave, and that you, my own government representative, are not going to lift a finger to help me? Are you telling me...?"

"I'm afraid that, yes, that's exactly what I am telling you. When you married Bahram, Barbara, you automatically became a Iranian citizen and must, therefore, abide by the Iranian marital laws, much as we despise and disrespect them. You're not the first American woman to whom I've had to tell this, and believe me it hurts me very much."

"HURTS YOU!" she screamed, "hurts you! Well, if it hurts you so much, why don't you...?"

Why didn't he what? She couldn't think of what she'd started to say to him; she couldn't think of anything. Her brain was chilled.

He said, "Barbara, we have counselors here at the Embassy to advise American women, many of whom are in your position...If you knew the number of American women who want nothing more than to escape their Iranian husbands, and yet...American women married to Iranians must abide by Iranian marital laws...Listen, please let me arrange an interview with a counselor..."

"These counselors," Barbara asked, "are they going to tell me what I need to do to get to America?"

"No, there's nothing they can tell you, nothing I can tell you...Iranian law states..."

"You've already told me what it states. And all I want to know from you now is, what about the American law that's supposed to protect me and my unborn child as American citizens?"

"Iran does not recognize dual-citizenship, Barbara. And since you became a Persian citizen when you married..."

"But what about you, Edward, what about America? Don't you recognize me as an American citizen?"

"You must know, Barbara, that it doesn't matter what I...we...recognize. Iran is our host country and, much as it hurts and goes against the grain, we, like you, must abide...Please believe that if there was anything in the world we could do to help you, we would."

His face was kind, he seemed concerned, yet Barbara turned on him. "All my life," she shrieked, "I was proud to be an American, proud of what I thought of as American compassion and mercy and justice. Well, now I can't believe in all that any more, and I tell you that to lose my belief is...I can't accept that America would leave me, leave any American woman to a life of..."

Edward reached out to take Barbara's hand, but she pulled away from him and rose stiffly from her seat. Her limbs felt as if all the juice in them had dried up, and she walked out of the room as if she were a cripple.

All the way home in the speeding taxi she held her head in her hands and felt ill, giddy, as though she were going to vomit. She would be Bahram's slave. And not only his, but also Hajji Khadivar's, Baba Bozorg's and every man's in that extended family.

Once Barbara arrived home she regained outward control of herself. She sought Bahram, and when she found him she told him of her discussion with Springer. "Now, I've no choice but to throw myself on your mercy and ask you, for the sake of whatever it was I once meant to you, to give me your written permission to return to America. I'll do anything if you'll only...In the name of common decency, say you'll let me go."

"No."

"My God, Bahram, why do you want to keep me here when...Look, you've made it clear that you don't give a damn about me, that you despise me, in fact. So I'm asking, I'm begging, I'm going on my knees for your permission."

"Get off your knees, Barbara, you don't crawl with style like some women do. Stop whining and let's talk like adults, all right?"

"Oh yes," she said, rising and looking him in the eye, "like adults. As one adult to another then, Bahram, just tell me what I can do that will melt your heart—excuse me, I mean, compel you to let me go. I'll do anything you want in return for my freedom."

If what Barbara meant by freedom was Bahram's giving her permission to return to America, he said no, that was out. For the time being anyway. He wanted, needed, her there to bear his son...his half-American son...as well as to serve as his hostess and companion at important functions.

These two services were all that he required of her, and he was willing to pay high for them. He would supply her with all of the clothes and jewels she wanted, as long as she dressed as he required whenever they appeared together publicly. She would have a home of her own and receive an allowance equivalent to five thousand American dollars a month, no strings attached, no questions asked about what she did with the money. She could return to school, travel anywhere she wanted within Iran, and after her baby was born, she could travel to Europe and even America. But she would have to leave the child behind, with him. She had Bahram's guarantee that he wouldn't interfere in any life she chose to lead, provided that she did not become an object of gossip or embarrassment to him. "Well, do you accept my bargain?"

Quietly, grimly, Barbara asked, "What's my alternative, Bahram?"

Bahram grinned as he said, "You don't really have one, do you, my dear?"

CHAPTER IX

The Wiping Out of Shame

For weeks after her "arrangement" with Bahram, Barbara felt hideously empty. She could not bear thinking about her life before Iran. And she didn't want to think about the future because it was too frightening. She lived one day at a time, and all that made each day bearable were Aysha and Farah and the loving attentions they gave to her.

Aysha carried through on the promise she'd made to Barbara on her wedding night, to teach her about the true Islam and Mohammed the Prophet, and the contemporary patriarchal interpretation of it. Barbara went every day to the fern-green, book-lined den of the flat Aysha shared with Peri, a friend, colleague and lover, as Barbara would later learn. Aysha, who happened to be a consummate actress as well as a superlative teacher, dramatized all of her lessons so that when they were done, Barbara felt that she knew Mohammed well—knew his Meccan city people and desert Bedouins personally. She was able to see, in her mind's eye, the scenes Aysha created for her.

Scene One: Day had come suddenly to the watering place in the great Nafud desert, where a dozen or so goat-hair tents had been pitched for three days to shelter a small Bedouin tribe. Now, in 110-degree heat, the people had to move on to a new watering place, because the sweet grass of this one was almost exhausted and the camels had to be fed. The move entailed a two-day march.

In front of each tent, lying in a loose semi-circle below the crown of the dunes, rose a column of blue smoke from a camel-dung fire where the women, with their veils loosened, prepared rice, bread and coffee to break the night's fast.

But the wheat and rice were running out, and there was no other food. Walid, the tribal sheik, a man of dignity in his cloak of fine brown camel's hair edged with gold, sang out, "I want you in front of my tent, O my people."

And when the people were gathered, he instructed the men to bring the baby girls to him; the men, in turn, instructed the women to bring them. And when the four baby girls, one newborn and the others less than a year old, were delivered to him, Walid strangled them, their arms and legs thrashing about, until they were dead. Then he cut off their arms and legs and chopped up the little bodies into small parts.

"And now bring me your sons, O my people," he commanded the men, and they commanded the women.

Six little boys came with their mothers to the sheik's tent and sat cross-legged in front of his fire to receive their shares of their sisters. They crammed the flesh into their mouths with bloodied fingers.

Scene Two: It was night in the bleak, barren country immediately outside the gates of Mecca. A mob of turbaned men, their beards gray with desert dust, their sun-browned faces filled with hate, surrounded a barefoot, bareheaded girl with eyes of terror highlighted by a leaping fire. One tall, powerful man stepped out of the crowd and shouted, "This is the woman taken in adultery! This is the abomination of our tribe!"

He kneeled, picked up a stone and threw it at the girl with force. Now that the first stone had been cast by their leader, the other men gathered ammunition and threw it 'til the girl became unconscious. Then the crowd broke loose and rushed to her fallen body, dropping on it rocks too heavy to have been thrown, until the girl was completely crushed.

"The wiping out of shame with blood"—such was the punishment for adultery, before the advent of Allah and Mohammed.

Barbara asked Aysha whether the Meccans, the people who lived in the city before Allah and Mohammed, were as ruthless toward their girls and women as the Bedouins.

Aysha answered that the Meccans *were* Bedouins who had come to the city looking for a better life, and having settled along important caravan routes, they became wealthy and didn't need, any longer, to feed their sons with their daughters' bodies or bury their girls before they became mouths to feed. The only reason for burying daughters now was shame. And some people, perhaps many, controlled their feelings and permitted girl-babies to live. But they continued to be as savage toward adulteresses as their desert brothers were. And they chipped away at the rights of their women who were not adulteresses or offenders against other traditions in a way the Bedouin men would never have dared to do.

In Bedouin tribal life, after all, the labor of women who lived to adulthood was as important to a clan's survival as the labor of men. Although the men were the fighters and traders, the women looked after the herds and produced the meat, wool, yogurt and cheese necessary for life. And many proved themselves men's equals in war as well, by fighting side by side with them. Then the Bedouins went to Mecca and the women experienced a tragic descent. Suddenly there wasn't any place anymore for independent, spirited women who could hold their own with men. Their work was no longer needed for survival; they became unnecessary. And the wealthy Meccans, the new patriarchs, turned them little by little into nonpeople. They were the ones with whom Mohammed had to battle on the women's account, and in the end, the ones he had to appease and placate.

"If not for those patriarchs and Mohammed's necessary subservience to their demands," Aysha said, "Moslem women might have been, since Mohammed's day, among the most liberated women in the world. If Mohammed had his way...But one must not think like that, because the truth is that if Mohammed had not compromised and played politics with them, the patriarchs would have destroyed him; there wouldn't have been any Islam at all."

Mohammed, Aysha continued, was twenty-five years old at the time Allah appeared to him, and was dark-haired, dark-eyed and very attractive to women. He worked in the caravan of the widow Khadija. Khadija was forty, good-looking, intelligent and as brave and independent as the most intrepid of the leaders among the Bedouin women. She administered her caravan herself, and many Meccan men, like it or not, had to take their orders from her. Mohammed and Khadija fell in love, and she asked him to marry her. This kind of independent behavior was, of course, hardly typical of Bedouin women who had, by then, yielded their freedom to the patriarchs in order to have a roof kept over their heads. But the Khadijas among them were still in a position to play by their own rules.

Mohammed and Khadija, for the twenty-five more years she lived, had the happiest of marriages during which six children were born. Mohammed never desired or even looked at another woman while Khadija lived. She was not only his lover, but also his friend. And she was, though never formally credited for it, Mohammed's co-founder of Islam. Although like all Meccans of the time, she had been born and raised to worship astral deities, through her business she had broad contact with Jewish merchants and Christian monks, and so had knowledge of their religions that she shared with Mohammed. And these discussions readied him spiritually so that when, while meditating in his cave overlooking Mecca, he heard a voice declaring that there was only one omnipotent God and commanding him to convey this to his people, he could define the voice as that of the Angel Gabriel.

The name of the new religion was Islam, meaning submission not to the ungenerous former deities who had to be bought off by blood sacrifices for so long, but to the one great God, Master and Creator of all the world. The great God's name was Allah, after the Zeus of the old Meccan and Greek gods. The converts were called Muslims (those who submit) not Mohammedans, since their fealty was to God, not his prophet.

The Koran is the revelation of God Himself, and of his plan for salvation. The Mojeb, Muslim code of ethics, is much like that of Judaism and Christianity and can, though the rituals are different, be summed up by the Ten Commandments. Islam preaches justice and goodness among all people. The Vajeb comprises Muslims' obligatory acts: to pray five times daily, to recite the creed ("There is no God but God, and Mohammed is His Prophet"), to give alms to the poor, to go, if one can afford it, at least once in one's lifetime to Mecca, and to keep the fast of Ramazan, the month in the lunar year when Mohammed received his first revelation.

A person must adhere to the Mojeb and Vajeb during his lifetime, and must not offend against the Haran that specifies the great sins of Islam, which are: idolatry, murder, adultery, false charges of adultery against women, wasting the estates of orphans, taking interest on money, deserting from holy wars, drinking wine and other spirits, and being insubordinate toward one's parents. If a person commits these offenses, his soul, upon his death, will be torn from his body and thrust into hell where it will be subjected to the most terrible of punishments until the coming of Judgment Day, when it will disintegrate into nothingness.

Meanwhile the souls of the heaven-worthy will be lifted gently out of their bodies and carried heavenward to a Paradise replete with exquisite young <u>houris</u> (as pictured in 17th century Persian miniatures, they await men in the Islamic heaven, catering to their every desire).

Aysha explained that this paradise was, in reality, a part of the political game Mohammed played with the patriarchs on the women's behalf. The men could have their houris in heaven so long as they did not interfere with his activities for advancing women's position on earth. Thus he, whose only living children were daughters whom he treasured as others did sons, was able to abolish men's right to bury their unwanted female children at birth. And in the matter of polygamy...Allah's permission to "marry women of your choice, two or three or four" was given, after all, at a time when men could take as many wives as they wished, and when men who could afford them had harems of hundreds or even thousands.

As for Mohammed's emphasis on women's virginity, it was as politically motivated as any single element of Islam. He had no choice except to assure the patriarchs that the new religion, far from threatening their system, would strengthen it. Keeping Islam's women virgins until they married was one way of reinforcing the patriarchal system. If Mohammed had not given the patriarchs that directive, they'd never have negotiated with him for other important rights for women, like the right to an education. He ruled that learning was "a duty incumbent upon every Muslim, male and female." And he insisted upon women's right to be recognized as legal heir to their fathers' property along with their brothers. True, daughters received only half the property that sons did, but there was a rationale for that—women were supported by their husbands.

Most important of all, though, Mohammed guaranteed certain rights for married women that had been denied them before. Although the men would not give up their old prerogative of divorcing their wives at will, they were now required to pay them a two-part dowry, such as Barbara herself had received. The smaller portion was to be given at marriage, and the much larger one, upon divorce. It was Mohammed's hope that such a monetary arrangement would serve as a deterrent to divorce, but even if it did not, the dowry would necessarily make a vast difference in the lives of the women of the time as it still does today. Farah and her sisters, for instance, would not have been the women they were if Soraya had not had her dowry money. Who would have educated them and made them independent if Soraya had not been able? Mohammed, the father? His sons and grandsons were "the lights of his life", and his daughters and granddaughters, including Farah and her sisters, could not have mattered less. Would Hajji Khadivar have helped? Baba Bozorg? Of course not.

Aysha did not mean to say that all Muslim men rejected their daughters and granddaughters as did the Mosallais under the aegis of Baba Bozorg. But the fact was that Muslim men, the mass of them anyway, assumed no responsibility for the wives and daughters who were repudiated; many women would have been homeless and starving without the dowry. And those with dowries were upper-class women like Soraya. Lower-class women whose dowries were small, and whose families were too poor to take them in when their husbands repudiated them, were starving and homeless.

Barbara asked Aysha whether women in Mohammed's day were free to choose their own husbands. Aysha answered that some people might say a definite "no" to that question, and some a tentative "yes". Aysha herself believed that Mohammed was "speaking out of both sides of his mouth" when he declared that "no one, not even the father and sovereign, can lawfully contract in marriage an adult woman of sound mind whether she be a virgin or not." The catch to this manifesto was that most so-called women were about eight when they became engaged, and ten or so when they moved into their husbands' homes. Therefore, they were neither adult nor could they be considered as being of sound minds. Their fathers, then, remained in a position to negotiate marriages.

In fact, Aysha, Mohammed's favorite wife after Khadija died...the one he respected so totally that he instructed followers to consult her on religious matters when he was out of reach...was only ten years old when he married her. She was eighteen when he died; she then became a political figure to be reckoned with.

And even while Mohammed lived, Aysha—in contrast to Barbara, who was required by Muslim tradition never to speak back to Bahram or to differ with him on any matter—spoke back to the prophet himself. For instance, when he first reported Allah's declaration that, as His prophet, Mohammed did not need to observe the limitation of four wives but could take as many as pleased him, Aysha retorted, "Indeed, Allah always responds immediately to *your* needs."

Barbara wondered, in view of Khadija's and Aysha's independence, why the veil and harem had come to be, and why she was not permitted to express an opinion to Bahram. Aysha told her that nowhere in the Koran is there any mention of the chador as it is worn today. "And say to the believing women," the Koran says, "that they should lower their gaze and guard their modesty; that they should not display their beauty and ornaments except what must ordinarily appear thereof; they should draw their veils over their bosoms..." Over their bosoms, not their faces. The face veil originated as a matter of fashion, not religion. The "beautiful people" of the Middle East, the trend-setters of the time, were the Byzantines and Persians. And since their beauties donned face veils, so did Mohammed's Muslims.

The harem similarly originated in aristocratic Byzantine and Persian society. Aysha's and Bahram's Sassanian ancestors, Kings Shahpur I and Shahpur II, reveled in their harems of not four, but hundreds of wives and courtesans who were both slave and freeborn. This was the case some three hundred years before Allah ever appeared to Mohammed. The Meccan patriarchs of Mohammed's day who kept their women secluded did so not because of enjoinment by the Koran, but in imitation of their elegant subject peoples.

And Mohammed's own first enjoinment to women to separate from men occurred in the late years of his life when he named his wives 'Mothers of Believers', and ordered them, as a matter of dignity, to remain in their quarters separated from the common herd. They could speak to unrelated men only from behind a curtain, and had to veil their bodies when they went out. But the independent wives like Aysha paid the seclusion rule very scant mind, and Mohammed, once he'd proclaimed it, did nothing to enforce it.

Barbara's ultimate question was why, despite women such as Khadija and Aysha, so many Islamic patriarchs consider their women to be their slaves? That was because as Mohammed grew older, richer and more set in his ways, the patriarch in him began receiving messages from Allah such as: "Men are the protectors and maintainers of women because God has given the one more strength than the other, and because they support them from their means. As to women on whose part ye fear disloyalty and ill conduct, (first) admonish them, (next) refuse to share their beds, (and lastly) beat them."

Also partly to blame was Aysha's defeat in the "Battle of the Camel" that occurred in 656 between Aysha, leading her forces of mostly men, and the caliph Ali, husband of Mohammed's favorite daughter, Fatima. Aysha was defeated, and Ali spared her life, but he commanded her to retire from politics and to "confess" that she regretted having gone to battle. "If I had it to do over again," she was ordered to tell, "I would have chosen to remain in my house. The wisdom of doing so would mean more to me than the honor of bearing ten noble and heroic sons to Mohammed."

And Aysha's defeat was, in a real sense, a defeat for all Islamic women.

One time, when Barbara's lessons with Aysha were nearly done, she voiced the question that had, of course, been much on her mind. Did Mohammed concern himself with the matter of women's sexual satisfaction?

"Mohammed," Aysha said, "was very much concerned with women's sexual satisfaction. He preached many sermons about it."

She took Barbara's hand and held it a minute to show she understood the reason for the question, then said, "Here is one of his sermons that comes to me offhand. 'You must not throw yourselves on your wives as do beasts, but first there must be a messenger between you,' Mohammed said one day. 'What messenger, O Prophet?' his followers asked. 'Sweet words and kisses,' he answered them."

And Barbara wondered to herself whether at least her sex life with Bahram would have been different if he'd adhered to this tenet of his religion, instead of his tradition that calls women objects to be used by men.

When Barbara was not with Aysha, she explored, with Farah as her guide, the Persia she'd had her heart set on seeing for so long, the panorama of Tehran that turned out to be even more intriguing and fascinating than she'd imagined. Farah and Barbara went often to the Tehran Bazaar because Barbara couldn't ever get her fill. This "shopping district" consists of six fascinating miles of roofed-over, open-fronted shops and booths threaded together by stone and dirt footpaths. Here were the grocer's kiosks and those of yogurt makers, fruit and vegetable vendors, and butchers; wool carders, coppersmiths and dyers with arms stained with tints from their steaming vats were here, along with sellers of sumptuous, voluptuous silks and satins of such quality that Barbara was amazed. Here too were the rug sellers sitting on piles of exquisite, expensive carpets thrown casually on the dirt floors of their kiosks, overflowing outside where passersbys could walk on them. Yet Barbara's favorite section was the jewelers...In the Tehran Bazaar there was no "junk jewelry"; everything was of pure gold and silver which was weighed on what looked like apothecary scales. Customers were charged for their pieces by the weight, to which charge was added the value the jeweler placed on his workmanship.

Barbara especially enjoyed watching Farah and the jewelers play the "bargaining game" in which all Persians delight.

Vendor, holding out a sample ruby necklace set in gold: "Is it not exquisite, Khanoum?"

Farah, wrinkling her nose: "Well, the quality...Anyway, it's not my kind of jewelry."

Vendor: "Ah, but it's exactly for you. It is as though your face had been before me when I modeled it. Your shining hair, your beautiful eyes. It is made for you Khanoum, only for you."

Farah: "I have seen many much more beautiful necklaces."

Vendor: "Khanoum, Khanoum, this is the most beautiful necklace in the world, and it would devastate me to see it dishonored...I could not bear to see this necklace of my deepest heart go to a homely woman. Here, Khanoum, honor me by wearing this necklace."

He sounded like he was giving it to her; and Farah, looking bored, waited for him to name his price.

Vendor: "Only for you, Khanoum...Give me seventeen hundred tomans, and this masterpiece of a necklace is yours."

Farah, laughing: "Baba, Baba, for seventeen hundred tomans, I could purchase nine such necklaces." She, followed by Barbara, began walking swiftly away.

Vendor, first in a small pretense of disinterest, and then breathless after allowing them to go a short distance: "The necklace is so beautiful, so..."

Farah: "For three hundred tomans, I would say that it is a fairly decent necklace."

Vendor: "Three hundred tomans for this necklace fit for a queen? All right, Khanoum, because it is you who will grace my necklace...Take it for twelve hundred tomans."

And so they went on for fifteen minutes, a half hour, until Farah and the vendor, having simultaneously tired of their game, settled at half the original asking price.

Fascinated as she was by the marvelous merchandise for sale and Farah's games with the vendors, Barbara's greatest enjoyment was in observing the people at the bazaar—the holy dervishes holding out their begging bowls; the mullahs with their flowing beards, fierce eyes and faces of maniacal intensity or cold passiveness; the city sophisticates and tribesmen in from the desert, alongside men dressed in every fashion from Saville Row suits to homespun shirts and bloomer-like trousers that were every color of the rainbow.

But the mysterious women in their chadors were more tantalizing to her than even the most colorful of the men. Were they old, young, sad, gay, plain, beautiful? She and Farah tried to read the women's characters and personalities in their eyes; Farah might have found the game boring, but to Barbara it was endlessly intriguing.

One day Barbara talked with Farah's fiancé, Mehrdad, about her enthusiasm for and obsession with the bazaar, and was startled at his response. He glared at her and shouted, "The bazaar is quaint to you, Barbara, quaint did you say, and like a fairy tale? Well, let me ask you a question then: Are the beggars who follow you around and whine at you, 'Khanoum, Khanoum, I am hungry. Khanoum, Khanoum, I am sick,' are they quaint? Do you see the blind children and crippled, desperate parents as characters out of fairy tales? They are not going to live happily ever after, you know."

Farah took hold of Mehrdad's hand to calm him, and asked him why he was picking on Barbara.

Mehrdad laughed, not good-naturedly, but in disgust; he withdrew his hand from Farah's and continued lambasting Barbara. "And what about the porters for hire in the bazaar, the men yoked like animals, the human donkeys? Do you call them quaint? Delightful? Charming? Do you 'ooh' and 'aah' over them as you do over your hennaed horses and cute little donkeys?"

This kind of raging attack was not something Barbara expected from the Mehrdad she knew: the handsome, dark young man with the slow smile and the soft voice, who glowed every time he looked at Farah and, by extension, at her. Perhaps, though, she should have expected it. Mehrdad belonged to one of Tehran's wealthiest industrial families with interests in oil, steel, hydroelectricity and textiles, and had a doctorate in sociology from New York University where he and Farah had met. Yet he worked as a labor organizer, and was a member of the outlawed Marxist Tudeh, dedicated to deposing the monarchy.

Barbara apologized to Mehrdad for her naiveté. "Surely," she said, "I should have realized the evils..."

Mehrdad then begged Barbara's pardon for his "unwarranted hostility," and offered to introduce her to places and people she never would meet without him. Then he, Barbara and Farah, dressed in cheap chadors they'd picked up in the bazaar, went into the slums of South Tehran and those just outside Tehran City. Even today, Barbara can't think of the people she met, or merely observed in passing, in the Tehran slums without becoming angry. She went into the hut of one woman of skin and bones who looked like a cadaver; Barbara thought her to be in her seventies. When Farah asked the woman her age, though, she said she believed herself to be somewhere in her early thirties.

One day Mehrdad took Barbara and Farah into a hut where seven children were ill with dysentery. They heard the children weeping and saw a trail of their bloody stools all over the small hut; they existed in mud and their own filth. Barbara looked at them, and looked away and flinched and looked again. Being in those childrens' harrowing presence was like a nightmare from which there was no escape. And when she, Farah and Mehrdad were finally back in her suite, she came apart, breaking into tears she couldn't control. All this comfort. All these luxuries. She thought of Baba Bozorg's mansion in Shiraz, and of the seventeen others he owned in other parts of Iran. She thought of the Shah's parties, and of the ones she'd attended at Toobah's and Khanoum-June's, and others of Bahram's friends and family, each one costing more money than thousands of poor people saw in a lifetime; and she hated the Shah, hated Bahram's wealthy family, and hated herself for being their beneficiary.

And when Mehrdad asked whether she understood now why "any thinking, feeling Iranian has no choice but to dedicate his life to overthrowing such a system as ours", she said that she did.

"If you understand, Barbara, I'd be grateful if you'd also help Farah to understand," Mehrdad added.

Farah, her face grim, tight and angry, said, "And I'd be grateful, Barbara, if you'd help Mehrdad to understand that I have this peculiar need to have the man I love by my side a long time, rather than die a hero in his prime."

Barbara, agonizing for them both, hastened to change the subject by asking Mehrdad whether there was any form of organized social service in Iran. He answered that there was not, but that "good Muslims take under their wings 'pet beggars' whose care they assume as their offering to Allah. These people come monthly to collect their living expenses, and then there is our good Shah's right hand, Princess Ashraf Pahlavi, and her 'Social Services Foundation'."

Barbara, under Mehrdad's guidance, saw for herself the activities of the "Princess Ashraf Social Services Foundation." It ran soup kitchens three times a week. The people fought one another for places on the lines of the "kitchens"; there were riots when the food ran out, as it invariably did.

There was also a "pediatric clinic" to which the mothers brought their children with dysentery, with worms, with impetigo, with malaria, with all of the ills resulting from their life conditions. And always the children had beriberi due to malnourishment and vitamin deficiency, a disease easily cured by a diet rich in protein and green vegetables. Such a cure was hardly possible for mothers who sometimes had nothing to feed their children except for roots they managed to dig out of the ground.

"There is, though," Mehrdad said, "one effective form of giving to the poor administered by the mullahs who do have a heart for poor people. And I say this although my fellow Tudeh members would condemn me for it. The mullahs, especially the mujtahids, and the ayatollahs use their huge sums of money...good Muslims contribute a fifth of their income to Allah...to help whole families, whole neighborhoods; they feed the people, shelter them, and above all, give them the feeling they and their children matter in the world. With no newspaper or television coverage, no fanfare.

"And I can tell you that the people are so grateful and devoted to them, they'll follow any place the mullahs lead. And where the mullahs are leading them is toward revolution against Mohammed Reza and his whole corrupt, degenerate, inhumane government."

"Mehrdad," Barbara said, "if such a revolution were to happen...Will the people be better off under the mullahs than they are under the Shah?"

He pondered the question for a long time and finally said, "O, my God, Barbara, how I wish I could answer that question; how I wish I could."

"Another question, Mehrdad," Barbara said, "is it really possible that such weak, sick, impotent people will, no matter who leads them, be summoned to revolt?"

"If you truly knew our people, Barbara...I'm talking about the middle class of professionals, workers and bazaaris, as well as the ones you've seen and met in the slums, and not the one thousand families or the Shah's nouveau riches who frequent your royal parties...If you once saw our people in their mosques—their total religious dedication, their love for their saints—you'd know that the power of Islam, the power of religion, the power of the mullahs..."

"Mehrdad," Farah interrupted, "why don't we let Barbara see for herself that power you're talking about. Why don't we take her to a mosque?"

Mehrdad shook his head.

"Well, why not?" Farah asked.

Mehrdad said, "You ought to know why not, Farah. It's dangerous for any unbeliever to be discovered in a mosque, and for an American unbeliever..."

"But how're they going to recognize her as either an American or an unbeliever under the chador?"

In the end Mehrdad yielded to Farah as he did in all matters except his politics, and agreed, albeit reluctantly, to go with them to the Mosque of Abdul Azim in the neighboring city of Rey. It is the shrine of a son of Hussein, Shiite Islam's foremost martyr saint.

Barbara felt immensely excited at her first sight of Abdul Azim, with its several minarets rising into a blue sky set above three domes of gold, not because it was the most beautiful mosque she'd ever seen from the outside, but because it was the first one she'd been privileged to go into. She, Farah and Mehrdad went through a courtyard with a large stone arch bearing the sign La-il-la-ha, Il-lal-la ("There is no Allah but one Allah"), that led into the mosque patio. Here were pools where men and women were performing their separate cleansing rituals before praying. Farah and Barbara, seeking to imitate the women around them, began to kneel by the women's pool but were roughly ordered up by Mehrdad.

"You girls had better not play any of your usual games in here, and I mean that," he whispered menacingly.

He led them into the checkroom, where a man behind the counter took the shoes they'd kicked off and handed them receipts. Stocking-footed, they padded down a corridor with small rooms where people lit candles or sat and prayed alone or chanted quietly to themselves. They then entered a room meant to accommodate perhaps five hundred people, that was brilliantly lighted and that had the same kinds of mirrors on its walls and ceilings as were in the Golestan Palace. It was crowded to suffocation with men and boys in front, and women and girls behind; even the littlest girls were chador-clad.

In the center of the far wall was a sunken cage surmounted by crisscrossed silver bars rising some ten feet above the floor, holding a black malachite sarcophagus where Abdul Azim's body lay in state. Barbara saw people kneeling against the walls that faced the tomb, weeping and beating their heads against the carpeted floor; to a person raised an American Methodist, the sight was startling...and terrifying. And even more unnerving were the sights and sounds of the masses of people who'd pushed and shoved and crushed one another to stand, finally, around the caged-in casket. They clung to the silver bars that protected the coffin, and strove to push their hands and heads through it.

Barbara saw those hands and heads bloodied in attempts to touch the coffin, and she saw people relishing their self-inflicted wounds. She thought as she stood watching that, yes, Mehrdad was right about the power of Islam being strong enough to move its adherents, even the sickest and weakest among them, to revolution; she was thinking as clearly and rationally as she had ever thought in her life.

Then, suddenly, she was not rational, not sane anymore. She knew she had to get out of the mosque; she could not take this wild, raw emotion; she knew herself and her vulnerability. "Monkey see, monkey do," her grandmother had said about her, and with good reason, from the time she was small. She had to run from these people's craziness before it engulfed her and she became a part of it herself.

She dashed out of the mosque, and didn't even look to see whether Farah and Mehrdad were following her. She stood in the crowd outside, trying to catch hold of herself and gasping for breath, when she heard Farah's voice, hysterical: "For God's sake, Barbara, pull your chador around yourself." Barbara hadn't even realized it had slipped in her panic. Her red hair and blue eyes, her American face, were there for everyone to see. Just as she'd succeeded in getting her chador around herself again, five mullahs with flowing beards rushed out of the crowd and bore down upon her, screaming MARGH BAR AMERIKA and other curses she could not understand. They beat her with their fists and spat at her; saliva from their lips ran down her face, from which the chador had again slipped. She stood paralyzed, sure the mullahs were going to kill her.

She saw Mehrdad and Farah rushing through the crowd and grabbing the mullahs, shouting at them to let Barbara go. The mullahs did let her go, but only in order to jump at Farah and Mehrdad, cursing and beating them. Barbara saw Farah rocking back and forth and crying, and then saw a mullah spitting into Farah's eye. That was the sight that caused Barbara, finally, to cry aloud.

Hearing her sobs, the mullah turned from Farah to her, shouting, "Margh bar Amerika! Margh bar Amerika!" He slapped her in the face many times...The last thought she had before she passed out was, "Please don't kick me in the stomach, please don't mutilate my baby."

Barbara woke in her own suite, in her own bed with Farah and Mehrdad sitting across from her. There were bruises on Mehrdad's face, a large deep one on his right cheek where the skin had been scraped away and one on his left temple, not large, but deep and bloody. Farah looked tiny and frail, her long hair hanging about her face nearly covering it, her eyes sunken in.

"Oh, Farah..." Barbara said. "Mehrdad, your face. Everything is my fault. I shouldn't have gone to the mosque."

"No, Barbara, nothing's your fault any more than ours. We'll be all right, dear, all of us," Farah said, and came to lie on Barbara's bed with her, while Mehrdad sat beside them. He said that Barbara would want to know how they'd made their escape. It was strange, miraculous. A mullah he knew slightly, "rather less fanatical and more intelligent than the rest," Mehrdad said, "happened to be in the crowd surrounding us. I looked out and caught his eye and next thing I knew there he was, running into the midst of the other mullahs who beat at us. I thought at first he was there to help them. I couldn't believe my ears when I heard him shout, 'Stop it, stop it, you fools. Don't you know that if you hurt the farangi and the ones with her, her government and their puppet, the Shah, will wreak terrible vengeance on us and our people? They'll take a thousand eyes for her one eye, and a thousand teeth for her one tooth...' And the other mullahs, startled by a challenge from one of their own, fell back for a long enough time to enable us to get away."

Barbara said, "What would have happened to us, Mehrdad, if that mullah hadn't intervened for us?"

He said, "We might be dead for all I know. The mullahs would not have killed us themselves, but they might well have incited the crowd to do it for them."

Barbara said, making a statement, not asking a question, "They would have incited the crowd to kill you because you tried to help me."

Mehrdad offered Barbara a cigarette and lit it for her; Farah kissed her, and lay her cheek against Barbara's. Neither one said anything, because what was there to say?

They sat looking at one another for a long time. Finally, Barbara said, "The crowd would have killed me...The mullahs would have led the crowd to kill me because I'm American, just for that reason." She rose from the bed and stood in front of the mirror; she examined herself from head to foot, paying special attention to her breasts and spreading stomach. She saw her face covered with sweat and her eyes full of terror. She looked down at her big belly, and thought to herself that she couldn't...she wouldn't bring a half-American child into a culture that would despise it for its nationality and might, someday, thirst for its blood as the mullahs had for hers.

CHAPTER X

The Giving up of the Dream

From that terrible day until three days after Roxanne's birth two months later, Barbara did not leave her suite. Those months were a nightmare. She lay awake nights, dizzy with the vision of the mullahs, their crazed voices rising in her memory. And the last month of her pregnancy was a physical hell on earth as well as emotionally devastating. Her body was so filled with pain that she could neither lie in bed nor sit, but had to pace the floor hour after hour. But the women of the family, not just Aysha and Farah and Khanoum-June, but all the women, even Toobah, even Mitrah, rallied round. They took care of her and comforted her. They talked to her when she needed to talk and sat silently when she needed quiet

Barbara's baby was delivered by Fatima, the midwife who delivered all the Mosallai babies; the women had great trust in her, more than in most doctors, and with good reason. She'd come to her profession with excellent training owing to the harem tradition that forbade any man, even a doctor, from touching a woman's body. She brought, besides, her woman's sensitivity as well as a kind of humility not generally shared by doctors, male or female. Unlike them, she felt it her responsibility to remain with Barbara through the whole fourteen hours of her difficult labor, easing her pains by predicting each one before it came; she became a partner in the birth of Barbara's baby.

All the women of the family were with Barbara when her labor began, and were still there when Fatima crowed in triumph, "Barbara, the baby is coming...now. You feel it, don't you? Push, push, come on Barbara, again, again; push. That's it. Now, wait."

At first Barbara had resented the women's presence at such a time; she believed them to be impinging upon her privacy. But when she heard them echoing Fatima with the most genuine concern and caring for her and her baby, she felt close to them in a way she'd felt toward few people, whether friends or family, even in America.

"Push, push, come on, Barbara junam, push."

Roxanne was very beautiful when she was born. She had a full head of red hair like Barbara's, but aside from that, when Barbara examined her for traces of family resemblance, the baby reminded her of lovely Khanoum-June. Holding her, Barbara felt an overwhelming love she'd never believed was in her to feel; she knew then that this little creature that came from her body and needed her for existence would, from that instant and forever, be the most important thing in her life.

Bahram did not come to see Barbara and her baby 'til three days after Roxanne's birth. He entered Barbara's room, grinning and waving from the doorway.

"Well," she said, "look who's finally come to visit. What are you doing here, Bahram, since our child's a daughter and not a son? You haven't come to celebrate or wish her and me well, have you?"

"No."

"Well, then..."

"I'm here," he smiled benevolently, "to tell you that I really do not hold Shit's birth against you."

"Who the hell are you calling Shit?"

"Your daughter, Barbara."

"GET OUT! GET OUT! GET OUT, SON OF A BITCH!" Barbara shrieked, jumping up from her bed.

"Tsk, tsk, temper, temper, Little Mother. Listen, Barbara, I'm also here to renegotiate our bargain. I still want a son, your son, and I still want to win election to the Majlis. And your reward for helping me achieve both these ambitions...I promise you that, once I win the election and have my son, you and your daughter will be free to travel back to America, or any place else you may wish. And you won't have to ask your grandparents for help, either; you'll be rich. Well, what do you say, when will you be ready to start working to give me my son?"

Give him a son, have sex with him again? The idea revolted Barbara. She nevertheless said, for Roxanne's sake, "If that's your price for Roxanne's and my freedom..."

When Bahram left, Barbara rushed into the nursery and stood

over Roxanne's crib watching her sleep flat on her back, tiny arms and legs spread. Barbara put her head next to the flower face, touched the red silk-like hair, and felt her heart suddenly begin pounding as she thought... What if? Oh God, what if she couldn't give Bahram a son? What if her hate and resentment toward him caused her to be unable to conceive at all? She thought, "God, please help me to give him his son so I can take my daughter and run with her."

Run with her daughter, and leave her son behind? Would she be able to leave him once he was born any more than she could ever leave Roxanne? Well, that was not something to be agonized over now. Roxanne was here, and her son was not; Roxanne was the one she had to protect and look out for now, no matter what could happen later.

She took Roxanne out of the crib and into her room, and lay with the baby curled on her stomach; she felt, after awhile, that she had caught some of the child's peacefulness.

Her calm did not last, though; she couldn't summon it at will, and especially not when Bahram and she were "working to make a son." She'd lie, eyes closed and teeth gritted, while he would place her in whatever position he wanted, enter her, come in a few minutes, get up, clean himself in the bowl of water Naila had left for him, and walk out the door. And always as she'd watch him go, Barbara would feel such a bitter rage boil up and threaten to gush over that she'd know she had to control it, or something terrible could happen. She'd grab up a bottle of the liquor that she had taken to stashing away in her suite and drink 'til the anger and despair were more or less gone.

In the morning, the rage would return. She'd look at her face in the mirror before even washing and dressing and be surprised at its grimness and melancholy. Would she ever be the same? she wondered. Beginning with her marriage, Bahram had taken a warm, loving, eighteen-year-old girl and made of her a mean and angry woman who had once thought of killing herself, but now thought only of killing him. Unless she and Roxanne somehow escaped him, Barbara was terrified that she might actually kill Bahram.

So one morning when Roxanne was six months old, Barbara got up before anyone else, dressed Roxanne, whom she'd kept in bed with her, packed a bag and drove her car to the airport where she got a flight to Isfahan. She and Roxanne hid out at an Isfahan hotel for three exhilarating days of freedom. Then while they were at lunch, three armed policemen in uniform came into the dining room...They had a warrant for Barbara's arrest for having "run away from your marital home and kidnapping the child, Roxanne, from her natural father."

Barbara and Roxanne were flown to Tehran and driven, in a police car with shrieking siren, to the Reformatory for Women. There they met the warden, Dr. Amir Humarabi. An immaculate, serious-faced man in his forties, dressed in a three-piece blue suit and white shirt, he spoke English well; he smiled at Barbara as he advised her to telephone Bahram and "to apologize for your crime against him."

"MY CRIME AGAINST HIM?" Barbara blurted out. Then she thought of Khanoum-June's advice to her to pay total obeisance to Bahram and all of the men in her life, because it was the only way she would survive in Iran. And Barbara told herself that if there'd ever been a time to take Khanoum-June's warning to heart, this was it. She had no choice except to beg Bahram's forgiveness. That was preferable, wasn't it, to rotting in jail?

Yes, but...no. To apologize to Bahram would be to admit to herself that she'd been, finally, defeated. It would mean giving up her dream that she and Roxanne would someday be free. She decided, therefore, to call Khanoum-June, not Bahram, and beg her to come for Roxanne and keep her for as long as Barbara would be in prison.

When Barbara told Warden Humarabi that she would call Khanoum-June to come for the child and would herself remain in jail, he said that so long as she was there Roxanne would have to be there with her.

"But why?...She's only six months old...You can't mean...She's only six months old, for God's sake!"

"It is exactly because of your baby's tender age, Sultaneh...our law, based upon our Koran, declares that children under three must be with their mothers wherever the mothers are."

Barbara remembered then what Aysha had said about Mohammed declaring that children had to remain with their mothers until the age of three, so that the patriarchs who repudiated women could not take them away while they were babies, and some still nursing. Surely, though, he hadn't meant the babies to languish in jail with the mothers. Such an instrument for control as this became, in the patriarchs' hands, "Do as I command, or I will jail not just you, but also your baby."

"Well, Sultaneh," Warden Humarabi asked, "will you call your husband or must I call my guards to bring you and your baby to the prison?"

For Roxanne's sake, then, Barbara swallowed her pride and called Bahram.

CHAPTER XI

The Beautiful Wife Goes One Night to Teymourtache

Back home, Barbara felt her enmity toward Bahram give way to a kind of hopelessness that was infinitely harder to deal with. Her hostility had, after all, had its positive aspects... It had enabled her to take some action that, although it had not yet done so, might eventually have eased her and Roxanne's situation. Her overwhelming feeling of futility, on the other hand, left her weak and unable even to think of any way out.

And then suddenly, one day, for a very strange reason, she recovered sufficiently to begin hoping again. Her reading of a book, one of the many written in English which her friends had bombarded her with in hopes of improving her spirit, had this positive result. The name of the book was *Two Queens of Baghdad*. The queens were Khayzuran (slender and graceful reed), and Zubadayeh, her daughter-in-law. Born into slavery, their early years were lived as slaves, yet they, perhaps more than anyone living in 9th century Baghdad, were ultimately responsible for their courts' historic splendor and magical glory.

Both women had realized early that they, being neither as beautiful nor as talented as many in the harem, would have to serve their masters in a different fashion from that of the other slaves. They therefore studied music, dance and poetry with the best teachers in the palace, not in order to compete with their gifted rivals, but rather so that they could draw attention to their artistry at the caliphs' many salons and entertainments.

They soon became the caliphs' official hostesses, and succeeded so admirably in those roles that their entertainments became the talk of the entire Muslim world, and were a source of inspiration for *The Arabian Nights*. As a reward for bringing them such fame, the caliphs eventually married them.

Barbara thought that she had much to learn from those wise and canny women. They hadn't battled their masters, but had instead transformed themselves into super-slaves able to give services the caliphs admired, needed and were willing to pay highly for. So highly, in fact, that they quit treating the women as possessions and recognized their personhood by crowning them queens.

And why couldn't Barbara do this with Bahram, who was, after all, her master, as Khazuran and Zubadayeh had done with their masters? Why couldn't she help him politically as he required, and thus put herself in a position to make demands of him?

Barbara's first party for Bahram was given in Baba Bozorg's and Khanoum-June's mansion in Shiraz, where Bahram planned to announce his campaign for the Majlis. Guests were chosen for their political usefulness and included members of the important industrial and professional families, and of the landed gentry, who were the "owners" of the villages around Shiraz and so commanded the votes of all the peasants who worked or sharecropped their land.

The guest of honor was Teymour Bahktiar. He, with American and Israeli help, had organized Savak two years earlier and was now its chief. A slim, stylish man in his forties, son of a noble Khan of the Bahktiari tribe, he'd been educated in French lycees and at Saint Cyr. Along with his close friend Queen Soraya, he was recognized among many of the rich and beautiful of Europe and America for his worldliness and charm. He was favored by the American Embassy and the CIA, and was on friendly terms with such highly placed Americans as presidential candidate John F. Kennedy. Iranians who knew him, though, believed that he was the most sadistic person in his whole sinister operation. They said that he took pleasure in personally observing the carrying out of the tortures he'd evolved. Barbara, like Aysha, Farah and Mehrdad, who lay awake nights in dread of him and Savak, hated him with a passion. Yet she was in no position to resist Bahram's command to invite—and cater to—him from whom Bahram and the whole family Mosallai had much to gain.

For this first party Barbara ordered the furniture in the Western dining room and salons to be replaced with the same kind of rug-

covered, low divans as were in the traditional rooms, so that all of
the guests could, as Khayzaran's and Zubadayeh's guests had done,
recline. And the pretty "slave girls", along with Fifi and Fufu,
looked as though they'd stepped out of *The Arabian Nights* as they
served the guests.

As at Khayzaran's and Zubadayeh's parties, musicians and
dancers entertained all through the night; Barbara had hired many
outstanding artists, including Sheherezade, who'd so enticed Baba
Bozorg at her and Bahram's wedding. Barbara directed her to dance
for a while in front of the other men guests, but to finish her shaking and wiggling before the guest of honor.

But Bahktiar did not seem pleased either by Sheherezade's performance or her attention; he revealed, instead, an impatience with
her, barely masked by courtesy. He'd glance for a moment at
Sheherezade, then close his eyes and open them again to stare at
Barbara in a way that made her feel like she was being stripped.
Bahram, delighted with Bahktiar's obvious attraction to Barbara,
told her that "he'll really be fascinated after your poetry contest is
finished."

Barbara's poetry contest, planned around those new young writers and reciters of traditional poetry that Khayzuran and Zubadayeh
had patronized, was also aimed to please the guest of honor, who
was himself a poet of distinction. He listened in silent absorption as
the top students in Persian literature and poetry from Tehran
University recited their own poems, as well as those of Saadi, Hafez,
Khayam and Rudaki.

When the readings were finished, Barbara recited in Persian, a
piece by Saadi which she'd carefully rehearsed with Aysha:

"I did not complain of my forlorn condition except on one occasion when my feet were bare, and I had not the wherewithal to shoe
them. Soon, after meeting a man without feet, I was thankful for the
bounty of Providence to myself, and, with perfect resignation,
accepted my want of shoes."

Now the applause would not be contained, and the guests,
including the guest of honor, declared that Barbara's party was the
most splendid event to have happened in Shiraz in fifty years.

Bahktiar rose from his place, came to Barbara, clicked his heels, smiled warmly and led her back to Bahram. "You have a marvelous wife," he told Bahram, "I don't know how much money you have, Bahram, but I think that you are the richest man in this room tonight."

There is a popular story called Ali and Bab that has been told for generations in Iranian bathhouses, or wherever women gather. "There was a time, and there wasn't a time," it says, "when there lived two close friends named Ali and Bab. Now Ali's wife was as ugly as sin, while Bab's wife was a beauty. One day Ali bet Bab many tomans that his beautiful wife was untrue to him and offered to prove it. 'Tonight,' Ali said, 'you must ask your wife whether she has always been faithful to you, and say to her that the devil will catch hold of her foot if she tells a lie.'

"So Bab asked his wife the question, and when she answered affirmatively, Ali, who had been hiding at the foot of Bab's bed, grabbed hold of her ankle. At that she cried out, 'I will tell you the truth, dear husband. The diamond necklace that I told you was a present from my mother was really given to me by a lover. But I swear that he was the only one and that now I am done with him.'

"Again Ali caught hold of her foot, and again she cried out, 'All right, I'll admit that I had one other lover, the one who gave me the ruby and gold bracelet I told you was a present from my sister.'

"And so it went all through the night with Bab's wife admitting that she'd had many lovers who'd given her jewels and other expensive gifts.

"In the morning Ali demanded payment of the bet, but Bab said that they must first test the faithfulness of Ali's own wife. So Bab hid at the foot of Ali's bed while Ali asked his wife whether she was faithful to him. She laughed as she asked, 'Oh, my dear, who except you would be so discerning as to see beneath this ugly face and form, and want to have me as a lover?'

"Ali was inclined to believe his wife, but Bab caught hold of her ankle and pinched it so hard that she cried out, 'Ali, I'll confess that our former cook took me before he left because I gave him one of your suits, and our present cook took me and takes me still because I give him your worn ties.'

"The next day, when Ali and Bab met, Bab said, 'You, Ali, have lost the bet, because while both our wives are indeed unfaithful, I reap profits from my wife's infidelities while you incur losses from yours.'"

The story of Ali and Bab is, in a very real sense, typical of the marital patterns and use of women by their husbands of some, if not many, upper-class Persian couples. The wives, finally out of the strait-jackets imposed by the need to remain virgins, and as often as not unfulfilled by their husbands, may engage in extramarital affairs. And the affairs may be tolerated, and even encouraged, by husbands who might, like Bab of Ali and Bab, have something to gain from them.

Throughout Persian history, there have been such tales as "Ali and Bab" that have been based on the perceived relationship among upper class husbands as ambitious as Bahram was for political appointments, their desirable wives, and those men in or out of the royal court in position to grant favors. Thus it was said in the days of Mohammed Reza's father, Reza Shah, that "the beautiful wife goes one night to Teymourtache (the Shah's chief councilor), and the next day the husband is elevated to high office." And in Mohammed Reza's own time it was speculated not only as idle gossip, but also by those in a position to know, that not only the Shah's courtiers but even the monarch himself...

Former U.N. Ambassador Fereydoun Hoveyda wrote in *The Fall of the Shah* that "one day while I was with the Foreign Ministry, I and some other colleagues were asked by our minister, Ardeshir Zahedi, to take a very pretty European out to dinner. These colleagues told me that Zahedi and Alam, then the Shah's minister of court, used to arrange entertainment for their master. I never managed to verify this, but the following year in New York I happened to meet a woman friend who had spent some time in Tehran teaching English. She told me that while she was there Alam had invited her to a cocktail party at his home. He greeted her amiably enough and showed her into the drawing room, which was empty. Alam withdrew and did not reappear. A door opened. It was the Shah. After a bland conversation, the young women asked to leave."

Barbara, like Hoveyda, never managed to verify the everlasting gossip about Mohammed Reza or other men of his close circle. But she knew for a fact that Bahktiar's reputation as the Teymourtache of his time was well-deserved. And when, after the Shiraz party, Barbara and Bahram were invited two weeks hence to dine with Bahktiar, Bahram, knowing the implications, was jubilant. Barbara, knowing them as well, was both angry and contemptuous. She screamed at Bahram that he and Bahktiar could have dinner if they wished, but without her, because she'd "contracted to be your hostess and breeding machine, not a prostitute to be pimped out to the highest bidder." At first, Bahram treated her adamance with indulgence, trying to cajole and tease and seduce her with presents. But when the two weeks were nearly over and she continued to be immovable, he intimidated her with the ultimate threat. If she wished to continue in Roxanne's life...

After dinner at Bahktiar's, Bahram, saying he'd return for Barbara in three hours, left on a pretend errand. And Bahktiar, without a word—because words were, after all, unnecessary in the face of the clear understanding among the three of them—led Barbara up the stairs to his bedroom. After the first time, she was picked up every Wednesday night at ten o'clock. She and Bahktiar would have dinner together, then have sex.

During the third month of Barbara's and Bahktiar's "relationship", he told her that he had solicited for Bahram the position of mayor of Rey. The very name of that city made Barbara shudder because it was there, at the Mosque of Abdul Azim, that the mullahs had attacked her and Farah. But Bahktiar considered the appointment a plum because its location as both a shrine city and burial ground for Tehranis assured its mayor of the most ample pishkesh (bribe). "And know, my darling Barbara, that it is to your credit, that without you..."

Barbara interrupted to say that if she had, indeed, pleased Bahktiar, he might see fit to give her the best recompense in the world: her and Roxanne's freedom. But Bahktiar acted as though he hadn't heard her appeal. And it was not that he didn't want to lose her; she was, after all, only one of many of his women. Rather, it was that her request, implying she wanted to get away from him as well as Bahram and Iran, was an insult to his ego.

Roxanne and Barbara did, though, receive certain advantages during the three years of her relationship with Bahktiar, which ended in 1962 when the Shah, who'd come to know Bahktiar as a rival for the throne, fired him. First of all, her life with Bahram was greatly eased. So long as she went with Bahktiar on Wednesday nights and continued producing surprises at her parties and Thursday night salons, she was in a position to get from Bahram everything money could buy. And, with the exception of his giving her permission to take Roxanne out of the country, an important thing money couldn't buy, he treated her and her child with consideration, not always, but most of the time.

Bahram told Barbara when she was having her house built in his name in Shemiran, not to worry about cost; she took him at his word. The house and its grounds were designed by one of Iran's most prestigious and expensive architects. Having lived and worked in Charleston, South Carolina, he created for Barbara a splendid, red brick edifice like those on that city's East Bay Street that reverent crowds of Americans pay admission to walk through and admire.

Barbara's pleasure in her house, even with a separate wing for Bahram, was enhanced when Mehrdad and Farah married and built a house so near to hers that the women could live as closely as they'd done when both had been residents in Toobah's house.

When the weather was good they spent whole days in each other's gardens, swimming, sipping iced tea and coffee, and watching Roxanne, whom Farah looked at with the same shiny eyes as Barbara did. For she, like Barbara, was convinced that there'd never been such beauty and cleverness and humor in any other child, as was in Roxanne.

Farah and Barbara dined together often during the week, Mehrdad joining them at times. Mostly, though, he was busy campaigning for his own election to the Majlis. Barbara took to stumping for him along with Farah, and soon began feeling as close to him as to her. So long as she had Farah and Mehrdad, and Roxanne, she did not desire or need any other recreation or company.

Barbara knew that some people, especially loving and beloved friends like Aysha, believed that her life was tedious. But, really, Barbara's life with Roxanne was anything but tedious; every day she spent with her was one of joy and wonder. And when Dawneh was born when Roxanne was nearly four, Barbara was even happier than she'd been at Roxanne's birth. Yet during the following months she became restless and thought that here she was, twenty-three years old, going on twenty-four, almost two years older than Betty and her other friends had been when they'd already graduated from college and become involved in careers. Barbara herself would have been into her second year of medical school if she'd remained in California, instead of coming to Iran and becoming a...what was she, anyhow? Well, a mother whose children were treasures. They were treasures, but what was she? The years of her life were passing and she was doing nothing with them...She'd allowed herself, no, caused herself to be obliterated by her children. That might make some sense, as Aysha often told her, if there'd been a need, if she'd been poor, for instance. But she was in a position, that God knows she'd paid heavily for, to have it all. Motherhood, and a career, and a life of her own.

She realized now that she wanted, needed, a career as passionately as she had before entering the University of California. Because of the years she had missed, she could not see her way clear to becoming a doctor, but she could still train to be of service to people.

On a warm September day in 1961, Barbara registered at the University of Tehran as a psychology major and a Persian poetry minor, under a program sponsored by the University of Pennsylvania. And if she hadn't known before that she was living in a police state, she'd have been bound to know it then. The heavy main gate of the high, green, steel-pike fence was guarded by four policemen with guns. Unless you were a visitor with written authorization, or a teacher or student with a proper identity card, the policemen would turn you away.

On the day she entered the University of Tehran, Barbara had a feeling that would only become intensified during the nearly eight years she'd remain there as both student and teacher: that its differences from Western universities were deep-rooted and fathomless. Her friendship with Aysha and other university teachers had caused her to envision a school with teachers eager to share their knowledge and students eager to absorb it. What she'd found instead was a school with all too many teachers who didn't care about teaching (they called their profession "eating chalk"), and students who'd come to college not to be educated, but only as a stepping stone to better jobs and higher status; the image, the "face" they projected to the world was what counted with them. Their prime interest in school was in passing final examinations with high grades, not only because of the matter of "face", but also because future jobs, especially in the government service that most were ambitious to enter, depended on it. Cheating during examinations was, therefore, a pattern in nearly every classroom. And it was often quite open. Some students turned to their seatmates for answers, and others exchanged signals with friends in other parts of the room. The teachers pretended they didn't see what was going on.

Barbara was also constantly amazed by the excuses with which students, fearing they had failed their examinations, covered themselves with their professors.

"My saintly mother is on her deathbed, Professor, I swear it on my life. I was too broken-up during these last weeks to have studied as I should have..." "A wild dog forced his way into my home yesterday, and ate all the sheets from which I was studying..."

And if neither excuses nor cheating secured students' "face-saving" grades, they could, in many cases, purchase them from teachers who happily accepted <u>pishkesh</u> (a bribe) when it was offered, and sought it out when it wasn't. At first Barbara could not fathom this, but soon came to recognize that the life of learning was, after all, no special bailiwick wherein high ideals had value. It was, rather, one single aspect of Iranian life. And, since the giving and receiving of pishkesh occurred everywhere else in Iran, there wasn't any reason to believe that the universities would be an exception.

Barbara herself paid implicit heed to the custom of pishkesh because if she had not, she wouldn't have survived long in Iran. She,

Farah, Toobah, Khanoum-June and everyone Barbara knew who ran a household expected her cook or whoever else did the marketing, and other servants who handled money, to steal a certain amount; she made provision for the thievery in her monthly budget. And she took for granted the fact that her chauffeur would not only present her with garage bills that included pishkesh for both him and his mechanic-confederate, but also would use her car as a taxi when she sent him on long errands. And she gave pishkesh to the post office clerk who sold her stamps, the gas station attendant, the dressmaker, the painter, the plumber, everyone...So, why not the university professor as well?

Barbara experienced her first taste of pishkesh within the university in her class in "Elementary Persian Poetry". It was taught by Professor Abbas Bozergan, a fifty-year-old man with a brush haircut and Ivy League clothes. His course of study included the poet Hafez, with whose works Barbara had fallen in love when she was introduced to them, first by Bahram and then by Aysha. Bozergan, though, taught Hafez by rote. Barbara condemned him for that, yet had to admit in fairness that even the best of teachers, like Aysha herself, could not have taught creatively in a classroom of seventy-four students of such diverse interests and backgrounds, who did not even have in their possession the books from which they were supposed to learn. Instead, Bozergan earned a second livelihood (most teachers held one, two or even three jobs in addition to their teaching loads) by mimeographing sheets of the assigned poems and selling them to the students for a couple of rials a page; he contracted separately with each purchaser. Barbara knew that she, as an American, was being grossly overcharged, and the fact rankled her, although she kept silent about it.

Then one day after class she told Bozergan that she very much wanted to own *The Complete Hafez* from which he mimeographed his sheets, and asked if he knew where she could buy it; it had been unavailable in all the bookstores she'd tried. Bozergan said that he had no idea where she could purchase the book.

Barbara said that in that case, she'd have to be satisfied with borrowing the book from the university library, and asked Bozergan how long she could keep it. He told her that students were not permitted to borrow books from the library. Barbara finally asked whether it would be possible for her to read the book in the library. Bozergan said it would not. The library always had to be ready for the inspection of visiting dignitaries; it would not do, therefore, to have books off the shelves where they belonged, or students "cluttering up the place."

Barbara began to leave the room when Bozergan stopped her; he said that since she was such a fine student and so interested in Hafez, it would be a pity if she were deprived...Out of his respect for her intellect, he would, himself, withdraw the Hafez book from the university library and give it to her to keep for as long as she wished. However, if he and she were "discovered", his "reputation would be forever sullied with colleagues and supervisors."

There was a silent pause, and he caught his breath and expelled it; then, "I must ask you, therefore, to think about, er, eh, well...my compensation. I will leave it to you to decide how much my services are worth to you."

And when Barbara offered him fifty tomans, he urged her to double the amount, which she agreed to do.

CHAPTER XII

The Unveiling

Fortunately for Barbara and the other students who really sought an education at Tehran University, there were also some brilliant, dedicated professors and teachers at opposite poles from the many Bozergans who feared and hated them for their creativity, commitment to teaching, and especially, refusal to play the pishkesh game. Among them were a number of women professors, including Shams Kia, a gentle, quiet, thoughtful person who taught "Advanced Persian Poetry and Literature" with such flair and zest and energy and passion as thrilled Barbara. Barbara consequently spent all the time she could with her, both in and out of the classroom.

And there was Maryam Machdavi, a chemistry and science professor. A tall, slender, attractive woman with green eyes shining brilliantly in the dark, taut face, she looked like the quintessential Persian aristocrat. She was, though, from a village family outside Shiraz; her father, claiming to be from a family of <u>seyids</u> descended from the Prophet Mohammed, taught in a religious school and was a total traditionalist. Maryam, youngest of three daughters and five sons, confounded her father from early childhood on with her brilliance. While his sons had to be driven to books she, who'd taught herself to read from her brothers' books when she was five, had to be driven away from them. Her grandmother, a superstitious woman, believed her to be a jinn (evil spirit), her traditionalist sisters were alien to her, and her brothers jealous of her. Only her mother admired, encouraged and harbored ambition for her, although necessarily in secret.

When Maryam was fifteen and tutoring her brothers at university out of their own books, a professor of one of them heard about her and came to call on her father. After two years of persuasion, the professor convinced her father to permit Maryam to take the national examination for university scholarship. She passed with such high honors that the father had to, albeit reluctantly, permit her to pursue her education.

Behdjat Goreschi taught philosophy and wrote on the subject. She was a tall, broad, handsome woman with bright black eyes who was nicknamed "the Female Ayatollah" because, as Aysha had informed Barbara, laughing, "She's a little gruff, very opinionated, and therefore absolute about everything, so sure she's right you'd think her messages came straight from Allah. And there's no sense arguing with Behdjat any more than there'd be in arguing with the ayatollahs. The point is, though, that she turns out to be so right so often that you find yourself thinking that she's entitled to her arrogance, even when it is giant-sized."

Finally, there were Aysha and Peri. Despite her thirty-six years, doctorates in both American and Persian poetry and literature, and travel around the world, Peri seemed, to the faculty men who judged her only by her sweet pretty face, to be fragile and innocent. They deplored her "loss to mankind" and often told her in ugly, plain words that they would enjoy teaching her the difference between men like themselves who were MEN and women like the female professors (except for her) who wished they were men. There was no question in their minds but that intellectual women, single and financially independent, were also lesbians.

Of course, very few of the single, financially independent women professors were lesbians, despite the men's wholesale labeling of them. But those who were, were attracted to the homosexual life for basically the same reasons that some were attracted to the single life. It began with their feelings about men who begrudged them their intellectuality, and feared them for their ability to defy their laws of female oppression. Even Princess Ashraf, the Shah's twin who, in the future, would reveal herself to be so fiercely independent that she'd be nicknamed "The Black Panther", was compelled at seventeen to marry a man her father had chosen whom she detested. Had she refused the marriage, Reza Shah would have disowned her and prohibited her mother, brothers and sisters from having any contact with her.

Shams, another professor Barbara admired greatly, who at sixteen found herself in the same position Ashraf had been in, refused to accede to her father's mandate and was quickly banned from his home. Fortunately her mother, whom the father repudiated years earlier, had become a secondary school teacher and so was able to take her daughter in. On her small teacher's salary and earnings from a second job as a couturier, she assumed the burden of Sham's education with no aid from her wealthy father.

Men's reprisals against women like Shams, Maryam, Behdjat, Aysha and Peri, who refused to knuckle under to the men, sometimes took such sadistic forms as were almost beyond the comprehension of a Western woman, even one who, like Barbara, had been initiated into male-female relations by Bahram and Baba Bozorg. Peri, for instance, related that when she was fourteen she woke up on a miserable, cold night while visiting her uncle's home in Mashad, to hear her cousin Cyrus ranting at Abassa, his elder sister, a music teacher. He called her a whore and screeched that she'd defiled the family honor and would be avenged by nothing short of her death.

When Peri, terrified, went to the room where her aunt and cousins were, she saw Abassa, glassy-eyed with fear. She saw Cyrus' fist arching toward Abassa's face, and Abassa trying to weave away. Then Cyrus' fist crashed into Abassa's jaw, and her mouth filled with blood. Next, Cyrus took a small, blunt-nosed gun out of his pants pocket, and put it against Abassa's head. She and her mother, Peri's Aunt Fatima, began screaming "NO, NO!", but Cyrus had passed the time for words. He pulled the trigger, the bullet piercing Abassa between the eye and the ear. Peri had to standby, watching the light of life leave her cousin. She learned, after going home to Tehran, that Cyrus had been tried for Abassa's murder and had gone free under Article 1979 of the Penal Code which stated that men would not be punished for killing wives they believed...believed...to be guilty of adultery. And so magnanimously was that law interpreted throughout Iran—and certainly in Mashad, the shrine city with its many mullahs and ten million pilgrimages a year—that Cyrus, although not Abassa's husband, and basing his evidence of her "adultery" on the fact he'd seen her get into a taxi with a man her mother knew to be a colleague, was held to be "not guilty".

All of Peri's later feelings about men were the direct result of her experience with Cyrus and Abassa. It was not that she hated men in general with the same intensity as she did Cyrus, she just believed fervently that most, if not all Iranian men, or farangi men for that matter, had a bit of Cyrus in them. Forever and ever, therefore, she would be terrified of men and want nothing to do with them on an intimate basis.

Aysha shared Peri's dread of men, and went a step further in that she did hate all men...All her life she'd known men who were oppressors and destroyers of women. Her Aunt Laylah, a brilliant woman, had nevertheless permitted herself to become emotionally as well as financially dependent on her husband. Then, when he not only repudiated her but also refused her contact with her children, she killed herself. And when Aysha's uncle's new wife, who was in her late teens—only two years older than his eldest daughter—rejected the children, he followed her lead and farmed them out to live with relatives who did not want them.

And the mother of Aysha's friend Sheherezade became a prostitute because there wasn't anything else she could do to support the three baby girls her husband threw out with her while he kept and indulged the two sons. There were so many stories like those, but what was the use of telling them one by one since they were all so tragically alike?

Ruined. So many women Aysha—and Peri, Shams, Maryam and Behdjat—had known all their lives had been destroyed by their men. What actually happened to those men, like the uncle who had driven Aysha's Aunt Laylah to her death, and to Sheherezade's father who'd turned her mother into a prostitute? The same as happened to the fathers and husbands of all the wrecked women. They took new wives, had more daughters and drove some of them to ruin. Those who lived long enough became patriarchs like Baba Bozorg, in positions of power with the ability to tyrannize their entire extended family; the women, though, naturally got the worst of it.

From the time Barbara first came to the university, she was fortunate to be accepted into the group, closer than any she'd ever known, comprised of Aysha, Peri, Shams, Maryam, Behdjat, and now including her. The six of them lived in a world of their own, one of such love and caring and warmth as enabled them to survive the anger, hatefulness and vindictiveness toward them that most men of their acquaintance displayed. This certainly included many of the professors' male colleagues who, though not possessed of half the women's spirit or intellect, treated them like fools or fractious children.

"The group", as the women called themselves, shared each other's problems and pains and miseries with the kind of openness that can only occur among people who would never censor one another or deny each other's truths. When one was in trouble, the others gathered round to lift her up. And they shared each other's joys as well as troubles. Any birthday or holiday or small triumph of one member signaled a reason for a party with lots of food, drink, music and laughter. They knew how to let their hair down and be light, knew how to celebrate life.

And celebrate they did at Barbara's party on Thanksgiving, 1961, not long after her entrance into Tehran University. Though a monotonous winter rain poured from the somber sky and pitted the mushy snow in the garden, "the group" and Behdjat's mother Khanoum Goreschi, as well as Shams' mother Khanoum Kia and grandmother Khanoum Azimi, were unperturbed by the weather. With the exception of Khanoum Azimi, who faithfully followed the Koran's ban on alcohol as she did all the laws of Islam, they all had downed several brandies on top of the pre-dinner drinks and they told silly jokes, laughing 'til they cried.

Suddenly Aysha changed the mood of the party when she repeated a series of acerbic and all-too-pointed "jokes" she'd heard at a recent meeting of psychologists who were depressed over Iran's police state mentality. The jokes were aimed at Mohammed Reza and his sister Ashraf. They caused Maryam and Behdjat to jump to Ashraf's defense, not because they did not realize her corruption, but rather because they knew her to be a champion of women's rights. They'd recently attended a meeting of her "High Council of Women's Organizations" and were impressed that Ashraf had secured the Shah's promise to give women the vote in the next election, scheduled for 1963.

"Isn't the cause of women's suffrage a good enough reason to get behind Ashraf and the Shah?" Maryam asked thoughtfully. And Behdjat, speaking in the fashion that had caused her friends to name her "The Female Ayatollah", added, "Speaking pragmatically for a minute...When will you women realize that you can't refute your most powerful allies, no matter how you may feel about them otherwise. Our cause is bigger and more important than all of us put together; we have no right to turn away from the Shah and Ashraf when...I'll challenge anyone here to prove to me that they are not solidly opposed to women's oppression."

Aysha, imitating Behdjat's voice and manner, said, "Speaking pragmatically then...Behdjat, Behdjat, when will you and Maryam realize that so long as you have human oppression, women's oppression cannot be overcome?"

This argument between Behdjat and Maryam on the one side, and Aysha, Peri and Shams on the other, was one that Barbara had heard often since her acceptance into "the group". And she'd heard it as well in other such groups of educated working women who, during the late fifties and early sixties, constantly debated the question: Can women's oppression be conquered in a country where human oppression reigns supreme? So long as the vast majority of Iranians do not have the essentials of daily life—food, water, housing, health care, education for themselves and their children—how much meaning can, for instance, the ideal of equal pay for equal work have for their women? And how significant is the ideal of universal suffrage to the women of a nation living in fear of Savak? Can women honestly believe that any advantage granted to them by the Shah, who can maintain his own position only by holding his people enslaved, is worth having? Don't they know that what the Shah will give them will be at best a sop, and will be taken back when it suits him? Hasn't history's lesson taught that the emancipation of women is inevitably tied to the cause of all people's liberation?

Now Behdjat's mother Khanoum Goreschi, and Shams' mother Khanoum Kia, joined the conversation. Both women were in their sixties with curled hair, wool suits and high-heeled shoes. And both declared that human rights in Iran would never be achieved without women's participation. How could women take their place in the battle for human rights, the two women asked, unless they first attained their own independence? In sponsoring women's suffrage despite the mullahs who fought him tooth and nail, Mohammed Reza was proving himself the best male friend they, and all women, could have; he was following in the courageous footsteps of his father, Reza Shah.

Reza Shah! Khanoum Goreschi and Khanoum Kia said that they would always honor his memory for all he had given to the suppressed women of their generation. Women of their daughters' generation couldn't possibly share the jubilance that they and many women like them had experienced at Reza Shah's firman (commandment) that raised the permissible marriage age for girls from nine to fifteen, forced men to tell prospective brides how many wives they already had, and initiated co-educational schools...Did the women realize that without Reza Shah, they wouldn't have been able to become educated, and so would not be in their present positions of independence?

Also, if not for Reza Shah's order to women to unveil, women not only of their time, but also of their daughters' would be cursed by having to wear the chador that would keep them out of the world.

Khanoum Kia turned to Shams and said, "You were eight years old, and I wonder...Do you remember how your Aunt Sheherezade and I sang and danced around the first time we left the house bareheaded? Do you remember how free we felt, how happy we were?"

"What I remember more than your and Aunt Sheherezade's happiness at the time, Mother, is my grandmother's misery." Shams went to Khanoum Azimi, took her white, slender hand in her own, held it for a moment against her cheek and asked gently whether she could bring herself to share with the group her feelings and experiences during the time of the unveiling.

Khanoum Azimi looked, with her huge, touching, wounded eyes set deep in her ravaged, patrician face, into the eyes of each of the women in turn. They were kind eyes. Good and loving eyes. She said to the women that, yes, she could share "this lowest, darkest time."

When Khanoum Azimi's daughters, Sheherezade and Soroor, read her the shah's unveiling firman, she (who had first donned her chador at eight and had never since then "committed the sin" of letting an unrelated man see her without it) could not believe it. How could the Shah dare to impose a law that was in defiance of God's law? And she went into isolation in order to think through how she would handle the command; whether she could...or would...accept it as most men she knew had done with the Shah's order to them to wear Western dress. Or whether she would defy it. She also found herself thinking about the years of her childhood in Mashad, hunting for clues about how to behave in the precarious present by examining and dissecting her life and attitudes in the safe and comfortable past.

She saw herself again as she was at eight and nine and ten in the short house veil she wore for her prayers at home, reciting the Arabic of the Koran she'd memorized and of which she'd someday learn the meaning. Performing her ablutions each time the call to prayer came. Imitating her mother's genuflections perfectly. Keeping the fasts as rigidly as her parents did on the Holy Days of Mourning for Islam's Martyrs. She had been so meticulous, so conscientious from the time she was small...She had always cleansed as an Islamic wife and mother should have; she'd given to the poor...she had done everything Allah required from her. And her feeling after the Shah's firman was that she did not intend, now that she was a forty-eight-year-old grandmother, to change her ways. Nothing the Shah could say, nothing he could do...She would rather die a martyr to her faith than live a traitor to it.

So Khanoum Azimi, clad in her chador, ventured out of her home for the first time in the five weeks since she'd heard about the firman. After she had been driven by the family chauffeur to Reza Shah Hospital, where her aunt was a patient, she sent him on errands, intending to take a cab or carriage home. When she tried to enter a cab, though, she was prevented by the driver who told her that he could not take her as a passenger because the Shah had ordered that all cabs and carriages refuse to carry veiled women. She waited, then, 'til she saw a carriage discharging two unveiled women, and while the driver was busy counting their fare, she entered and told him, in her grandest tone, to take her home.

Turning and seeing her veil, he said that he was under orders never to carry a veiled woman again. Tough and grim, she told him to take her to the nearest police station where she would report him for insolence.

"Khanoum," he said, "I will lose my license if I take you even one block."

She finally had to call for her sister's carriage and driver to come and bring her home. There she found Azadeh the cook in tears...There would, she sobbed, be no dinner tonight: The keepers of the meat shop, the vegetable and fruit shop, the bread shop, all had said that they could no longer trade with veiled women.

"Stop the tears, Azadeh, put on your street chador and come with me," Khanoum Azimi commanded. "We are going to find out whether those shopkeepers will refuse to sell to this veiled lady as they did to you."

Khanoum Azimi returned home from her shopping in a state of shock. True, the tradespeople, being among the most faithful of Muslims, had been as angered as she by the Shah's firman; they had extended to her their heartfelt apologies. And some had been in tears...She'd found herself having to give them comfort. Yet she'd never been so insulted and demeaned in her life as she had by the few unveiled women as well as men customers who'd said that it did not matter whether she was mistress or servant, a lady of quality, or an uncouth nobody...Women in veils were felons, because that was what the Shah had named them.

Every woman, by the time she reaches the age Khanoum Azimi was when the unveiling first came to pass, has a day she'll always remember as being the worst of her life. Hers was a cold Thursday in January of 1935, some six months after the unveiling was announced. She, accompanied by her personal bath servant, Shamsi, arrived at the bath-house for her Thursday night bath. The narrow street on which it was located was crowded with weeping, wailing women. They told Khanoum Azimi that the bath man, acting on orders from Reza Shah, had refused to admit them because they were veiled.

Khanoum Azimi leaned on Shamsi, who put her arms around her. They were not mistress and servant today; they were two women of Islam caught in the same nightmare. Well, Khanoum Azimi would find a way to deliver herself, and also Shamsi, Azadeh and all of the women at home who looked to her to lead them.

Six policemen in full uniform swaggered into the midst of the women; they ordered them to go home before they were shot or clubbed or...and this idea caused them to laugh uproariously...had their veils cut off.

Khanoum Azimi called upon Allah for direction about what to do. His answer came in a flash: "Remember Aysha, the Prophet's wife, and do what she would surely have done were she in your place today. Remember Safiya, the Prophet's aunt, who at seventy years old stood lone guard over Medina, and do what you know she would do in your position."

Khanoum Azimi, feeling bathed in the sight and sound of Allah, called out to the policemen, "In the sacred names of God and His Prophet, I command you to escort these women of Islam into the bath-house. If you do not...I warn that, if you do not, all of your souls are going to BURN THROUGHOUT ETERNITY."

"You," the policeman who seemed to be the leader screamed out, "You woman, who has dared speak to His Majesty's policemen in such a fashion...Come and repeat your brazen words to our faces!"

Khanoum Azimi, with Shamsi behind, made her way through the crowd to stand magnificently before the policemen. "In the sacred names of God and His Prophet..."

The leader gave a signal to his second, who walked slowly toward Khanoum Azimi. He stood before her with his face contorted into a sneer. His hand reached into his pocket for a butcher knife. But policemen didn't carry butcher knives, and if this one did...Khanoum Azimi prayed desperately, "Over and over I whisper to You, dear God, PLEASE GOD, DON'T LET HIM CUT OFF MY CHADOR."

Khanoum Azimi, followed by a frenzied Shamsi, flew into the andarum where her daughters and the servants were gathered for tea. She thrust her fists in the air and screamed, "Oh my God, let me die, please kill me before...I can't stand this life any more..."

She ran to the kitchen, Soroor and Sheherezade behind her. She pulled open a drawer and took out a knife, brandishing it and screaming that she wanted to die while "there is still a chance of saving my eternal soul that the Shah and his policemen have dishonored." Sheherezade finally managed to pry the knife away from Khanoum Azimi while Soroor held her close.

Khanoum Azimi was suicidal for six months after the cutting off of her chador, during which time Soroor or Sheherezade or another member of the family had to be with her constantly. She only recovered after she realized that she was not forced to kill herself in order to escape the Shah's firman; she had only to remain at home until "the evil law" would be lifted as it had to be eventually, and almost was in 1941. When Mohammed Reza succeeded his father to the throne, he did not formally repeal Reza Shah's law, but made it clear that it would no longer be enforced; thus Khanoum Azimi was able, for the first time in six years, to leave her home. And she, as Aysha explained to Barbara, was typical of a large number of such aristocratic women who remained in voluntary isolation during the years 1935 to 1941. "And many poor women who could not afford to hide themselves away killed themselves, or tried to."

There was a silence after Aysha's explanation, broken finally by Barbara, who first expressed her sympathy to Khanoum Azimi and her repulsion at Reza Shah's sacrifice of women like her for the sake of Westernization, then said, "I would like to ask you, Khanoum Azimi, what did you think about most during those years?"

Khanoum Azimi's hands were knotted so hard the knuckles were blue, and she kept smashing them into her knee. "I thought most often of Reza Shah, of his ghastly sins committed not only against women but also against the holy mullahs who spoke out against his unveiling firman. Every day my husband returned from the mosque with another piece of terrible news: 'Today Reza Shah ordered his generals to pull Tehran's mullahs' turbans off their heads and then to cut off their beards.' Last week they'd subjected the Shiraz mullahs to the same fate. And America, America encouraged his heinous crimes...THE SHAH HORSEWHIPPED THE MULLAHS; AND AMERICA SAID, GOOD, GOOD, WHIP THEM SOME MORE!"

Her outburst concluded, Khanoum Azimi, always the epitome of polite Iranian womanhood, apologized to Barbara over and over again. She said that she didn't know what had gotten into her to have talked as she had about America to Barbara, whom she loved as she did all of Shams' friends. She was a stupid old woman who, if Barbara didn't forgive her, would never forgive herself. And so on and so on, while Barbara put her arms around her and held her 'til she was more or less comforted.

Yet Barbara herself was both troubled and frightened, not so much by what Khanoum Azimi had said about America as by the look that had been in her eyes before she'd recovered herself. Khanoum Azimi's eyes, even if only for a moment, had flashed such hatred toward Barbara as an American that it reminded Barbara of the mullahs outside the Mosque of Abdul Azim, and the students in the demonstration who would have wished to see her dead.

CHAPTER XIII

The Shah's Secret Police

For days, Barbara brooded about Khanoum Azimi's hostility toward America. Finally she brought her concern to Aysha, who could look at such hatred with Western as well as with Iranian eyes and would examine for Barbara the reasons behind it.

To begin with, Aysha said, Khanoum Azimi's declaration that America had encouraged Reza Shah in his punitiveness toward the mullahs had no basis in fact. And even the mosque gossip of the time didn't claim that it did. Khanoum Azimi was quoting present mosque rumors that hold America responsible for every evil thing that occurs in Iran. Those rumors, though, did not begin to spread until perhaps 1951. Before that, America was seen not as a Satan but rather a savior of the people from both Iran's ruling class and from British and Russian domination.

There was even an authentic American martyr-hero, Howard C. Baskerville. He, in 1909, resigned his job as a mission schoolteacher in Tabriz in order to fight side-by-side with the "Constitutional Revolutionaries" against Russia, Britain and the Quajar Shahs, who sold out their country to them. Leading his untrained battalion, newly recruited out of his classroom, against a powerful royal battalion, he was shot and killed, and his funeral turned into a nationalist demonstration. More than 3,000 people sobbed and wailed with the same kind of wild bereavement they'd afford any Persian martyr-hero.

There was also Morgan Shuster, who came to be the country's financial advisor in 1920. He fought, until his expulsion, against "the Persian enemies of the people who are themselves Persian, and the British and Russians who are carving up their country." And Arthur Millspaugh, who came in 1922 as head of a mission of American financial advisers and was also expelled for being on the people's side.

And then, finally, came Franklin Delano Roosevelt. In December of 1943, at his urging, Churchill and Stalin joined with him in sign-ing the "Tehran Declaration" that bound the Allied powers to pre-serve Iran's independence and to aid her development. But in August of '45, Russia, defying its former allies, inaugurated the "independent republics" of Aberbijan and Kurdistan.

Although Russia's short-term goal in taking Aberbijan and Kurdistan might have been, as she declared it, the creation of "buffer zones" in northern Iran, there was no question but that she intended, eventually, to make a puppet state also of Tehran in order to ensure direct access to the Persian Gulf. This would threaten American oil holdings in Kuwait, Bahrain and Saudi Arabia.

America's alleged advocacy of "Iranian rights", her "willingness to go to the brink of war for the preservation of Iranian sovereignty" could no longer even be considered to be based on the vaunted "unselfish American idealism". Rather, it had to be recognized as a fight to the finish for her own "rights" against the new enemy, Soviet Russia. Mohammed Reza, impotent and ineffectual as America knew he was at the time, nevertheless had to be sustained and nurtured.

Which led Aysha, finally, to one of two basic reasons for Iranians' hatred of America and Americans.

When in early 1951, Aysha, twenty-four, and Peri, twenty-three, returned to Iran after five years of study at Columbia University in New York, they were thrilled by all that had gone on in their absence. Dr. Mossadegh...Dr. Mossadegh. His name was on every-one's lips, and his picture was displayed by almost every bazaari in Iran. As Oil Minister, and with the backing of the National Front Party, composed at the time of bazaaris, mullahs, labor union leaders and workers, doctors, lawyers, teachers, writers, poets, university professors and students...nearly everyone who yearned for freedom from foreign domination...he had confronted the big powers of the world by declaring that Iranian oil must be nationalized and Western imperialists driven out of the country.

Aysha told Barbara she would never forget the Majlis meeting on January 21, 1951, at which the Shah's Prime Minister Ali Razmara and Mossadegh locked horns. Mossadegh was seventy years old, gaunt and beak-nosed, with an eagle-bald head, and dressed as was his wont in a rumpled, ill-fitting suit. He arrived at the Majlis building with its paneled, dark wood walls, crystal chandeliers and resplendent rugs, to shouts from outside of: <u>Zendabad Mossadegh</u>! (Long live Mossadegh!).

Now came Prime Minister Razmara. He was in his fifties, a handsome man who looked, in his decorated uniform, like the four-star general that he was. He was also at the time in high favor with America and Britain, because he was responsible for the suppression of the Russian-inspired revolts in Aberbijan and Kurdistan. He challenged Mossadegh, declaring that Iran did not have the expertise to run the oil industry, and that nationalization would only bring on hunger and even famine, especially among the poor.

And what, Mossadegh asked, did Razmara consider an alternative to nationalization?

"I advise that the Oil Commission start immediately to arbitrate with Anglo-Iranians for a new contract granting Iran 50% of profits," he replied.

Mossadegh, appearing very thin and fragile beside Razmara, recited the history, from its inception, of the Anglo-Iranian Oil Company as "irrefutable proof" that further attempts by Iran to negotiate with the British would be both painful and in vain.

Oil was struck in Iran in commercial quantities by the British Petroleum Company in 1908. It was renamed the Anglo-Iranian Oil Company and, with the British government as majority shareholder, it laid claim to all the oil in south Iran, granting Iran 30% of profits, payable from the net, not the gross income. And there was not one Iranian director, not one Iranian person who could demand to inspect the company books.

"I have to ask you, Mr. Prime Minister, how you can...how you dare..after all that we have suffered at their bloody hands... YOU WOULD HAVE US ABASE OURSELVES BY GOING ON OUR KNEES TO THAT COMPANY?" Mossadegh screamed those words, then fell to the floor in a faint. Two aides, physicians and Majlis members, accustomed by now to this behavior of his, worked at reviving him, albeit slowly.

When he finally recovered, Mossadegh seemed a changed person from the one he was before the blackout. He was very composed and collected as he reminded Razmara that the Anglo-Iranian was, as of the latest record taken in 1949, the largest oil-producing company in the world; its wells spouted more than 700,000 barrels of oil a day, a third of the whole Middle East production. And although a new consciousness in the "underdeveloped" countries had already forced companies in Saudi Arabia and Venezuela to move toward a fifty-fifty split, Anglo-Iranian had refused to negotiate with Iran for more than its old 70-30 arrangement. And now that Anglo-Iranian was willing to split 50-50 with Iran, Mossadegh had a message he wished Razmara would deliver to the directors:

"THEY ARE DUMB ASSES, NOT TO HAVE RECKONED WITH OUR IRANIAN PRIDE. If they had offered the same arrangement to us at the same time that the other companies did to Saudi Arabia and Venezuela, we would have accepted. But now that they have tried to steal our dignity by behaving as though ours is a lower form of nation...Tell them that, before we would grant them even five percent of our oil, even two percent, we would call in the camels from all over Iran and cause them to defecate until the wells would be drowned."

So, Aysha said, Barbara must realize that Mossadegh was ruled by instinct, by passion, by his loving heart. For this reason he had always walked along a thin, precarious edge of control. But this, far from having caused his people to turn from him, had rather wakened in them an incredible, indescribable tenderness toward him. Yet the Western media "including the American media that surpassed all of the others" mocked at Mossadegh...They called him "Iran's Willie-the-Weeper Statesman", "The Persian Fainting Wonder" and "The New Menace."

Aysha, Peri and all of their colleagues were enraged by the naiveté of America and its media, not only about Mossadegh (who happened to be the third richest landowner in Iran), but also about Iran's political culture. If they'd probed even somewhat, they would have realized Mossadegh, in great contrast to Western perceptions, was as beloved in Iran as Ghandi was in India.

On May 2, 1951, Mossadegh, now Prime Minister, announced the nationalization of the Anglo-Iranian Oil Company, and its wonderful new name, THE NATIONAL IRANIAN OIL COMPANY.

Voice choking, and joyous tears flowing, he said that if a good genie would offer him three wishes, his first wish, his only wish really, would be for his life to freeze at this exhilarating moment, the summit of his years. Now, though, turning from emotional expressions to practical considerations, he wanted the Majlis informed that he and his financial advisers believed that, although the National Iranian Oil Company might not extract and sell as much oil as Anglo-Iranian had done, they should be able not only to satisfy their own needs, but also to secure at least the revenues presently received from Anglo-Iranian. And, perhaps most important of all, the untapped oil might be kept in the ground until future generations of Iranians would benefit from it, instead of its being squandered on the enemy British .

The whole room, Majlis and observers, many weeping along with Mossadegh, rose to give him the most rousing, thunderous ovation they'd ever given him or anyone else before. The nationalization had given them and all the Persian people a validation, a new, prestigious identity. It said "No"; it shouted out to the world that IRAN WAS NO LONGER A POWERLESS PAWN TO BE USED AND ABUSED BY THE WESTERN NATIONS, but rather was their equal, and due to the oil she owned and they needed, perhaps even their superior.

But the world did not, as Mossadegh had expected, come begging for Iranian oil. Instead, Britain and its six sister international oil companies which included the American Aramco, doubled their production in Saudi-Arabia, Kuwait and Iraq, so that Iran's oil was not missed either by the British public or by former customers of AIOC. And in Iran itself, the oil industry came to a practical halt, and created an ever-deepening depression. By early 1953, the hunger and famine that Razmara had predicted had, indeed, happened.

On May 28th, 1953, a desperate Mossadegh appealed to President Eisenhower for aid. He had been counting on the favor of an America which earlier, under President Harry Truman and

Secretary of State Dean Acheson, had inveighed often against both British "intransigence" and the cruel boycott of Iran by the "Seven Sisters oil cartel".

"And Eisenhower did not respond to Mossadegh for a month," Aysha continued, "and when he did...'America can no longer continue to bail Iran out,' Eisenhower wrote, 'and you would not need help, Mr. Prime Minister, if you would resolve your problems with Britain and get your oil fields operating again.'"

Of course Aysha hadn't realized at the time that the Eisenhower letter was a warning to Iran that America's political climate—and its empathy for such nationalist third-world leaders as Mossadegh—was different now from what it had been under Roosevelt and Truman. It was also a prelude to the covert "Operation Ajax", conceived by Churchill, Eisenhower and Eisenhower's intensely anti-Soviet Secretary of State John Foster Dulles to overthrow Mossadegh.

"Operation Ajax" occurred on July 24, 1959, under the aegis of the then six year old CIA. It was headed by Kermit Roosevelt, grandson of Theodore, Chief of the Middle East Division of the CIA and an oil expert in high favor with the British. Earlier, with a million dollars of CIA money, he had bribed army officers and corrupt mullahs to spread rumors in the mosques and among the bazaaris that Mossadegh had sold out to Tudeh and to the Russian communists. And he gave Shaban (Brainless) Snafiari, head of the South Tehran sports clubs known for their criminal activities, a hundred thousand dollars to distribute to his members, which he did. And thousands of those members, armed with guns, knives and iron bars, followed his order to flood central Tehran. They screamed, "God save the Shah" and "Death to Mossadegh"; they beat up pro-Mossadegh demonstrators, turned over cars, burned office buildings and stormed through the gates of Mossadegh's home. He was arrested and sentenced to death for treason. The Shah, though, commuted his sentence to house arrest for the remainder of his life. "That way," Aysha said, "although he would be as lost to his followers as though he were indeed dead, Mohammed Reza didn't need to be concerned about the effect his martyrdom would have in Iran."

Aysha was silent a long while with her eyes closed. Finally, she said in a quiet, though bitter tone, "And the Shah, more repressive than ever since he had so powerful a friend and ally, sat more comfortably upon his throne than he'd been able to do before, while America—'Imperialist America'—now took the place of 'Imperialist Britain,' in the minds and hearts of the Iranian people."

Barbara, committed as she was to Aysha, totally accepted her interpretation of the CIA as Mossadegh's destroyer. She would not perceive until after she'd returned to America that the CIA could not, on its own, have overthrown Mossadegh. By the time "Operation Ajax" was effected, his position, due to the depression, was changed from what it had been. There had emerged outspoken anti-Mossadegh forces in the Majlis, not only among the royalists, but also the disillusioned middle class and civil servants. And when he attempted to override the chaos they created by dissolving the Majlis and taking dictatorial powers for himself, he made even more powerful enemies, especially among the religious, who had formerly backed him.

There is no question that by August 1953, Iran was in terrible trouble, and the Tudeh Party, sometimes with the encouragement of an increasingly desperate Mossadegh, grew in power as his National Front Party declined.

Even after she would learn these facts, though, Barbara would remain cynical and ashamed of her country. The fact was that America, whatever the circumstances were, helped to put the Shah back on the throne and to overthrow Iran's most beloved nationalist hero.

Now Aysha discussed with Barbara the second basic reason for Iranian hatred of America. Barbara already knew that, five years after Mossadegh's deposal, the CIA helped to organize Savak, and to train its operatives. But Aysha had never before detailed the specifics to her. To begin with, she said, not only enemies of the Shah, but all Iranians had been, from its inception, terrified of Savak. This was because of the belief, deliberately fostered, that SAVAK HAS GOT ITS EYE ON YOU AND IS GOING TO KNOW WHATEVER YOU SAY, OR DO, OR THINK. Aysha said that as teachers, she and Peri were aware that at least two students in each of their classrooms were Savakan informants. "And the reason there are two or more is that Savak doesn't even trust its own agents...The spies are assigned also to spy on one another."

The same was true in business and industry and on the farms as it was in the high schools and colleges. People with even minor influence could be certain that their every act, their every word was being weighed and considered by the spies in their midst. They knew that they'd either confess to anything they were accused of, or suffer under Savakan instruments of torture. These included electric prods on their genitals, clubs and heavy weights for breaking their bones and then re-breaking them once they were partially healed, soft-drink bottles for forcing up their rectums, vaginas and sometimes both, and bedsprings for them to be tied down upon while the wires were heated from warm to hot and finally, to temperatures hot enough to sear the skin.

"And, if you stay silent through all of this, why then, they have another technique that is practically guaranteed to break you down," Aysha continued. "They will bring your wife, husband, lover, children, parents before you, and force you to watch them tortured...They will rape your children, babies included, in front of you. If nothing else does, that'll force you to do as they want. Then they may offer you a job you'd better not turn down if you want to live free again. So far as they are concerned, you can live the rest of your life in prison if you refuse their order to spy, not on strangers, but on the people to whom you have the most immediate access...YOUR FAMILY AND FRIENDS. I often think to myself that, of all the many horrors the Savak has inflicted upon us, the worst one is that they've caused us to doubt and fear our nearest and dearest.

"And I sometimes wonder whether I...I'd have the courage to stand against Savak, no matter how I'd be tortured by them. Then I think of Peri, and also Khanoum-June. And I know that if I saw Peri tied down on one of their bedsprings, or Khanoum-June lying face down on the floor with one of their bottles stuck inside her, I would give up and cry out, I'LL DO ANYTHING, NO MATTER HOW ABHORRENT, SO LONG AS YOU LET HER GO!"

Sḥiites vs. Sunnis

Barbara had occasion to remember her conversation with Aysha about Savak when, two years later, she and Farah sat in a long, narrow jail-like room waiting for Fatemeh, the famed folgar (soothsayer and healer). There was an odd mingling of bad smells in the room. Tobacco and urine, with which Fatemeh was reputed to heal wounds doctors called "hopeless"; souring milk she used for calling up her spirits; and the high, bitter smell of the anxiety of people who had, for the past forty years, brought her their problems.

Barbara, holding Farah's sweating hand in hers, could hardly believe they were here for the reason that they were. A week earlier Farah, having been immensely depressed and having avoided Barbara for many weeks now, telephoned to say that she needed to see her right away. When Barbara arrived at Farah's before ten o'clock in the morning, she found Farah, who seldom touched alcohol, very nearly drunk.

"Thanks for coming, Barbara." Farah's beautiful eyes were lusterless, and there were deep circles under them. Her mouth was twitching. "Mehrdad wants to divorce me," she said.

"But he adores you...my God, Farah, why?"

"He says...It's exactly because he loves me so much that he can't bear...He's going to divorce me for my sake, he says."

"Do you know what he means?" Barbara asked gently, and Farah nodded as tears began to splash down her cheeks. She said that what he meant...Barbara had known for as long as she and Farah had been friends how she had always been terrified for Mehrdad because of his anti-Shah politics and membership in Tudeh. Always before, though, she'd managed to keep her fear under control; however, it had become more consuming in recent months. Every time Mehrdad came home later than he said he would, she felt herself being driven crazy by her mind's horrendous pictures. She envisioned Mehrdad in a hospital, his head covered with bandages, looking up at the faces of Savakan agents who were prying for the information he'd die before releasing to them, i.e. the identities of his Tudeh colleagues. Or she saw him crushed beneath a Savakan car. Or flattened under a Savakan tank.

And then came the night Farah believed heralded the breakdown of her and Mehrdad's relationship. It was twenty minutes past twelve, and Mehrdad had faithfully promised he'd be home at eleven. No question now but that he was lost to Farah. MEHRDAD WAS DEAD.

No, he wasn't, he couldn't be. God couldn't be so cruel.

What God? If ever a person needed to believe, to be able to pray..."Protect and save this good man, this fine man, God," Farah prayed, although with little faith or hope. Yet she'd barely finished her prayer when, miraculously, there was Mehrdad, leaning over her where she lay shivering on the bed, kissing and caressing her while she stayed passive, letting the flood of his love wash over her. And then suddenly, against all her instincts, she heard herself screeching out: "WHERE IN THE HELL HAVE YOU BEEN SO LATE, BASTARD?"

Now Farah put her head into her hands, and Barbara saw her shoulders heave with sobs, but she soon composed herself.

"Why did I do that? Why did I sound like a bitch, when all I wanted to do was let Mehrdad know how happy I was at his being home?"

"Mehrdad knew what you meant, Farah."

"No. No, he didn't."

From that night on, Farah's and Mehrdad's relationship began to deteriorate and become more difficult with each passing day. She could not keep herself from weeping whenever he left, and pleading with him not to go. Nor could she keep from showing her resentment when he ignored her importuning and went anyway. And he was constantly angry at her for trying to prevent him from doing what he saw as his duty.

And when they agreed that he would phone her whenever he found the chance, in the hope it might lighten her fear, she, despite her constant warnings to herself, wept on the telephone as she did in person, and begged him to come home. On more than one occasion he slammed the phone down with a force that smacked of punishment. Farah had felt a threat from him then, frighteningly palpable although unspoken: Someday you will go too far with your tears and pleading, and I will do more than bang down a receiver; I WILL LEAVE.

Mehrdad apologized profusely after the first time he hung up on her, and he and Farah kissed and held one another for a long time. But when he took off his clothes, he was not erect for her, and although she attempted with her hand and mouth, she could not help him to achieve an erection. And many times after that, although he was able to penetrate her, he did not come to orgasm, and neither did she.

She'd see his expression of failure and feel her head aching with tears. "It's all my fault, Mehrdad...If I didn't cry so much, and nag..."

"No, Sweetheart."

"Yes. I know. Listen, I'm going to change...You'll see. Well, I'm going to TRY to change."

"Sure, dearest, and I'm going to try..."

Try what, Farah wondered, but never asked.

Day by day, Farah and Mehrdad grew farther apart, although she didn't cry any more in his presence. Now she walked him to the door in the morning and waited to cry 'til it closed behind him. "And one morning, Barbara, he came back unexpectedly, and...He took one look at me and he began...It was almost as though we both began crying at the same moment. It was sad, but also beautiful. We sat a long time crying and holding hands, and then I said, 'Maybe you could give up Tudeh, and...Oh God, how I wish that I could be enough for you, that our children and I could be enough. The way that you love Dawneh and Rocky, Mehrdad, think how it would be to have our own. And he said...'" Farah twisted her mouth and sipped her drink.

"And he said...?"

Farah looked away from Barbara and stared at her drink. "He said, 'A child would be one more instrument for you to use against Tudeh...against me.'"

"Surely he didn't mean..."

"No. He said he was sorry the minute the words were out of his mouth. And he said he loved me even more now than he had before we were married, and...he said that he understood and sympathized with my longing for a child, but that he had promised himself long ago that he would never bring a child into Mohammed Reza's rotten, cruel world. Besides, his revolutionary commitment precluded his becoming a father, since you never know how long you'll live in that situation.

"And suddenly, I...It's so humiliating, embarrassing to have been...Barbara, I suddenly felt myself being eaten up alive by my jealousy toward all those members of Tudeh, who knew a part of my husband that had always been closed to me, and to whom...His commitment to them was greater than to me, that's the way it seemed at the time, and I said, 'You shouldn't have married me or any woman, Mehrdad...YOU SHOULD HAVE MARRIED TUDEH.' I kept pounding on him, demanding he choose between me and his 'other wife'... 'It's me or Tudeh, Mehrdad,' I screamed, although I knew it was crazy; I thought I was going crazy, maybe I had already gone crazy.

"And that was when Mehrdad said that he loved me too much to see me so hurt, and that he was going to divorce me for my good. He was sobbing, and he screamed out, 'I must be the only man in Iran...or anywhere...who's divorcing a wife out of love, not hate.'"

Farah came to where Barbara sat, buried her head in Barbara's lap and cried. They were like that for a long time. Barbara had never heard anyone cry so long, so hard.

Eventually, Farah's sobs subsided. She stood up and went to her dressing room. When she returned she seemed somewhat calmed as she said quietly, "I called you today because...Remember when you said that I'd always been there when you needed me, and that you...THIS TIME I NEED YOU, Barbara. I want you to come with me to Fatemeh, the folgar. If she foresees Mehrdad's life as being long, or at least not ending in the near future...Don't look at me that way...It isn't that I have that much faith in Fatemeh, but...How do you know she doesn't see into the future? I mean, really, how do you KNOW?"

Barbara had learned by now that many Persians, including not just the likes of Toobah, Mitrah, Khanoum-June and, yes, Hajji Khadivar and even Baba Bozorg himself, but also graduates of Western universities with doctorate degrees, patronize folgars, and pay serious heed to their predictions and "cures". She therefore said, "When, Farah, shall we go to Fatemeh's?"

Fatemeh's appearance came as a surprise to Barbara. She had a flat face with one eye clouded by a cataract, a lumbering body, fat legs and swollen feet in men's shoes with the toes cut out.

Farah and Barbara sat facing Fatemeh as she clapped her hands for her assistant, Sherezade, a crooked little lady who looked like a gnome as she limped in to hand Fatemeh a Koran and a pot full of souring milk. Fatemeh dipped her hand into the pot, then rubbed her fingers over Farah's and Barbara's faces. Next, she poured the milk over their heads.

Then Fatemeh kissed the Koran and handed it to Farah and Barbara to kiss; she sat with her good eye closed, rubbing the Koran with her right hand. She then placed Barbara's hand under her own on the Koran; Barbara instinctively withdrew her hand, saying that since she was here on Farah's account, she hoped that Farah's communication would take precedence here. Fatemeh informed her that HER SPIRITS, NOT THE SUPPLICANT'S, guided her and her message-delivery time. If Barbara didn't like that, found it too difficult to submit, YES, SUBMIT TO THE SPIRITS' DIRECTION, why, then...Barbara, responding to the importunement in Farah's eyes, apologized to Fatemeh and placed her hand back on the Koran. After a few minutes, Fatemeh removed her hand from underneath Barbara's, swung away from her, rose up and, followed by Sheherezade, walked out.

Soon Farah and Barbara heard marching music coming eerily over a loudspeaker as an accompaniment to Fatemeh's shrieking. "Farah, and Bar-ba-ra, farangi, YOU TWO WILL LIVE TO EXPERIENCE THE COMING OF THE HIDDEN IMMAM HIMSELF."

The concept of the Hidden Immam, one of the most significant in all of Iranian Islam, cannot be comprehended without knowledge of Islamic history from the time the Prophet Mohammed died in

634. Two parties arose then, and battled one another for power and the right of their leaders to replace Mohammed. The majority sect, the Sunnis–Moslems of the Right Path–was led by Abu Bakr, the Prophet's long-term lieutenant, his dearest friend, and the father of his beloved Aysha. The Sunnis declared that, since Mohammed had left no orders for choosing his successor, by all rights he had to be elected. The minority faction, Shiat Ali (Partisans of Ali), believed that the Prophet's son-in-law, and his sons after him, were Mohammed's only legitimate heirs.

The Sunnis triumphed, electing Abu Bakr caliph to take Mohammed's place. And when Abu Bakr died after two years, the Sunni warrior, Omar, assumed office. He was stabbed to death by a Shiite slave; his successor, Omar Sunni, was also killed by Shiites.

Now, at last, Ali the Shiite succeeded to the throne; he was assassinated by the Sunnis. So was Ali's son, Hussein, who, like Jesus, is believed to have sacrificed himself for the good of mankind, and is Shiah Islam's premier saint.

Shiah became the established religion of Iran at the beginning of the 16th century, and was the faith, as it is today, of 90% of its people. About four-fifths of the world's Shiites are Iranians with small numbers living in Iraq, Pakistan, Afghanistan and the two Yemens. Worldwide, though, there is no numeric comparison between them and the Sunnis. Six hundred million strong in Turkey, the Arab countries and Pakistan, as well as in Bangladesh, Malaysia, Indonesia and much of black Africa, Sunnis outnumber Shiites fifteen to one.

Perhaps the most bitter discord between Sunnis and Shiites occurs around the concepts of the Moslem Immamate and the Hidden Immam. To the Sunnis, the Immams are the prayer leaders of the people, while to the Shiites this function is reserved for the twelve saints of the religion—limited to Ali, Hussein and their descendants. And the Shiites' "Hidden Immam" is the last of the saints, the twelfth one. He, in the year 784 at the age of four or five, went into hiding and is still alive in Iran, though unknown to his fellows. Someday, this Hidden Immam will reappear and bring about the triumph of justice and virtue, just as the world will seem to be nearing its end.

It is for the Hidden Immam's sake, more than because of the Shah's Westernization or even his denial of human rights, that the faithful of Shiah Islam were up in arms against Mohammed Reza. For their holy truth declares that the Hidden Immam is the only legitimate ruler of Iran.And it states that until he reappears, the country must be ruled not by any ordinary man like Mohammed Reza, but by the Immam's surrogate, chosen from among all the ayatollahs as being the most godlike and pure of heart.

Fatemeh continued shrieking that Farah and Barbara would witness the world nearly coming to an end and the Immam's coming. Barbara, moved in spite of herself, glanced at Farah, whose whole body was taut. She tried to take Farah's hand, but couldn't because the fingers of her two hands were wrung too tightly together.

Now Fatemeh's voice calmed somewhat. "The signs of the appearance of the Immam are many, as the Hadith (true sayings of the Prophet, compiled from the time of his death to the present) tells us. So know you, Farah, and you, Bar-ba-ra, although you are farangi, that the first sign of the Immam's advent according to the Hadith will be the coming of the Daijol, a one-eyed man who is skilled in the magics.

"And, although you two will not ever meet the Daijol in person, you already have met his female representative. For I, Fatemeh, am also one-eyed and skilled in the magics...And, as the female representative of the Daijol, I say to you, Farah and Bar-ba-ra, that you will hear shouting in the sky like thunder: 'THE HIDDEN IMMAM HAS ARRIVED, AND THE RIGHTEOUSNESS IS COME.' Such an IMMOLATION will there be in Iran, such a HOLOCAUST. All of Iran will be turned into A SHOOTING GALLERY. People will be murdered by the thousands...And you, Bar-ba-ra, will lose your three best friends, although not during, but sometime after the holocaust."

When Fatemeh's gory omen was concluded, Barbara told herself over and over that she didn't believe a word the crazy woman had spoken. Why, then, did she need to keep repeating that to herself? And why did she feel such panic? Her mind was so confused. "You came here as an American, scoffing at such things," she said to herself, "and now, suddenly, you feel like a Persian born and bred."...For an instant Barbara entered into Farah's mind, thinking like her, believing as she did, in a part of herself anyway, that Fatemeh's predictions were very much to be reckoned with.

Barbara got up, went to Farah whose face was buried in her hands, stroked her hair and said softly, "Even if Fatemeh's prediction...She couldn't have meant Mehrdad when she was talking to me, not you, and about my three best friends, not your husband."

Farah took her face out of her hands, and flung her head back. "Well, I consider...Mehrdad's one of your best friends, Barbara."

"But remember, Fatemeh said my three best friends."

"Yes, your three...Aysha, Peri and me, not Mehrdad at all."

The relieved expression on Farah's face caused Barbara to think to herself...You are SOME LADY, Farah. If you were given the choice between Mehrdad's salvation and your own, you'd settle on his, wouldn't you? Suddenly she felt a jealousy toward Farah like a hot stone in her stomach. Will I ever feel for anyone the all-consuming love she does for Mehrdad?

Now Fatemeh, followed by Sheherezade, came back into the room, her good eye wide open and a kind of smile on her face. "I am sorry, Farah," she said, "that I was unable...that the spirits would not contact me on your behalf. Another day, perhaps...And, meanwhile, much that has been shown to be...The kismet of Bar-ba-ra, the farangi, is in some ways also applicable to you."

She motioned to Sheherezade, who put into her hand two ornately embroidered sacks the size of tea bags, which she then gave to Farah and Barbara. "You must wear these always, never be without them."

"What are they, Fatemeh?" Barbara asked.

"Good luck amulets."

"But what use...Can they save my friends?"

"THEY CAN, IF ANYTHING CAN."

Iran's faithful said about the Ayatollah Borujerdi, surrogate for the "Hidden Immam" and leader of Shiite Islam worldwide from 1950 'til his death in 1961, that he was the best of men—a living picture of the Prophet Himself. They said that, even if you'd never had the honor of being a member of his personal audience, but had only seen him in a crowd, you would have felt the warmth in him. And, although he had every opportunity to become as rich as the "worldly ayatollah", Jomeh, who had been educated in Lausanne, spoke fluent French, wore European clothes and was so closely aligned with Mohammed Reza that he was known as "the Shah's Boy". Although many, from the faithful bazaaris to the Shah himself, would have exulted in the chance to contribute to Borujerdi's personal well-being, he accepted everything for the poor but nothing for himself; he died possessed of a single samovar.

After the death of the Ayatollah Borujerdi, the faithful wondered which one of the Ayatollahs would be sufficiently without fault or flaw to take his place. The Ayatollah Ruhollah Khomeini was only one of several candidates, and not necessarily the front-runner. But when God, whose ways are not comprehensible to ordinary people, uplifted Khomeini to be the replacement for the Ayatollah Borujerdi, there was no question but that THEY WOULD LOVE HIM as they had his predecessor.

What did it matter that he was, in almost every way, the exact opposite of the Ayatollah Borujerdi? To know the Ayatollah Khomeini was to know that he wore the impress of the murder of his father (also an ayatollah) by the governor of Khomein, the town from which he took his name, etched indelibly upon his consciousness. This was one of many reasons why, while the less-troubled Ayatollah Borujerdi gave out an aura of softness and gentility, the atmosphere around the Ayatollah Khomeini was one of anger and fury...although toward the people's enemies, never the people.

How often had the Ayatollah Khomeini, from youngest manhood on, not preached openly against "the unjust, carnal-minded godless Pahlavis, a family full of looters whose arms are sunk in the blood of the innocent." The people were "the innocent" for whom their ayatollah demanded justice. He was ready to give his life for the lives of their children and them. The question they had to have asked themselves, therefore, was: Were they ready to give their lives for him and for God's righteousness on earth? And they always had to remember that when they said "him" they meant not only the

Ayatollah Khomeini in his body, but also the Hidden Immam, Hussein and Hassan, the martyr saints, Mohammed the Prophet and Allah himself.

The answer to the question was–in fact had to have been–Yes, certainly I would die for the Ayatollah Khomeini. Meaning I would die for God. Such a death would be the greatest honor in the world and would assure me a place close to the Prophet Himself at the heavenly table as well as my pick of the most beautiful of the heavenly houris.

As it happened, great numbers of the faithful would be granted, only some two years after his ascendancy, the opportunity to fight and die for the Ayatollah Khomeini.

It was five o'clock in the morning on June 4, 1963...Two hours earlier, a dozen armed soldiers had invaded the home of the Ayatollah Khomeini, and placed him under arrest. Khomeini was arrested for organizing anti-government riots after the Shah's announcement of his "White Revolution", whose most important feature was land reform. This took an immense amount of arable land from both the traditional landlords and the Islamic Church, and distributed it to the peasants. And the fact was that Khomeini, "reflection of Allah" though he was, was also among the wealthiest landholders in Iran, and thus fought with every weapon at his command against the land reform.

By nine o'clock that morning, the faithful of Tehran, Shiraz, Meshed and Mashad, having been informed over the private telephone systems of the mosques and bazaars of what had taken place in Quom, gathered in front of their mosques. And they were joined by Tudehists, National Frontiers and many of the urban middle class and even upper class young. These people, though they might have rejected Khomeini's fanatic religiosity, nevertheless respected him for his dedicated campaign against the absence of freedom of speech, press and assembly in their high schools and colleges.

Mehrdad, Aysha and Peri were at the Tehran demonstration, and mercifully came through it alive and uninjured, though over a thousand in Tehran who came along, and at least four thousand nationally, were killed by the Shah's soldiers.

Their faces tense and all of them, even Mehrdad, on the edge of hysteria, Aysha, Peri and Mehrdad told Barbara and Farah how the killings had happened. Their reports jumbled in Barbara's brain and melded hideously with her recollections of Fatemeh's portent: "Such an immolation will there be in Iran, such a holocaust...People will be murdered by the scores, and hundreds and thousands...THE DEAD AND WOUNDED WILL LITTER THE STREETS..."

All had happened according to Fatemeh's predictions. "And you, Bar-ba-ra, the farangi," she had declared with such sinister assurance, "will lose your three best friends, although not during, but after the holocaust."

And Barbara thought, "Now is after the holocaust, God, and I'm in mortal fear for Farah and Peri and Aysha...As crazy as that may seem."

CHAPTER XIV

The Lowest Year

The weeks and months after the June demonstration were immensely significant ones in Iran, and also for its "ally" America, which presaged a change in the countries' relationships. President Kennedy, who deplored Eisenhower's tactics in Iran and tried to force the Shah to adopt human rights reforms by making certain arms sales dependent upon them, was assassinated. And Iranians, even those who despised America, mourned for him.

Mohammed Reza, during the updating of an old bilateral agreement, granted United States military advisors immunity from prosecution under the Iranian law. Khomeini thundered out that the decree "places the Iranian people under American bondage...because America is the land of the dollar, and the Shah needs dollars."

President Johnson was too occupied with the Vietnam War and his own "Great Society" to continue Kennedy's pattern of prodding Mohammed Reza for reform. And a 1963 West German poll showed that 85% of young Iranians perceived American aid as "working to make the rich richer."

Yet Barbara's friends flourished. And the time came when, certainly, she and even Farah could smile at the thought of Fatemeh's predictions. And both Barbara, who'd gone on wearing her amulet for Farah's sake, and Farah herself, unceremoniously removed them.

This took place on November 25, 1963. Three days later, on Thanksgiving, which was, of course, not a holiday in Iran, Barbara's phone rang at two o'clock in the morning. It was Maryam. "I just heard, Barbara, Aysha is dead," she said flatly.

Aysha was dead...It happened while Peri was away to see her grandmother, who was dying in Meshed. Maryam and Behdjat were accustomed to lunching with Aysha every day while Peri was gone. Two days ago, though, she hadn't shown up for lunch, and they found she'd not been in her classes either.

They phoned her all though the day and night and, receiving no answer, went to her flat the next morning. Their knocking attracted the attention of the building superintendent's wife, Shamsi, who told them that Aysha was not at home.

"Do you know where she is, Shamsi?" Maryam asked.

"I don't know where...They didn't say where they were taking her, Khanoum."

Behdjat asked, "Who took her, Shamsi?"

Shamsi began to cry and remonstrate with them...She begged them to please not force her to answer that question, because her husband would beat her if she did. And the National Police would come back and kill her and her family.

Behdjat and Maryam knew that if the National Police had come for Aysha, she'd been fingered by Savak. Therefore they solicited Cyrus, Maryam's brother, to accompany them to the Tehran Hilton Hotel where many Savakan officials ate and drank. They believed, in their panic, that they might eavesdrop on some useful information about Aysha, and so stayed at the Hilton 'til nearly midnight, eating and downing drinks they didn't want. Then they went together to Maryam's where their colleague, Farah Mansur, had been awaiting them for hours. She showed them a memorandum, typed on university stationery but unsigned, that had been distributed to all the faculty.

"For Your Information: Killer and terrorist Dr. Aysha Quasam, formerly of this faculty, is dead at her own hand. Surrounded yesterday by the National Police in her South Tehran hideout, she blew herself and her headquarters up with a hand grenade."

Barbara sat frozen on the opposite side from Maryam and Behdjat in Aysha's study, recalling all the times that she'd sat there in trouble and been uplifted. She read and reread the shocking words "...blew herself and her headquarters up with a hand grenade." Aysha, so vivid with her thick dark hair flowing loose, her eyes dark and alive, her infectious laughter, the quickness of her marvelous mind...Aysha, Barbara's beloved mentor and guide, was dead. There was one thing, though, that Barbara knew as clearly as she knew anything: Aysha had not blown herself up. She loved Peri too much. And life. Barbara remembered back to her last conversation with Aysha about Savak. Aysha had said that when the officials wanted it known that their victims were dead, they portrayed them as either pulling guns or grenades on arresting policemen, who then had no choice except to kill them in self-defense, or else as so stupid or frightened of the records of their terrorists being revealed as to blow themselves up with their own hand grenades.

Well, Aysha was neither stupid nor a terrorist. Barbara knew that she wouldn't have blown either herself or anyone else up. Yet Barbara couldn't drive out of her head another conversation with Aysha about Mossadegh and murder and terrorism in Iran. Aysha had admitted–no, declared proudly–that she'd have killed if either Mossadegh or she had judged it necessary for achieving the people's freedom. Facing up to that fact then, Barbara said to herself, or rather to Aysha, "Know this then, dear Aysha...Just as you believed that whatever Mossadegh did or contemplated doing, murder not excepted, was for the good of the people, so I believe it about you. And I know that if you did kill, if you did, as they say, terrorize, you were driven not by any evil but by your goodness, compassion and love of people."

Maryam told Barbara that her brother Cyrus had gone in Aysha's place to the airport to meet Peri's three a.m. plane, and should be back with her any minute.

"My God," Barbara asked, "Who's going to tell Peri?"

Before anyone else could answer, Peri came through the door, Cyrus behind her, and Barbara knew that no one would have to tell her. She came over to Barbara and put her arms around her.

"Oh, God, I'm so sorry, Peri," Barbara whispered.

"Did you see her, Barbara, before... Savak got her, didn't they?"

"Yes. Oh Peri..."

"I ought to place a call to Aysha's mother. It'll be easier for her to hear it from me," Peri said.

She went into her own study, shut the door and didn't come out for half an hour. Then she went to Behdjat and Maryam and embraced them. "It's so good of you to be here at this hour. I don't know what I would have done otherwise... my God."

She looked at Cyrus who was standing there. "Forgive me for

not thanking you sooner for picking me up. I was too surprised to see you instead of..." She stood now between Maryam and Behdjat, their eyes red. She touched their cheeks gently, in turn. "I suppose...I suppose you two were the last to see her alive. I want to ask you so many questions, how she looked, how she felt..."

Only then did she put her head in her hands and weep. "There were so many nights," she gasped out, "when I awoke in a panic, believing that something would happen to take Aysha and the love we shared away. And I told myself then as I am doing now...I feel, today, that I am one of the world's most fortunate ones to have had so much of her for so long. For twenty years we were the center of one another's lives, and...knowing all that Aysha's done for so many over the years, I feel so proud of her that I could burst."

And Barbara, as all of "the group" did, took her cue from Peri, celebrating Aysha's life in the midst of mourning her death.

1963 was the darkest year, the lowest year for Barbara's friends, and therefore for her as well. Less than a month after Savak's killing of Aysha, Mehrdad vanished. Farah and everyone who loved him believed, necessarily, that he too had been killed by Savak, or else was being held in prison.

Thanksgiving and Christmas would always, from then on, be nightmarish times for Barbara. As she'd learned about Aysha's death on Thanksgiving Day, so she was faced with Mehrdad's disappearance on Christmas Eve. Knowing that Barbara would be especially homesick on that night, he'd arranged to take her and Farah to dinner, but hadn't come home then...or ever. During the first months of Farah's mourning, she cried a great deal, declaring over and over that if only she could know what had happened to Mehrdad she could, as Peri had, make some kind of adjustment. If she only knew he was dead. Day after day she, accompanied sometimes by Soraya, sometimes by Barbara and sometimes by both of them, went to the Hilton Hotel to eavesdrop on Savakan officials, though knowing its futility all the time, as Behdjat and Maryam had.

But the time came when Farah, with no urging from Soraya or Barbara, gave up her vigil and exhibited, in place of the constant crying and mourning, an eerie calm. From morning on, heavily made up and dressed elaborately in the kind of clothes she used to ridicule, she held court in her company salon for relatives and friends. She talked earnestly and sincerely about them and their interests, never about Mehrdad, not even when she was pointedly questioned. And when she'd had her fill of their company, she thanked them for coming in a cold, sing-song voice that was entirely bereft of her usual warmth, and made it clear she wanted them gone.

She treated Barbara as politely, coolly...and unbendingly...as she did her other "guests." She turned away from any conversation about Mehrdad or the feelings she used to share so totally with Barbara, and asked her over and over not only about Rocky and Dawn but also about her life at the university. She'd sit, hands folded in her lap, looking into Barbara's face and eagerly awaiting her answers. And when Barbara, only partly joking, once remarked that Farah had phrased her questions about the university as though they were momentous, Farah had smiled gently, and said that, to her, everything about Barbara was momentous. Translation, as Barbara perceived it: You are more important to me than I am to you. A posture that was as foreign to the old Farah as her new, high-pitched voice.

The third phase of Farah's mourning began in June, some six months after Mehrdad's disappearance. Soraya, frightened for her daughter to live alone, had begged to be allowed to come and stay with her; Farah had always said an unyielding no to her appeals. Now, though, Farah asked her mother to come to stay and, when she did, rushed into her arms as though she'd not seen her for a long time.

"Oh, Mother..."

They held each other, rocking back and forth and crying, and then Soraya held Farah at arm's length. She looked into her face, almost skeletal as a result of her near-starvation, and her hollow, huge eyes, and pushed back her hair.

"Will you do something for me, Sweetheart?" Soraya asked.

In a small voice: "Yes, Mother, certainly." Then intensely, anxiously: "What...What do you want me to do?"

"Will you eat some dinner with Barbara and me?"

Farah nodded. "Yes. I'd like that."

They sat down then to a dinner of Farah's favorite foods: yogurt soup, chelo kebab and broiled pumpkin. At first Soraya fed Farah like a baby, a spoonful of soup, a forkful of kebab. But Farah soon began eating by herself, like the starving person she was. And afterward, she, after having been unable to sleep and dreading going to bed for months, excused herself soon after dinner because she wanted to rest. Seeing this, Soraya and Barbara shared a feeling of relief and even hope for her.

But the following afternoon, while Barbara was at tea with Soraya and Farah who, she thought wistfully, was less tense, the doorbell rang and Dr. Mohammed Amuzegar, one of Tehran's most prestigious physicians, was shown into the family salon.

"Which one of you ladies summoned me, please?"

A luminous smile from Farah. "I did, Doctor."

"I came as soon as I could."

"And I thank you very much."

"Can you tell me the nature of your husband's injury, Khanoum?"

Quietly, very quietly: "I would prefer for you to see him for yourself, Doctor."

They went, with Farah in the lead, to her and Mehrdad's bedroom.

Soraya lurched forward in her chair as if she'd been shot from behind. "Aaah, God, Barbara, just when everything seemed to be going so well..."

Barbara and Soraya were sitting in miserable silence when Dr. Amuzegar, followed by a wild-eyed Farah, came out of the bedroom. Farah pointed at him, a small, plump man in his sixties, and said, "Look at this...this doctor, ha...this pouter pigeon of a so-called doctor dared say to me...I told him, 'You, Dr. Pouter-Pigeon, must be blind not to see a man lying in the bed in front of your eyes.'"

Suddenly she became silent, and looked and kept on looking at Barbara, Soraya and Amuzegar, pulling all of them into her huge suffering eyes. Then she said, "I'm going to my bedroom if you will pardon me." And spitefully to Dr. Amuzegar: "My husband's and my bedroom."

Soraya, staring at Amuzegar, apologized for her daughter. He stopped her with a compassionate smile and lifting of his small pudgy hand. (My God, he really does look a pouter pigeon, Barbara thought, but such a kindly, good pigeon, Farah.) He said to Soraya, "Khanoum, Khanoum, I don't believe that we can begin to know the hell that poor girl is going through."

Soraya made a small, helpless gesture with her hands. "Yes, and I was hoping...Is there any medication that will give her some relief?"

"I can give her tranquilizers that may offer some temporary relief, but basically...She should be put under psychiatric care as soon as possible. As an in-patient."

Soraya looked at him in panic. What did he mean by those words "psychiatric care" and "in-patient"? She'd heard the words before, and what they really meant were "crazy" and "lunatic asylum." And she knew what the Tehran asylum was like because she'd once visited an old servant there. She'd been shown into a kind of huge cage behind a locked door where her servant and seven other mindless women sat on the floor in their own excrement, looking as though waiting for the release that only death would bring.

No. Not that for her child, her baby. She shook her head fiercely, her hand pressed to her mouth. "Oh no, Doctor, Farah is not crazy, and even if...She will never go to an asylum as long as I'm alive."

Amuzegar patted Soraya's arm soothingly, and explained that he was talking not about Iran's asylums, but about European or American private psychiatric facilities. There, people in such trouble as Farah, not crazy people but ones with life's problems that seem beyond them, are helped to work the problems through. Or to learn to live with them with the least amount of pain. He did not mind telling Soraya that while he was a student at the University of Kansas he, who'd had minor depressions from childhood on, had a major breakdown and had been over a year at perhaps the most highly regarded psychiatric hospital in America, the Menninger Clinic.

"What my time there did for me...The short version of it is that I've come to know myself in a way I didn't before, and therefore I'm a more fulfilled, happier person. And I'll be glad, Khanoum, to give you the long version—all the details you may find applicable to your daughter's situation—at your convenience."

Soraya, with a wry smile, replied, "Yes, well, thank you Doctor, I may take advantage of your generous offer." And thought to herself, and later told Barbara, that she'd have nothing further to do with him.

When Amuzegar left, Soraya and Barbara went to Farah who, from bed, looked at them with such incredible misery as was unbearable, and caused them to turn from her for a moment. When they turned back, they saw Farah leap up and run into her dressing room. They went after her, but she'd locked the door. In answer to their banging and pleading with her to come out or allow them in, she screamed nonsense words with whooping sounds that began low but grew louder and fuller all the time. She emerged in about a half-hour; she'd scratched her face with her long nails until it bled.

Soraya, having spent hours with Amuzegar and, at his suggestion, on the telephone with a Menninger Clinic psychiatrist after Farah's last acts, became convinced that she could, indeed, benefit from going there. And miraculously, Farah, temporarily calmed by tranquilizers, had herself declared after a conversation with the doctor that she knew Mehrdad would urge her to seek help if he could. She was therefore eager to go to the Menninger Clinic for as long as would be necessary for her recovery.

The problem, though, was money. Soraya had none, and all of Mehrdad's assets, including his and Farah's home, as well as her promised dowry, were administered by his father. And he was either lying or had truly persuaded himself that Farah had led Mehrdad into Tudeh and was, therefore, responsible for his (the father's) tragedy. Further, he'd declared to Soraya that Farah, "like all those American-educated men-women," had not borne him grandsons to comfort him in his old age now that his son was gone. How, then, could Soraya expect him to lift a finger to help the woman who'd destroyed his son?

"Finally," Soraya told Barbara, "I went to Farah's father and...Oh God, Barbara, Mohammed said, 'If what you're telling me, Soraya, is that your daughter has gone crazy, you don't have to spend all that money to send her to an American lunatic asylum when there's one right here in Tehran.'"

Hearing Soraya, Barbara wondered why she'd been so stupid as to have permitted Soraya even to start out on her humiliating mission. Why hadn't she realized that she could supply her and Farah with whatever money they'd need? True, she didn't have much cash immediately available, but since she was servicing (yes, servicing was still the word) Bahram to his satisfaction, she had only to ask for more money to have him give it.

So Soraya, laughing and gay, told Farah that they'd leave for America soon; their money problem, thanks to Barbara, was resolved.

Farah stared at Barbara coldly, then spoke through tight lips to Soraya. "I do not want to take her money, Mother."

Barbara was hurt, but tried to smile at Farah. "I guess you don't understand, Farah. It'll be Bahram's money, not mine...All I'll have to do..."

Farah spoke only to Soraya. "I mean it, Mother, I do not want her dirty, imperialist money. She believes that she can pay for her and her country's crimes with money, thinks she can pay for Mehrdad's killing or imprisonment with money...I don't want her money, Mother, and I don't want her favors!"

CHAPTER XVI

The Gift of Laughter

Only days after her harrowing time with Farah, Barbara had to appear the involved hostess at yet another of her interminable salons. But this time the guests, who had always, in her perception, ranged from dull to obnoxious, included three newcomers who stood out as different.

The first was Dr. Amir Abbas Hoveyda, Minister of Finance, who would in the following year become prime minister. He must have been in his middle forties at the time, short and already balding, but with almost black eyes that looked at you in a way that made you feel as though you were the most important person in his world.

To Barbara he appeared like a writer or poet or reformer, but not a politician. And he was, as it turned out, not very different from Barbara's first judgment of him. A poet and strong democrat, he would never have joined the Shah's government if he had not believed, as did many liberals at the time, that the agrarian reform instituted by Mohammed Reza's "White Revolution" heralded a democratization of Iran.

One of the most brilliant, charming, sophisticated people Barbara would meet in Iran or anywhere, Hoveyda was the son of a diplomat who had lived with his family in Egypt, Syria, Saudi Arabia, Palestine and Yemen. His secondary school had been the Lycée Français in Beirut, and his colleges were the Université Libre in Brussels where he took his M.A. in political science, and the Sorbonne where he got his doctorate in history. His favorite city was Paris, where his friends included Jean Paul Sartre, Simon de Beauvior, George Bidault and Juliette Greco.

"So you can imagine, Barbara, that my cultural life here in Iran isn't...hugely soul-satisfying." He confided this in a tone that bordered on amusement with himself.

But Barbara, the needy part of Barbara, reacted only to

Hoveyda's words, not his lighthearted mood. "Does that mean you might go away? Back to Paris?"

"No, Barbara, not so long as there's a job for me to do for my people. And I want to tell you now that you can count on me for...Listen, there's something you should know about me. Several men of my family are married to foreign women, and my contact with them has given me a kind of insight into the special problems they face in Iran. And I do believe, in humility, that I've been able to help some of them. My door has always been open to them, as it also is now to you, my dear. If there's ever anything that I can do..."

In the future Barbara would call upon Hoveyda often, not just for help as a foreign wife, but also because being in his presence was not only stimulating but comfortable...She could voice to him her inner feelings she necessarily kept hidden from most others. And he responded by the sharing of himself, especially his hopes for a new democratic Iran for which he'd happily give his life.

The other strangers at Barbara's salon, both close friends of Hoveyda, were Edward Brohden and Yah Yah Sharif. Edward, an American educational expert, had been asked by Hoveyda, with the Shah's approval, to research Iran's educational facilities such as they were. And Yah Yah was, like Hoveyda, a poet. He was the only son of the wealthy industrialist Aga Mohammed Sharif. He was handsome with a strong, yet sensitive face. And there was something beyond just his good looks that touched Barbara. He looked like someone who'd felt deeply, suffered deeply. Or was she, out of her neediness now that Aysha and Farah were lost to her, making up a person of depth who might, in a way, take their place in her life? And who, being a man besides, might also...She was twenty-six years old, Barbara thought in a sudden spurt of self-pity, and had never known a man's love or true friendship.

Barbara and Yah Yah sat alone together long after the other guests had gone and Bahram had retired to bed. And after four o'clock in the morning, when she found herself in his car on the way to his home in Shiraz, she didn't really know whose idea it had been, or whether indeed it had not been anyone's idea, but rather a simple, singular purpose. They laughed during the whole twelve hours of the trip, and they continued laughing as Yah Yah, both arms around Barbara, fumbled with his key and took a long time to open the door. And they laughed as they sat close and drank brandy. But the laughter died when Yah Yah said softly, "I knew from the first moment that I saw you that I had...that you and I..." And suddenly they stood together, clinging, clutching, caressing, kissing, ripping off one another's clothes. And when they reached Yah Yah's bed, a trip which seemed to Barbara to have taken an eternity, he searched her face as he thrust and arched his body over hers, for expression of her pleasure, her readiness. There were only bodies then, only sensation, both Yah Yah's and Barbara's bodies and faces already wet as he entered and stayed with her, inside her, 'til the ecstasy was nearly unbearable. She held him fast as her heart pumped, and her mind escaped...All those dreams she'd had on her wedding night had finally, seven years later, become reality.

Barbara and Yah Yah fell asleep in each other's arms. And when they woke, they lay close and relaxed while Barbara answered Yah Yah's questions about her childhood, her young girlhood, her whole life 'til the day of their meeting. He was greedy to know everything about her. Women sometimes asked such questions as Yah Yah asked Barbara, but she'd never have thought a man would. For an hour, two hours, she talked as intimately to him as she ever had to Aysha or Farah, or Betty and Ann, for that matter.

Now came Yah Yah's turn to open himself up to Barbara. He told her that he'd been married for twenty-one years to a woman he'd never loved, a cousin his father chose for the same reason her father had chosen him, to keep the fortune in the family. He'd known of several affairs his wife had over the years and had "only hoped that she'd get from her lovers all that she'd been denied by me." He had two daughters of nineteen and twenty, one studying in the States, the other in London. He, himself, had had several mistresses, but none who'd been important to him, and he, like Barbara, was hungry for a meaningful life.

For the lovers, the months after their coming together were, despite the complications of their lives, a time of floating from day to idyllic day. They met daily either at the flat they'd taken in Tehran or at Barbara's home, where they spent time with Dawn and Rocky (Barbara's daughters and Sharif were soon caught up in a mutual love affair). And on Thursday nights and Fridays they stayed at Sharif's Shiraz home, now stocked with their favorite books, records, liquors and food that Barbara and Yah Yah, now servantless, cooked together.

In a sense, Barbara and Yah Yah were prisoners in Shiraz, for they dared not see other people, except for Edward whom Barbara had come to care about as much as Yah Yah did. The three of them, or two when Edward wasn't there, were sufficient unto themselves and wouldn't have had anyone else around even if they'd been able. They played games like poker, gin rummy, backgammon and chess, and talked, talked, talked about everything. Also, they were light-hearted together as they never were with anyone but each other. Of all the many gifts Yah Yah gave Barbara, the one for which she was most grateful was the gift of laughter. He taught her to laugh honestly, and from deep within her, as she'd not done since her first days in Iran.

And one night while resting in Yah Yah's arms, Barbara let come out in the open a feeling she'd had numerous times before but had managed to restrain...However hard her life might become because of it, she wanted to have Yah Yah's child.

Teymour, born when Roxanne was nearly six and Dawneh nearly two, was a beautiful baby, long and slender, and with a quaff of black hair. He looked, Barbara thought, altogether like Yah Yah. Yet when Bahram, bringing Barbara a pearl and gold necklace as a reward for having brought forth "his" son, came to see her and Teymour only minutes after the birth, he was as thrilled as if the baby had actually been his. After a while he took him from Barbara, placed him on his pillow in the crook of his arm and kept looking into the perfect little face with such pleasure as caused Barbara to wonder whether he was playing a role, or had really deluded himself into believing that Teymour was his, not Yah Yah's, natural child.

Watching his every expression like a scientist watching a specimen, Barbara finally concluded that Bahram was not acting, but had, indeed, deceived himself.

The months after Teymour's birth went by, then a year, then time rushed to the second year's end. Roxanne, with a face of delicate porcelain beauty, was sometimes a lady to her fingertips, already in love with clothes. Other times she was a hellion who easily climbed the highest trees and garden walls. Either way, she was a constant delight. And Dawneh, always giggling and laughing, was also. And Teymour was even more beautiful than he'd given promise of being when he was born.

Barbara's life with Bahram continued quietly. She served as his hostess and accompanied him to public functions, and he did not interfere with anything she did. Her children interested her passionately. And the excitement, the high dramatic moments with Yah Yah did not lessen with time. Perhaps even more important, she knew that no matter what would happen, she could always look to him for sweetness and comfort and succor.

As she did on the terrible night when she learned of her grandmother's death. When Yah Yah came less than an hour after Barbara's call to him, he found her in still, silent shock, her face drained of color. He kneeled at one side of her chair and took her cold hands in his. She slipped from the chair and crawled into his arms, pillowed her head on his chest and closed her eyes. Though he, himself, was feverish and had a bad cold, he held and rocked her on the floor for the rest of the night while she thought about and talked about her grandmother. Her comfort and confidence, her humor and wisdom...Everything, all that had made Barbara what she was and that she would carry with her throughout her life, were gone from her. There were things, inner things, she should have talked to her grandmother about, and had also thought there would be time to do. She'd died, God, without ever seeing Barbara's children. Bahram didn't permit Barbara to take them to America, and Barbara didn't want her grandmother to glean the realities of her life in Iran, so she had never invited her there.

Such a bleak event, orchestrated top to bottom by Barbara's mother, was her grandmother's funeral. The church was her parents' church and contained mostly friends of her mother. The eulogy was a dispassionate statement professionally delivered by Barbara's parents' flat-voiced, pale minister, who knew no more about his subject than what he'd been told by her unloving daughter-in-law.

And the gathering at home—Barbara's parents' home—was presided over by her mother, all in black, who received mostly her friends coming to condole with her over her bereavement. This death, Barbara found herself thinking bitterly, has made my mother's week, maybe her year, a social success.

Barbara sat in a corner with her grandfather, who looked pale and blank and helpless. Over and over in a shaking voice, he said, "She's gone, Barbara, I don't know what to do...Everyone, everyone, they're all gone except for you...and your children. She died...Her last wish was that...She didn't want to die before she'd seen Roxanne and Dawneh and Teymour. And now she's gone, and I don't know what to do or how I'm going to live without her."

There was a sweetness in Barbara's grandfather's face, such a sweetness as caused her to think superstitiously that he was not going to have to live without her grandmother very long. And what Barbara wanted for him was the same as she'd wanted for her grandmother. Serenity. If he had to die, she wanted him to die peacefully, not feeling bereft of her and her children.

"Listen, Grandfather," she said, "I want you to come to Iran with me." Yet she knew, even as she spoke the words, that he was too frail to make the trip. *So you, too, dear Grandfather, will die while longing for the sight of my children. And there is, God, not a damn thing I can do about it.*

Back in Iran, Barbara's plane was met by her children and Bahram, not Yah Yah. And her husband, relishing every word, informed her that her lover had died, two days earlier, of pneumonia.

CHAPTER XVII

Children of the Clan

For two months after Yah Yah's death, Barbara was numb with the shock. It was as though she had died, too, when Bahram had told her; she didn't even cry the tears she knew her husband was waiting to see, and she didn't cry, either, after he was gone. More like an automaton than her former self, she carried out her daily activities, continuing courses at the university while also teaching English there, supervising her household, taking her children on outings and to join their relatives in Shiraz on weekends.

The only obligation she could not bring herself to resume was the one as Bahram's party planner and hostess. She did, though, keep assuring him that if he would bear with her for another month, another week, another couple of days, she'd regain enough strength to give him even bigger and better parties than she had in the past. She, as well as he, believed that at the time, and it might have happened in reality if the numbness of her shock had continued as it had been. But she began, little by little, to feel again. And, before three months had passed since her grandmother's and Yah Yah's deaths, not only was it impossible for Barbara to even think about the resumption of her salons, but she also could not bring herself to pursue any of her former routines. By the end of the third month she'd changed so much physically that when she looked in the mirror, she hardly recognized the woman in the glass who stared accusingly back at her...She looked old and ugly to herself. And she felt a nervous wreck, pretty nearly unable to leave her bed. She couldn't eat; food nauseated her. She couldn't sleep for fear she would dream of a different Yah Yah than the warm and gentle one she'd always known. This Yah Yah's eyes flickered out at Barbara and caught her in their stare, while he accused her angrily of having caused his death. She'd known he was feverish and sick, and had been too self-centered to even tell him to go to bed and take care of himself. All she'd cared about was herself and her problems.

She woke up one night screaming long, wailing screams. Her daughters heard her and came running from their rooms; Bahram heard her all the way from his quarters, and also came running. She took her terrified children into bed with her and yelled at Bahram to go back to his wing of the house and leave her and her children in peace.

Bahram was drunk, and he was mad. How dare Barbara order him out of any place in this house his money paid for? Who did she think she was, anyhow? Well, in case she didn't know, he'd tell her...She was an American fuck-up, that's who. She wasn't even pretty anymore because of the way she'd let herself go since Yah Yah and her grandmother died.

Suddenly he came to the bed, dragged Barbara out from where she lay between Rocky and Dawn, stood her on the floor, and caught her full in the face with a backhanded slap. "YOU BITCH, YOU DUMB GODDAMN BITCH!" He held her by the hair with one hand, shaking her violently back and forth and slapping her face over and over again.

Barbara did not remember afterward much more that happened on that night. She only knew that she woke up the next day with the taste of blood in her mouth. She dragged herself out of bed and made it to the bathroom before she threw up. And when she returned to her bedroom, shaking and feeling she was losing her already slender hold on reality, she found Rocky, Dawn and Bahram there. He ordered her to stand between her daughters, and he, facing them, called Barbara a whore, a slut, a bitch. And after a while he turned to Roxanne and Dawneh...bitches, whores and sluts like their American mother. Then came the beatings, with Bahram's pushing Barbara and the girls against the wall, slapping them across their faces, bloodying their mouths and slamming them with his belt.

And this was not a one-time thing, but rather the beginning of a pattern that had its basis, as Barbara would come to realize, in yet another change in her and Bahram's relationship. First he'd courted her with such tenderness and indulgence as had been irresistible. Then, when they'd come to Iran where Baba Bozorg and Hajji

Khadivar had been his role models, he'd believed he could mold her into the kind of slave-wife his mother had been to his father. And when she'd revealed herself to be unmoldable, he'd been both disappointed and infuriated. More than that, it had brought to the fore his love-hate relationship with America, as Barbara exemplified it. He loved her for what he perceived as her "American superiority", though he'd never defined to her or himself what the words really meant to him. But the point was that he did love her for that inherent quality, whatever it was...so long as he could feel that he owned her...and it. And he would have gone on loving her in his fashion (giving her every material thing she could want) if she had gratified his ego by behaving as his possession whose prime function was to do his bidding.

But when she'd shown herself to be an independent person, he'd equated her independence and desire for personhood with her nationality. And since he could not totally possess her, he had no choice but to crush her before she, as he perceived it, would crush his manhood. Therefore, he indulged in the labeling of her and even his own half-American daughters as sluts and whores. And he subjected Barbara to the obscenities, the filthy nature of his and her sexual relationship, including his flaunting of Mohammed.

Then Barbara, knowing she had to bend if she intended to survive, had made herself into an ideal hostess on Bahram's behalf; she'd become, overtly anyhow, the "proper" Persian slave-wife. His "manhood" had, after all, triumphed over her. And so he'd not only stashed his former furies, but also had again "loved" her, meaning he'd indulged her as he had in their courting days.

Now, though, Barbara was no longer a source of pleasure or service. And so, all of the anger that had never really been forgotten, but only stashed away during the years she'd pleased him, reasserted itself. And it reappeared also against "her" daughters, future half-American women, and maybe more than half since their prime allegiance had always been to their American mother, not their Persian father. That was why he needed to annihilate Roxanne and Dawneh as well as Barbara.

Barbara, too weak and sick to do anything about Bahram's abuse of either her or her daughters, could sometimes close herself off from his treatment of her, becoming almost unconscious of its happening. But what she could never overcome was having to watch Rocky and Dawn destroyed in front of her eyes. Dawn, always the cheeriest, friendliest, most loving of all her children became, during these months, gruff and irritable and hostile. She wanted nothing to do with anyone, and spent all her time away from school in her room. She did not come to Barbara's suite unless she was summoned. Barbara tried to comfort her by telling her that Mama would get well soon and get her and Roxanne away from Bahram. In response, Dawn would stare at her out of the dim, small room that was her pain, furiously and with contempt, then snap, "You are a fool, Mama, not to know that...No, you'll never get better, and I'll never get out of here." Then she would break into bitter tears, throw herself into Barbara's arms and tell her she loved her very much even if...Even if what, Barbara would ask. But Dawneh would only shake her head. And Barbara would torture herself with the excruciating thought that what her child meant was, "I love you very much, Mama, even if you are inadequate and hardly worth loving."

Rocky's anguish was altogether more latent than Dawn's, and in fact, only exhibited itself at night. During the day she hid herself behind a smooth and polite surface and seemed, if anything, to be more outgoing and communicative than ever before. At night, though...she awakened every night, screaming, "HELP ME! HELP ME! PLEASE HELP ME!" She was dreaming and had the same dream all the time. In the dream, not just Bahram, but dozens of other men like him shouted hatred at her, then fell on her in a venomous pack. Every night her father and his cohorts became more violent, and Rocky's appeals for help more desperate. Her screams became louder night after night, filling Barbara's bedroom where Barbara had taken her to sleep, filling the house.

Once awake, though, she would resume her calm and behave with her mother as though she, Rocky, were the mother and Barbara, the young girl in trouble. She kept assuring Barbara over and over that she, unlike Dawn, believed in her promise that she would soon recover her strength and be enabled to help her and her sister escape their father's abuse. And she begged Barbara not to worry in the meanwhile, but to take care of herself and try to sleep and eat, and maybe see her friends.

Barbara hadn't seen or talked to Behdjat, Shams, Maryam, Peri or Edward since her deep depression had begun. They phoned often, even though she refused to take their calls. And they sometimes came to visit, though Naila, on Barbara's order, turned them away at the door.

Then one day Peri, literally subduing Naila physically, entered the house and found her way to Barbara's bedroom.

Barbara ran to Peri when she saw her; they embraced one another tightly and stood together for a long time.

"Barbara, Barbara, you should have let me come sooner, you owed it to our friendship, to your and Aysha's friendship, don't you even know...?"

"Yes, Peri," Barbara said, gazing into her face.

First Peri gave Barbara a half-full glass of scotch out of the bottle she'd brought with her. Then she ran a bath and helped Barbara into the tub. And after Barbara was bathed and dressed in a fresh nightgown, Peri tucked her into bed and sat on the bedside combing her hair for her, just combing and combing it while Barbara told her everything that had happened since they'd last seen one another.

After Peri's coming, Barbara's other university friends also came, as did Edward Brohden, who she knew had reported to Hoveyda about her. Their intense caring for her caused her to begin caring for herself again, and at least think in terms of a future. And, although all of her friends were thinking this, Edward was the first to say, "The first thing we've got to do, Barbara, is to get you a divorce."

"And how will we accomplish that little feat? Since I'm a Persian citizen...Have you ever heard of a Persian wife who instituted divorce proceedings, and won, no matter how much right was on her side? Sure, if I were truly Persian and surrounded by a big, loving extended family who'd negotiate with Bahram's family for my rights, I wouldn't need a law that'd be fair to women. But, as it is..."

"We'll find a way, Barbara." Edward kissed her on the cheek, and left the house. He returned three days later to inform her that everything was settled; Bahram had agreed to divorce her and to allow her to keep her merieh money. Barbara intuited, though Edward didn't say so, that Hoveyda had a hand in the arrangement.

"Your and Bahram's agreement must certainly...He's giving me my kids, too, Edward," Barbara said, but her words sounded more like prayer than conviction. "He can't believe that I'd accept the divorce without...He knows I'm not about to leave this house unless my children come with me. You must have made it clear that I..."

"Barbara, I assure you I tried, but Bahram would not..."

"Edward, you're crazy if you think...I can't leave my daughters to bear Bahram's beatings alone. And as for Teymour, Bahram's whole purpose in life is to turn my sweet, beautiful baby into a complacent, selfish, arrogant Muslim man. No, Edward, I couldn't even dream of escaping this life by myself while leaving my kids...What the hell kind of mother would you, yourself, consider me if I...?"

"Barbara, you may hate me for this, but I have to tell you that you're so sick physically and emotionally that you're not even able to think straight. Your being here the way you are is hurting your kids worse than if you weren't here. Don't you see that you've got to help yourself before you can even hope to help them?"

Barbara had to face the fact that Edward was right. But how could she go away and leave her children behind? She knew Bahram, and knew that he would tell them she'd abandoned them, tell them she was crazy; he'd be happy to tear them up as long as it tore her up, too. But she had to go anyway.

Barbara had to get drunk before she could bring herself to explain to her children the need for her to leave them temporarily, in order to arrange their being with her permanently. Ten-year-old Roxanne, lying on her bed when Barbara told her, lifted up on her elbow and stared at her mother. "So Dawn and I will be the only ones who'll be around to take our father's beatings, while you'll be away from us all, Mama." But even as she said that in a cool voice, she clutched Barbara to her and asked, "When'll you be back for us, Mama? O, we'll be waiting for you." Six-year-old Dawneh stared out the window all the time Barbara talked to her. Her little hands were balled into tiny fists and crushed together into her lap.

"Dawneh, Sweetheart, do you understand everything Mama's saying to you? Don't you have any questions you want to ask me?"

Dawneh rubbed her head and shook it. Then suddenly, "Yes, Mama, there's this question...Why won't you get me a divorce from my father when you get yours?"

Teymour, of course, was too little for talk, but during the whole night before she left the house Barbara sat by his bed while he slept, and did not take her eyes off him. "I will not fail this child. I will not fail him," she repeated to herself.

Barbara might have sought help from Hoveyda in her pursuit for her children's custody. But at the time, he was under the most intense criticism from the strangest of all bedfellows, the aristocrats and the religious. Both censured him as "in truth a foreigner, not an Iranian." Their reason was his compassion for, and sometimes open championship of, certain foreign wives of Iranian men who, like Barbara, were on their way to being destroyed by their husbands and the husbands' families.

To the aristocrats who made up the majority of the husbands of foreign wives, Hoveyda's expressions represented, first of all, the most offensive interference in their lives. Also, they derogated him for his lack of macho, as they perceived it. No "true man" would be concerned, as he was, with the so-called rights of women, foreign women at that. And the mullahs accused him of "immorality with those foreign whores, those spawns of the devil he cherishes." And according to Edward, the Shah, intent on not stimulating the constantly seething hostility of the religious, had warned Hoveyda away from further activity on the women's behalf.

Barbara's custody battle for her children therefore had to begin with Khanoum-June. She went to the Shiraz mansion by appointment, and Khanoum-June herself opened the door and embraced her warmly.

"Barbara, junam, I'm so happy you came to me in spite of...I thought I'd never see you again, and it hurt me deeply." Her guileless eyes appraised Barbara lovingly, and Barbara laid her head against her cheek and let her stroke the back of her head.

"Khanoum-June," she said, "I come to you today as I would come to my own mother or grandmother..."

"Barbara junam, you want to come back into the family, and you want for me to intercede for you with Bahram, Hajji Khadivar and Baba Bozorg. It's a happy task you're giving me."

Barbara explained that her and Bahram's differences could never be resolved and that she had come to Khanoum-June to help her gain custody of her children.

Khanoum-June stared at Barbara with shock and incredulity. "How can you ask me...How can I ask Bahram to give his children up to you, when the Koran itself says that a man's children..." Barbara's thoughts drifted as she gave up all hope of getting help from Khanoum-June.

The next logical second step in her fight, one that of necessity had to precede any court action, was a confrontation with Hajji Khadiva and, even more importantly, with Baba Bozorg himself. She spent many days preparing herself, studying under Peri, the whole rigidly structured fabric of the patriarchal Iranian extended family as exemplified by Bahram and his literally hundreds of concerned relatives.

She came to realize, first of all, that according to patriarchs like Baba Bozorg, her children did not belong exclusively to Bahram any more than they did to her. Rather, they were the children of the whole huge Mosallai clan. Their true guardian, therefore, was Baba Bozorg, as the clan head. Had Barbara been a member of a Persian extended family, her grandmother, representing her grandfather, would have negotiated with Khanoum-June, representing Baba Bozorg for her rights. And it might even have been possible that the families' respect for one another, their need to remain on friendly terms, might have resulted in a more or less equitable arrangement for Barbara as well as Bahram.

"But what can someone like me, with no family, and a farangi besides, do in order to secure a just arrangement–from Baba Bozorg?" Barbara asked in desperation.

Peri said that she didn't really know the answer to Barbara's question; she did, though, have an intuition for a kind of strategy. However, it could hurt Barbara's case as much as help it, and therefore had to be used only as a last resort. Baba Bozorg was as concerned as any patriarch with "family face", and it might be that if Barbara threatened to reveal in open court all the ugly details of Bahram's moral unfitness as a father, he'd be intimidated into negotiating with her.

"I repeat, though, Barbara, only use such a threat as a last resort, because you can't ever tell how Baba Bozorg's going to react to it. Since he's a man who enjoys a battle, even though he may seem to be on the losing side..."

Baba Bozorg, Hajji Khadivar, Bahram and a young nephew, Hussein, an attorney who'd taken his undergraduate work at Yale and legal training at Harvard, and whom Barbara knew by reputation as the most brilliant and prestigious of all the younger Mosallai men, sat together smoking cigars on a comfortable sofa in Hajji Khadivar's suite. Barbara sat across from them on a straight, hard chair.

"Why are we here, Barbara? What do you want from us?" Baba Bozorg's voice rang out in the room.

"What I want...I want my son and my daughters. As the children's mother I am entitled..."

"You are entitled to nothing except what I choose to grant you. And it may be that what you will receive from me will be the same as what other such farangi wives have received from their Persian families...A one-way ticket home...without your children."

"That...Baba Bozorg, I...Right is on my side and...I intend to fight for my children, Baba Bozorg."

"And exactly where do you propose to fight?" This question was asked by self-assured Hussein, wearing his sweater with a Yale University emblem.

"I...I propose to fight in open court, Hussein, and..." Barbara turned to Baba Bozorg, "I can present ample proof, Baba Bozorg, that Bahram is an unfit father."

Baba Bozorg sipped from a glass of water, and flung what was left in Barbara's face. Then he, followed by Hajji Khadivar and Bahram, stormed out of the room, leaving Barbara alone with Hussein.

"You should know, Barbara," Hussein said, "that any attempt on your part to prove Bahram unfit will hurt you, not us."

CHAPTER XVIII

A Woman's Testimony...

No matter how much one may disapprove of Princess Ashraf for a host of reasons, she must be praised for her contributions in the field of women's rights, even though they were made out of a desire to westernize rather than true commitment. In 1975, after the International Women's Conference in Mexico, she, with the Shah's backing, succeeding in passing the Family Protection Act. This gave Iran's women, on paper at least, the most sweeping civil rights in the whole Middle East except for Israel. It limited a man to one wife, although indirectly in the face of the Koran's permission to take four. In order to take a second wife, he had to have the first wife agree; had to prove that she was incurably ill or sterile; and had to have the financial means to support two households equally.

Beyond this, the act aspired to cause husbands to recognize wives as equal partners in planning their futures and those of their children. Also, men's right to casual and unreasonable divorce was denied, and the same clearly defined grounds for divorce were required for both husbands and wives.

Most important of all, the children's custody was granted to "the deserving parent". And machinery was set up whereby the mother, if chosen as "the deserving one", could seek alimony and child support.

It would, of course, be revealed in future years that tradition would triumph over law, that few husbands would recognize their wives as equal partners and that hardly any mothers would be chosen over fathers as "deserving" by the Family Court judges. Further, very few divorces and custody arrangements would actually reach the courts. Most would continue to be negotiated by the family patriarchs.

All the same, due to the Family Protection Act the circumstances of Barbara's court fight for her children's custody might have been somewhat less appalling after 1975 than they were in 1971.

It took Barbara over three months to find an attorney. Everyone to whom she went must have previously been contacted by Hussein, because they all knew her story before she even opened her mouth to explain herself. Finally, through Peri, she met Mohammed Zahedi. He was young, a couple of years younger than Barbara, but with an air of great maturity and warmth. Though he made Barbara aware of all that militated against her winning of custody, he said that "if by some strange turn of events you...we do win, it will be a victory for all the women of Iran. And I'd like to feel I had something to do with helping it to happen."

Less than a week after Zahedi had agreed to take Barbara's case, her phone rang at three o'clock in the morning. "Mama, Mama." It was Rocky, trying to get out words but unable to because she was crying so hard. Then, "Mama," again, then the bitter weeping, making speech impossible.

"Rocky, Sweetheart, try to tell me...No, don't...Listen, darling, go back to your room and wait for me there. I'm coming right now." Fortunately, Barbara had held onto a key to the front door of her former house, and so was able to let herself in. Rocky was sitting on the edge of her bed when Barbara came into her room. Her whole face was red and swollen, and the blood that had trickled in thin lines down from her nostrils had caked on her chin and neck.

Barbara put her arms around Rocky and held her while she sobbed wildly; then she asked, after a long time, "Do you want to tell me now what happened, baby?"

"It was Shirley Kashani, Mama, my father and her..."

Shirley, Rocky's best friend since age five when they'd met in their private school, had come to spend the afternoon and evening. The servants had, as usual when Shirley came to visit, muttered under their breath because they didn't like Rocky's having a Jewish guest. However, their prejudice, that Barbara had explained long ago was based on ignorance, hadn't bothered either Rocky or Shirley.

At eight o'clock, having tired of all the toys in Rocky's and Dawn's playroom as well as of Dawn's insistent company, Rocky and Shirley went into the garden and sat by the goldfish pool. It was so quiet, so peaceful with just the fish, the orange moon, the stars glittering overhead, and the two of them together, best friends.

Then, suddenly, Naila appeared to say that Bahram wanted to see them in his study. Rocky couldn't imagine why her father would want to see Shirley, since he'd never before taken any interest in her friends. And she prayed to God to please keep him from humiliating her in Shirley's presence.

When Shirley and Rocky entered his study, Bahram signaled them to be seated, and he came to stand in front of them. He began talking about the man called Hitler whom Rocky knew little about, yet hated in her heart. He said that Hitler, far from being the villain stupid people like Barbara believed him to be, was a hero who'd almost succeeded in ridding the world of Jews. He talked about Hitler for so long that Rocky almost stopped paying attention. He got her attention back in a hurry, though, when he started on Shirley, calling her "dog shit" and other evil names because she was a Jew.

And then, suddenly, Rocky saw him doing that awful, awful thing; no, he couldn't be doing that, but her eyes were telling her that was exactly what he was doing. He was doing it right in front of her eyes; she couldn't believe it, but it was happening. Her father dragged her friend off the sofa and threw her onto the floor, then turned to Rocky, laughing and yelling that "the only thing your little Jew friend is good for, Rocky, is to have men's dicks jammed up her cunt." And next thing Rocky heard was all that screaming. It was like an animal's screaming; it was like she imagined a devil's screaming would be, it was the worst screaming she'd ever heard. And it wasn't coming from Shirley, who was lying so still she looked like she'd fainted, but from her, Rocky.

And then she stopped screaming, because that didn't stop her father from doing it. The screaming seemed to make him want to do it harder, make him want to hurt Shirley more. Rocky ran and got a knife and waved it at Bahram, and said she'd cut him if he didn't let Shirley go. And he finally did let her go. Rocky then saw her run out of the room and knew with relief that she'd now go to her family's chauffeur who'd been waiting for her all evening, and so Bahram wouldn't be able to hurt her anymore. There was no way, though, to prevent his hurting Rocky.

First he twisted her arm so hard that she had to let the knife drop, and then he picked it up and held it against her throat as though he would slit it. She told him to go ahead and slit her throat, she didn't care. And he threw the knife down and stood for a while, just looking and laughing at her. Then he stopped laughing and started slapping her around, and punching her and smashing her against the wall and calling her all the terrible names he'd called Shirley, so she had to think that he hated her, his daughter, as much as he did her friend. And maybe he even hated her more than he did Shirley, and had only hurt Shirley in order to punish her. She didn't know why he needed to punish her in such a terrible way, but then she never knew why he needed to beat her and Dawn and Barbara all the time, either. It was just something he needed to do; it was just the way he was.

Yet he'd hurt her worse through Shirley than he'd ever hurt her and Dawn and Barbara through his beatings. Why had he needed to do that to her? What had Rocky done that was so awful to have made him do what he'd done to Shirley?

Barbara held Rocky against her, Rocky's head on her shoulder, her cheek against hers while she struggled to find the words for convincing her daughter that she was in no way to blame for her father's cruelty because, as she herself had said, that was the way he was.

In the morning Barbara, true to her promise to Rocky, sat in the family salon of the Kashani mansion across from Shirley's mother and repeated over and over again, "I'm so sorry, Khanoum. Oh God, I'm so sorry."

Khanoum Kashani, with a sweet, gentle face like Shirley's own, sat with her shoulders hunched over as if they would protect her heart. She cried quietly, wearily. She was unable even to get up to find a dry handkerchief or to ring for a servant to bring her one. The one with which she was trying to dry her face was so wet it looked like she could squeeze the tears out of it.

Barbara gave her own handkerchief to Khanoum while she kept repeating "sorry, sorry, sorry," feeling helpless to stop herself and wondering when, or if, she'd ever find the words for expressing the misery that thickened her tongue. Wondering what to say to a mother whose good and gentle child had been savaged by her child's father.

She cried out, finally, "That you, Khanoum Kashani, should have been willing to receive me after the monstrous crime perpetrated by my...husband!"

Khanoum Kashani, speaking through her bitter crying, said that her whole family had always loved Rocky.

Now the tears poured down Barbara's own face as she begged the Kashanis to go on loving her child. "She wanted to kill her father for what he did to Shirley, Khanoum Kashani; indeed, she tried to kill him."

Khanoum Kashani raised an anguished face to Barbara, and looking straight at her for the first time said that Rocky must not become embittered, and she would do everything in her power to make sure Shirley would not either. "I know, Sultaneh," she said softly, "that you are fighting that...monster for your children's custody. And I wish...believe me that if we, as Jews, did not have so much to fear from...people like him...If I were not frightened for my family's lives, I would help you by appearing as a witness, and telling about what he...You understand, though, why I can't, don't you?"

Barbara said that of course she understood. She embraced Khanoum Kashani, who embraced her in return and said, "And please tell Rocky that we do not blame her for her father, and that we'll always love her in spite of him. Tell her that from our hearts; our hearts, Sultaneh."

Barbara thought often of Khanoum Kashani and Shirley during the days and weeks that she and Zahedi sat in the lobby of the Tehran Court House waiting for their call to trial. The Court building was marble-walled and high-ceilinged; architecturally, it was more Germanic than Persian, since it had been built by German workmen and utilized German stone brought from the Rhine. It had been Hitler's gift, given soon after he came to power, to Reza Shah. It might have been impressive in its day, but had turned gray and shabby by the time Barbara came to know it. And the obnoxious odor of urine (men relieved themselves against the marble walls and in the overflowing Western toilets that Hitler had installed and that the people did not know how to use) contracted Barbara's stomach.

All manner of trials except for political ones occurred in the Tehran court building, and all kinds of people crowded the lobby. There were alleged thieves, chained and dragged in. Rapists whose shaven heads signified their crimes. Prostitutes who'd dared escape their walled city in South Tehran to solicit in the streets outside, and the madams who exhibited them like objects for customers' selection.

Sitting away from the prostitutes were numbers of chador-clad wives from the South Tehran slums, whose husbands had become displeased with them and had come to court to declare them prostitutes. These women didn't socialize as the prostitutes did. Some wept softly to themselves; one begged her husband to drop his charges, promising she'd be good and obedient and would do everything the husband said.

The husbands clustered in noisy groups, laughing and cracking watermelon seeds. They made comments they didn't know Barbara understood, about her "sweet ass that went tick-tock, tick-tock" when she walked. And when, on occasion, she had to pass them by, they tried to touch her backside.

The crowding and the smells and the noise could somehow be endured, but the leering, sneering men kept Barbara in a constant panic.

On January 8, 1971, nearly four months after they'd first brought suit, Barbara and Zahedi sat in the court lobby with Rocky and Dawn, who were here though it was not one of their regular visiting days with their mother; Naila had sneaked them out of the house. Rocky's face was red and swollen, and Dawneh's left eye was black and blue.

While Barbara was comforting her children, a guard appeared and summoned her, Zahedi and the children to the courtroom of Judge Amir Amuzegar. He informed them that they'd be coming to trial immediately.

Bahram, flanked not only by Hussein as his attorney but also by

Hajji Khadivar, Baba Bozorg and a large entourage of young and older men whom Barbara did not know but assumed to be more Mosallai extended family, entered the courtroom from the judge's chambers. They'd obviously been spared the ordeal of awaiting trial in the public lobby.

Judge Amuzegar was a short, lean, angular man in his late sixties or early seventies. Although he was dressed under his judge's robes in a conservative Western three-piece suit, white shirt and wine-colored tie, his face reminded Barbara of the mullahs she'd come to know in Baba Bozorg's villages and their surrounding towns. And the reason why he was reminiscent of village and town mullahs...Barbara knew from Zahedi that Judge Amuzegar had, indeed, been a mullah in the year 1940. That was when Reza Shah, having organized Iran's legal system along Western lines and staffed his courts partially with Western-oriented judges, nevertheless also chose others who were Shariah-oriented, of whom Amuzegar was one. They presided in their courtrooms much as they had done in their villages, as adjudicators according to religious, not Western, law.

Judge Amuzegar—not Zahedi—personally questioned Barbara. Why, he asked, did she believe her children would be better off with her than with their father and his family? When she told him that Bahram beat and abused her daughters, he, though seeing Roxanne's swollen face and Dawneh's eye, asked for "proof of your allegations."

Barbara said, "If you will just ask my children, Your Honor, they can tell you...Young as they are, they've lived through so much, and...If you will ask them..."

"I'll ask them when, and if, I deem it necessary. And I wish you also to be informed that this court does not put a great deal of credence in children's testimony."

"Your Honor," Zahedi said, "we have outside, objective witnesses to the children's abuse by their father, and respectfully urge you to hear..."

"Who are these witnesses?"

"They are professors at Tehran University."

"Women professors?"

"Yes, Your Honor."

Amuzegar asked irritably, "Are you not aware...Do you, an attorney, not know that, according to our law of Islam, a woman's testimony is worth only half that of a man?"

Zahedi said, "I do know it, Your Honor, and...I would wish, with your kind permission, to call four women witnesses in place of two men who..."

"No, I will not waste the court's time in such a fashion."

"But, Your Honor, my client has a right under the law to have her witnesses..."

"Don't you tell me about the law, Mr. Zahedi," Judge Amuzegar rasped out, "because in this courtroom, I AM THE LAW." With an uplifting of his hand he commanded Barbara and Zahedi to take their seats, and Dawn and Rocky to stand before him. They came, Dawn holding tight to Rocky's hand and trembling violently. Amuzegar asked them whether they were good and obedient children. Before they had time to answer, he said that it was his opinion that they were not as good and obedient as they should have been. And that their father, following the dictates of the Koran, had beaten them to make them better.

Barbara could not help herself; she cried out, "Please, Your Honor, realize that my children...Their father..."

Judge Amuzegar turned to Zahedi. "One more such outburst from your client will result in my holding her—and you—in contempt of court."

"I'm sorry, Your Honor," Barbara stammered from her seat. "Please overlook my outburst, and see into my mother's heart and..."

"On your feet and stand at attention when you address a judge of His Imperial Majesty," Judge Amuzegar bellowed as Barbara sprang to her feet. "And let me tell you that if your husband had not, in his wisdom, already seen fit to divorce you, I would say to him that...Sometimes men do well to beat their wives, as well as their children, into goodness." It is, therefore, the ruling of this court..."

Barbara, knowing all too well what Amuzegar's ruling would be, felt impelled, no matter what would happen, to make one last attempt to change the inevitable by at least setting the record straight. Taking a deep breath, she brought out the whole sickening story of Bahram and Shirley Kashani.

Hussein declared that Barbara was "a vicious liar." And Rocky, her face white and anguished, screamed out, "My mother's not a liar...I was right there in the room when my father did that to Shirley, and...Her mother would be here today, too, to tell you about it if she wasn't afraid that my father'd do other terrible things to her and her family."

"You be still," Amuzegar thundered out, "and remember that your being a child won't save you from prison if you keep behaving in contempt of this court."

Rocky looked at Amuzegar with frightened eyes, and Dawn began to cry. Barbara asked the judge's permission to go to her children, which he granted. From her place between Rocky and Dawn, she fought to stay composed while she listened to Mohammed, Bahram's lover, whom Hussein called "an objective witness to combat the farangi's lies." He said that Bahram was the best of fathers, and that Barbara's accusations "would be laughable if they weren't so tragic." He was then ordered off the stand by Amuzegar. And when Zahedi claimed his right to cross-examine Mohammed, the judge roared out that there would be no cross-examination in this case. And when Zahedi objected, Amuzegar warned that if he didn't look out, both he and his client would end up behind bars. He then asked Hussein whether "the family Mosallai wishes the farangi and her attorney jailed for her slanderous attack on your face."

Hussein conferred for a minute with Baba Bozorg, then said, "We do not, for now, wish Miss Srader or Attorney Zahedi jailed. We do, however, request...Your Honor is aware that the Family Mosallai, out of its good-heartedness, has permitted this farangi visitation rights with its minor children, and you know for yourself how she has returned this favor. We therefore intend—with your blessing, of course—to deny her further contact with our beloved children."

Amuzegar lifted an arm in the blessing-motion and said in a mullah's, not a judge's voice, "Family Mosallai, you have my blessing."

Now Barbara thought, yet again, not of asking for the help she knew Hoveyda was forbidden to give, but only for his ear. Just to sit across from him and bask in his warmth and caring, his true regard for her, would have been comfort under the circumstances. But she condemned herself for even thinking of trying to involve Hoveyda in her problem, on whatever level. There was, then, one last person to whom she might turn; the Shah himself. A week to the day after her courtroom defeat, she sat awaiting Mohammed Reza in the saffron-silk reception room off his office in the Saadabad Palace. Her audience had been scheduled for ten in the morning, but the Shah was not there at eleven or twelve, or twelve-thirty. Meanwhile, she drank cup after cup of tea brought by a tailcoated butler. Occasionally, to give herself courage, she spiked her tea with scotch she'd hidden in her purse.

The Shah came at ten minutes past two, four hours and ten minutes after his Minister of Court expected him. He led Barbara into his office and informed her that he had ten minutes to spare; he then asked whether she was in trouble.

"In trouble?" Barbara repeated. "Oh God, my children and I are in so much trouble, Your Majesty." She handed Mohammed Reza a packet of pictures of her daughters taken by Naila. First Dawneh, her backside bloody from being beaten with Bahram's uniform sword, then Roxanne, on crutches after Bahram broke her leg while in one of his drunken furies, and last, another of Dawneh, her knees bloodied from the time Bahram ordered her to crawl all over the house and garden.

Barbara's eyes rested, aching, on Mohammed Reza as he looked at the pictures. As he handed them back, he merely asked why she had come to him.

She sat staring at him, appalled that after seeing those pictures of Rocky and Dawn, he'd need to ask such a question.

"It's...Bahram's killing my children, Your Majesty, and I'm here to beg you to give me their custody before he..."

The Shah said then that, even though he might wish to, as a good Muslim he could not possibly grant Barbara's request. Allah had, after all, declared to Mohammed that children's fathers and male relatives...The words echoed, in Barbara's mind, the voices of Khanoum-June and Baba Bozorg and Hajji Khadivar and Judge Amuzegar. And she had to respect the fact that they all spoke out of the depths of their consecrated hearts. Mohammed Reza, though, had a disdain for the ideals of Islam that he showed clearly when in the company of Westerners, or Westernized Iranians. At how many parties for visiting American or European diplomats had Barbara not witnessed the television cameras photographing the guests drinking their toasts to the Shah and Iran, but focusing elsewhere when he drank his to them. He was so contemptuous of people that he supposed he was fooling the faithful, by such a ruse, into believing that he observed the Koran's interdiction against alcohol. This, despite the fact that they had to have known that he profited from the manufacture of beer, wine and liquor by fully forty Iranian companies. And, although they did not attend the high-priced restaurants and nightclubs frequented by farangis and rich Persians, they were aware of the open drinking that occurred in them, as well as of their "entertainment"—nude dancing to the accompaniment of Western music.

Barbara knew that Mohammed Reza was deaf and blind to his moral isolation from his people. He took them at their fawning face value whenever they were in his presence. He believed, truly, that they did not discern his hypocrisy when he declared to them in writings and speeches that he'd been possessed, since age seven, of such a rich religious inner life as had enabled him to meet all the Shiite saints.

Thinking thus, the scotch Barbara had downed in her tea while waiting for the Shah caught up with her. And her half-drunkenness, coupled with what she knew about Mohammed Reza's colossal ego and ability at self-deception, gave her what she believed at the time to be a brilliant idea. She would flatter Mohammed Reza into giving her the children. She, therefore, told him about her study of Islam without naming Aysha as her teacher, and declared that she'd always recognized the similarity of Mohammed Reza, the Shah, to Mohammed the Prophet.

"There is so much in you, Your Majesty: your love of justice, and caring for people, especially those who are most vulnerable...To my mind, you are the incarnation of...YOU ARE MOHAMMED THE PROPHET OF THE MODERN WORLD, and so I come to you..."

Almost as suddenly as her craziness had come upon her, Barbara came back to herself. And she saw the Shah standing with a hand uplifted, like a traffic cop ordering stop.

"So you, Barbara, believe me to be an idiot who can be taken in by...It is strange that you, who ought to know I have never been misled by others infinitely wiser than you, could believe me an idiot whom you could take in." Mohammed Reza's voice was relaxed, intimate and devoid of menace. Certainly, it did not match either his words or the threatening look on his face. "An idiot who can be taken in," he repeated in the same soothing tone.

Then, with a shout that must have been heard throughout the palace, he screamed, "WHO DO YOU THINK YOU ARE, FARANGI BITCH? And do you believe that your being American will save you from the punishment you deserve for having conde-scended to me?"

He turned and walked out of his office, leaving Barbara huddled and crying.

Two palace guards came in after the Shah left. They did not talk to Barbara, and one backhanded the top of her head as she sat, smacking it again as the hand came back the other way. Then both guards carried her, struggling, into the back seat of a car driven by a third guard.

CHAPTER XIX

Imprisoned

Ears ringing, heart thumping, Barbara was escorted by the palace guards through the iron gate and high-walled courtyard of the Tehran Reformatory for Women, where she and Rocky had been taken after she'd tried to run away from Bahram. Warden Humarabi, fourteen years older, was still there, still dressed in a three-piece blue suit and white shirt with a stiffly starched collar.

He read Barbara's commitment papers for a long time, then told her that he had no information about how long she would remain in the prison, and could only advise her to "make up your mind that you will, for however long it may be, do as you are told, be good, obey."

She asked whether she could telephone a friend, and he said she couldn't. She then asked if she could call the American Embassy; he shook his head.

"My God, if I can't even...How am I going to...Doesn't every prisoner, don't I have the right to make even one phone call to inform my people of...?"

"In simple words, Sultaneh, every prisoner does have the right, but you do not. And now if you will give me your watch, earrings and necklace for safekeeping, and if you will empty the contents of your purse..."

He took all of Barbara's money as well as her cigarettes, silver lighter, leftover Scotch in its silver and leather flask and a nearly full atomizer of perfume, as well as the purse itself; he handed her a brown paper bag for carrying her cosmetics, the only possessions outside of the clothes on her back that she was permitted to keep. She begged also for the packet of pictures of Rocky and Dawn and, strangely, Humarabi let her have them.

Next came a pair of prison guards to escort Barbara to the Women's Reformatory, a single decaying room where some fifty women and three girl children of two to four years were held. Toilet facilities consisted of two latrine buckets and a "urinal corner". A dozen or so buckets of water, delivered daily for drinking and bathing, were apportioned among all the women and children. And a special amenity, courtesy of Warden Humarabi, provided a supply of rags about the size of small tea towels, one for every three inmates, to be used during menstruation.

Meals consisted mostly of rancid rice and weak tea, with the occasional addition of a piece of rotten fruit or hard bread, and once in a while also a hard-boiled egg.

To Barbara, the true horror of life at the Women's Reformatory was that the other inmates, the mass of them anyway, felt no horror at it. The Reformatory was, after all, no worse that the homes from which they had come, and they accepted its routines as resignedly as they did the whole of their lives. The mass of the women were prostitutes who were, in the main, like the ones Barbara had seen while awaiting trial, in their tight jeans or flashy clothes now filthy and falling apart from having been worn day and night. They were mostly between twelve and twenty years old, and already full of a bleak hopelessness and acceptance of their kismets that came through in every exchange they had with one another.

"...I told my madam that I should get more than two tomans (twelve cents) for every 'visitor' that I have," one woman related, "and she said, 'Why? Already I am losing money on you, girl. Figure this: The most a visitor will pay for a worn-out whore like you...you are not a new face, you know...is five tomans, out of which I must pay the police. And if you don't realize that I'm losing money on you, you ought to try free-lance whoring.'

"I ran away then and went to Maiden Ferdowsi (a main square of Tehran frequented by streetwalkers), but I could not bring myself to work naked under my chador, and so did not lure sufficient customers. And those who did come with me put all manner of hats on my head. 'Oh, come with us now, little girl, and we'll pay you well later.' Then when later came: 'Buro, buro, dirty prostitute, get out and stop troubling us before we bring you to the police and have you put in jail.'

"And one customer—a good Muslim he was, too, going with

me on Thursday afternoon so he could purify himself afterward at the bath before he'd pray on Friday—said to me, 'Little girl, do you know that it is written in the Koran that a man does a noble thing if he marries a prostitute and delivers her from her kismet?' And his voice made me believe that, oh, maybe, maybe...So I did all that I could to please him.

"Afterward, he laughed in my face and said, 'Oh, did I put a hat on your head, stupid little whore. Here you thought I might marry you, and all the time I used you while knowing that I didn't even intend to pay you for your services. Ah, isn't that a funny joke?'

"I said, 'Well, I don't think it's funny.' That is all that I said, 'I don't think it's funny.' I did not make any more of a fuss than that. Yet he dragged me before a policeman screaming that 'this whore daughter of donkeys is an abomination to our city and must be put away to where she will not be able, anymore, to solicit and corrupt our men.' Then he took me again, as the policeman also did, and they both beat me before bringing me to the judge who sentenced me here. And the judge said, 'You, young prostitute, had better not be seen around the Maiden Ferdowsi one more time after you are released from the prison, because if you are and are brought before me, I'll sentence you back there for the rest of your life.'

"So I know now that I must never again fight against, and try to change, my kismet, and make my own way out of a house and away from a madam, no matter how cruel she may be."

The younger prostitutes, many of whom were also imprisoned for having run away from their houses and attempting to free-lance, had not yet totally embraced the philosophy of the older ones that "the house (and cruel madam) is my kismet and I've no choice but to return there." These girls were thirteen and twelve, and one, with peroxided hair, a pointy bra jutting out from an improbable position on her chest and a dirty orange sweater, was eleven.

The "elderly" prostitutes, the true has-beens of the profession in their thirties and forties were, of course, the most persuaded fatalists in the prison. They knew that now that their madams no longer wanted them (their kismets had decreed this would be the case long before they'd ever entered or been sold into their houses), they would, when their time came, die in lonely misery, despised by everyone. That was the way it was for the woman in her forties, whom the other prostitutes, shuddering and spitting when they passed her, called "Putrid Shit." Bald and almost blind from what must have been advanced syphilis, she lay, her body jerking up and down on her segregated bit of floor, and waited for death.

Some of the inmates, though, were not prostitutes but opium sellers, thieves and drunks. And others, though treated as criminals, were victims in reality. There was Shayla, not quite eighteen, a clumsy, gawky girl with a face that might have been homely had it not been for the eyes that gave away an unusual intelligence. She had been a hardworking and highly efficient housemaid to a mistress who, fearing she'd quit and go on to a better job, connived with her husband to take her as a zighe under a ten-year contract. From then on, she needed her "husband's" permission to make a move out of his household and the dominion of his wife. And when she, less timorous than many of her station, tried to run away, she was apprehended and jailed "'til the time comes when you recover your good sense."

Ootah, fifteen, an exquisite girl with a pale, oval, classically Persian face and a long slender body, was a daughter, granddaughter and great granddaughter of mullahs and mujtahids. Engaged by her great grandfather to his colleague, who'd been recently widowed and was more that fifty years her senior, she'd run away from home. Caught on her first morning out, she had been in prison some three months by the time Barbara arrived there. Her mother or aunts visited every week, bringing gifts of food and assurances from the father and grandfathers that her release could be effected any time she would apologize for her "stubbornness" and agree to marry the would-be husband. She never apologized, and always gave her food to the children.

The mothers of the children (four-year-old Zarah and Soraya, and three-year-old Mahede) were timid, pathetic young women, hardly more than children themselves. They never uttered a word above a whisper during the time that Barbara knew them. They were in the Reformatory because, finding themselves finally unable to bear their husbands' and mother-in-laws' abuse of them and their baby daughters, they performed what must have been the bravest act of their lives and ran away with the children. Now, though, they had as little courage or ability to cope with the prison conditions as the children themselves. Zarah, Soraya and Mahede already looked beaten down and always behaved in a manner of unchildlike submissiveness. They must have known that though their mothers loved them dearly, they could not be depended upon for safety or support or any other kind of help.

Fortunately, though, there was one inmate on whom the children could and did rely, whose love helped make their ghastly world a better place. Khanoum Efshat Mahdari was in her fifties, large and soft and lovable in both body and soul. She weighed easily two hundred and fifty pounds—the better, she laughed, for enfolding all of "her" three children at a time to her capacious bosom. In this embrace she would tell them stories, sing them songs, and feed them grapes, bananas and other pieces of fruit she managed, only God knew how, to smuggle in for them.

Khanoum Mahdari, a native of the city of Tabriz, was a high school teacher and children's rights activist, in the contemporary Western rather than Iranian sense. She'd been arrested for the fourth time in as many years, because as a member of the "Tabriz Committee for Protection of Children in the Carpet Factories", a branch of a national organization, she had led demonstrations of teachers and students on the worker-children's behalf.

Barbara's friendship with Khanoum Mahdari began on her first morning in the jail, when she woke to the sight of several of her fellow inmates swarming around her. They screamed and shook their fists at her. She, hardly knowing what she was doing, shook her fists back at them. Then suddenly, Khanoum Mahdari assumed her place like a mountain in the midst of the overwrought women and dispersed them with dignity and gentleness. She declared, while she shooed them from the piece of floor on which Barbara cowered, that she, Khanoum Mahdari, would give them her sacred word that Barbara was not the evil spirit they perceived her; she was a mortal woman in trouble. Therefore, as good Muslims, they should treat her with kindness–not despite, but rather because of her being a farangi, a guest in their country.

Barbara was constantly with Khanoum Mahdari after her intervention, causing the women thereafter to behave toward her, if not kindly, then at least in a way that alleviated her fear of them.

Khanoum Mahdari often talked to her about the lives that must surely be unbelievable to a Westerner, those of the child weavers to whom she'd devoted her own life from the time she was twenty years old. In order for Barbara to even begin to perceive their plight, Khanoum Mahdari said, she had to let her imagination run riot to where she could visualize the daily life of a single weaver-child, such as Farah Ghorabaji. At six years old, Farah, tiny for her age and so frail that even her young fellow workers had nicknamed her "Matchstick", rose every morning at five o'clock, ate her breakfast of tea and cold rice, and walked four miles to the Yazdi Carpet Factory. In summer she went barefoot, and in winter, her legs bound in heavy rags, she dressed in everything she owned.

The Yazdi Carpet Factory, like many other factories in Tabriz and other weaving cities where children were employed, was a barn-like room, sweltering in summer, freezing cold in winter. It was brilliant with the colors of half-completed carpets hanging from giant racks on looms about twelve feet high and perhaps twice as wide. Across from the looms were boards suspended like scaffolding, where Farah and some sixty other children, barefoot even on the coldest winter days because their foot bindings would have impeded their climbing up to their places, squatted from sunup to sundown in tailors' position—with aching knees out and stiff necks bent— while they worked on the looms; the carpets' patterns, worked out on paper by the master weavers, were propped up in front of them. Many of the young workers were Farah's age, some were older, but none were over ten. This was because older children's fingers would have become too large to tie the knots, forty to sixty to the square centimeter, as rapidly as was necessary. Farah was able to tie 14,000 knots in an ordinary workday, for which she received twenty rials, eqivalent to about thirty-two cents.

The most poignant thing about Farah and all the children, to

Khanoum Mahdari and others who knew them...At some point during their first day, their first week at work, these seemingly fragile children (though possessed, in reality, of immense tenacity, an inconceivable inner toughness) followed the example of those others who'd been in the factory longer. They made the simple, awesome decision that not only would they survive their work conditions, but also that they would create an atmosphere of gaiety, laughter, exuberance. And so they bantered, told jokes and funny stories, and sang while they worked. "Pass me the green yarn, the green yarn, pass me the green yarn now. Now the red yarn, the red, the red, please pass me the red yarn now..."

First a row of girls burst into song, then a row of boys: "Pass me the blue yarn, the blue, the blue, please pass me the blue yarn now...Pass me the yellow yarn, the pretty yellow yard that reminds me of the sun shining so bright."

Tragedy came and went in the Yazdi Factory. Old friends sickened, died and were replaced by new ones. But Farah and the others went on singing. And no one who had ever heard the sound of those children's voices singing—with nothing to sing for—had been able to forget it. Khanoum Mahdari knew that if their songs and the life stories of ones like Farah Ghorabaji could be broadcast to the outside world, hearts would be broken and good people would rise up in anger. They would declare to the factory owners, declare to the Shah that they would no longer buy Persian carpets because to walk on them would be akin to walking on children's lives.

No doubt government representatives would say, in answer to such foreign advocates, that there were no more Farah Ghorabajis in modern, progressive Iran, with its universal education and child labor laws. But how much meaning can such laws, though written into the books, have in a country where hunger is rampant and where the few rials the children earn can mean the difference between their families' living and dying? And where, besides, pishkesh is such an acceptable part of life? Truly, the prime beneficiaries of the child labor and education laws had been, from their inception, the inspector-bureaucrats to whom the factory owners paid substantial pishkesh. The only difference in the children's condition since the laws' passage was that, while the factories had formerly been open to farangi customers who wished to tour them, they were now closed.

And Khanoum Mahdari lived her whole life in and out of jail for the purpose of disproving the government's "big lie" to America, and to other nations that would certainly condemn such a denial of human rights to little children. For years she'd been crying out the tragedy of the child weavers in uncountable numbers of communications to such people as Secretary of State Henry Kissinger, and Dean Rusk before him. She had, so far, been ignored by them, or perhaps (as her colleagues, most more astute and politically sophisticated than she, maintained) dismissed as a "lunatic" or "eccentric" by those Americans who were infatuated with the Shah.

Khanoum Mahdari, as much Barbara's support and source of strength in the prison as she was Mahede's and Zarah's and Soraya's, was also full of hope for her and her children, convinced that some way, somehow, she would achieve their custody.

Some way, somehow...Through the Empress Farah perhaps. Strangely, Barbara herself had never thought of making contact with Farah, although she'd admired her since the time of their first meeting at a party held shortly after the royal wedding. She'd not been as fascinated by Farah as by Queen Soraya, even though they'd only met once, perhaps because Farah was less glamorous than Soraya, not cultured in the European fashion. But Barbara had recognized a quality of humaneness in her that Soraya, in her self-absorption, had not possessed, and that was the very opposite of her husband's sternness, remoteness, coldness. Certainly she would not react to the horror of Bahram's abuse of his daughters with the callous disregard the Shah had exhibited. Barbara determined that, as soon as she was free, she would write Farah the whole terrible story of Bahram, Roxanne and Dawneh, and would enclose the sickening pictures.

March 21 was Norooz, New Year's Day in Iran, and Barbara's seventh day of imprisonment—Khanoum Nahdari joyously informed her that today there would be a surprise for all the women and children, and tomorrow or the next day or, at the latest, the day after that, there would be a special surprise for her.

The women's and children's surprise occurred at noon. Khanoum Mahdari's three sisters, all living pictures of her, burst into the Women's Reformatory with laughter, loving words for everyone and baskets full of hard-boiled eggs, cheese, cold meats, bread and fruit, as well as candies, cookies and flowers...Flowers!

Everyone ate their fill, but the children, the children ate throughout the day. They didn't stop eating 'til late at night, when Khanoum Mahdari engulfed them in the folds of her bosom and assured them that there'd be food in the morning, and they didn't need to eat it all that night. As for the surprise Khanoum Mahdari promised Barbara...

Early in the morning after the beginning of Norooz, the Reformatory guards, transformed suddenly into creatures of utmost humility who bowed low before Barbara with trembling hands upon their chests, came to bring her to the office of Warden Humarabi. The warden also groveled as he opened the door to an inner office, and saw Hoveyda, smoking his everlasting pipe with its Dunhill Royal Pipe Mixture...He had come to help her despite the Shah's warning.

"Amir Abbas," Barbara screamed, running to him. Then, while he smiled, she said, "I...My God, Amir Abbas, I was drunk during an audience with the Shah, and I tried to fool him into..."

"So rumor has it," Hoveyda said lightly. "I heard it from..." He hesitated, and Barbara knew he'd heard it through one of Khanoum Mahdari's sisters, who'd heard it from Khanoum Mahdari. Both women had been willing to risk their lives for her. She felt tears in her eyes as she said, "I think I must be crazy, to have gotten so drunk before an audience with the Shah that I would...My God, do you think I'm crazy, Amir Abbas?"

Hoveyda made light of her question, grinning and shaking his head. He said, "Let's get out of here, Barbara, unless of course you've grown so attached to the place...Now that warrants a smile, so let's see one, please."

Barbara tried to tell Hoveyda how rare a thing his sort of kindness was, but he turned her thanks away, saying, "One of the happier returns of my often unhappy position is the opportunity to rescue pretty farangis in distress."

CHAPTER XX

Escape to America

Barbara's kismet seemed to have undergone an all-out transformation from the day Hoveyda rescued her from prison. She was hardly done writing her letter to the Empress, her first act on returning to her flat, when her servant Shamsi announced that she had a new suitor. He was, of all people, Mohammed, royal chauffeur to Her Imperial Majesty. And yes, Shamsi would be seeing Mohammed tonight, Barbara's schedule permitting. Of course, he would personally deliver Barbara's letter to the Queen.

Only three days after Shamsi gave Mohammed Barbara's letter, her bell rang at two o'clock in the afternoon. The woman at the door was young, tall and very slender with long, shiny black hair. Barbara knew that she was Sheherezade Najafi, a good friend of Barbnara and a lady-in-waiting to the Queen. She told Barbara that Farah had cried when she'd read the letter and seen the pictures. "And she sent me to tell you that you will have your daughters' custody."

Barbara was aware of the blood rushing in her ears as she heard Khanoum Najafi out, of her heart beating, of the tiny pulse in her neck, the veins as they stood out on her hands...Of the fact that she was living out, on that day, one of the most wonderful times of her life.

The only thing that she was not aware of was that Khanoum Najafi had told her that the Queen would grant her custody of her daughters, but made no mention of her son.

Khanoum Najafi had, she said, already seen Judge Cyrus Rabii of the Supreme Court and delivered the Queen's order to him. "He has summoned your husband, with your daughters, to appear before him at two o'clock tomorrow afternoon. Your letter and your daughters' pictures are in his possession. Once he hears your testimony, you and your daughters will be free to go home together."

"And my son...Will...?" Barbara's voice rose, "When and how will I get my son?"

Khanoum Najafi looked at Barbara, and her expression had everything in it—understanding, compassion, the sharing of her pain—when she said, "I am sorry, Barbara, but the Queen...You must know, after all, that sons in Iran...Even the Queen..."

Barbara and Zahedi were already seated in Judge Rabii's walnut-paneled courtroom when the judge, quite young and with a Western look, entered. Minutes later came Bahram. Believing this trial to be a sham like the previous one and the judge a Mosallai family tool, he was in the court without Baba Bozorg, Hajji Khadivar and all the uncles, cousins or whoever, who'd flanked him at the earlier trial. And even without his lawyer, Hussein. He was accompanied only by Dawn, Rocky, Mohammed and Mohammed's pretty twenty-year-old sister, Esmat. Barbara's former wardrobe mistress, Esmat was now Bahram's fiancee, and she flaunted an engagement diamond that looked as big as one of Barbara's knuckles.

Judge Rabii greeted Dawn and Rocky kindly and asked them to wait in an adjoining room 'til he would send for them. He then turned to Bahram and forced him to examine the packet of pictures one by one. "To hurt your own daughters as you have done...Your own daughters. I am ashamed in the presence of this American mother to admit that I too am an Iranian man. As for your daughters, you'd just as well have killed them outright as little by little. And I would, if I legally could, sentence you to where you can do no more harm for the rest of your life. But since I cannot...I am granting your daughters' custody to their mother, and ordering you to stay away from them and make no further problems. Do you understand?"

Bahram, as Barbara could have predicted would happen, went mad with rage. He slammed his hand on the table and screamed obscenities at both Barbara and Judge Rabii. He finally had to be dragged from the courtroom by a clerk and two policemen.

After long minutes, considerately calculated to permit Barbara to regain her poise, Rocky and Dawn were brought in and stood in front of Judge Rabii. "I hope," he said, "that you young ladies will approve my decision to give your mother custody. It means that you will, from now on, be living in her home, not your father's home."

Barbara and her daughters ran to each other. Her arms went around them, and she held them tight as she'd dreamed of doing during the time, only days, really, but days that seemed like years, since they'd been taken from her.

As soon as she had Dawn and Rocky temporarily settled (with only the clothes on their backs since Bahram had refused to let them have any of their possessions), Barbara went to her former home at an hour when she knew Bahram and Mohammed would be away. She was received by Esmat in the company salon.

"Hello," Esmat said. "Would you like some tea, dear?"

"No tea. And don't call me dear anymore, okay? Where is my son?"

"I'm sorry, but my orders from Bahram...You may not see Teymour, Barbara."

"My child. What the hell do you mean, I may not see him?" Barbara leaped around Esmat, out into the hall and up the stairs to the children's playroom. Teymour rushed into her arms. Immediately, two menservants came and pulled her away from him, and she went quietly in order to save her child the sight and sound of his mother being further abused by his father's servants.

In the morning Dawn, knowing that Barbara had gone the night before to try and see Teymour, and having heard her weeping through the night, said to her, "Mama, my father's home is not the only place where Tey...He spends as much time at school as at home. I think that if you talked to his principal, offered her enough pishkesh..."(only eleven, Barbara thought, and she already knows the significance of pishkesh!) "...she will let you see Teymour, maybe every day for lunch,"

"Dawn, of course. You're brilliant, do you know it, darling?"

Teymour's principal, Khanoum Jahanjiri, was tall, with snow white hair and her mien cool, polite and aloof. Her eyes seemed to bore into Barbara as she declared that she must surely understand that what she was asking of her...Bahram would have her job, certainly, if he ever discovered her to be aiding Barbara. And there was no telling what else he might do–have her imprisoned, anything. It sounded as though she was readying to request substantial pishkesh, which Barbara would have happily paid, and had it on the tip of her tongue to offer.

Yet something, some fortunate intuition, kept Barbara silent while Khanoum Jahanjiri seemed lost in thought. She rose after a while and went to stand so close to Barbara that she could see the pulse in her throat, see a glistening of tears in her eyes as she said softly, "Oh, my dear, how could I, a mother who has had no contact with my own children since my husband divorced me twenty-one years ago, not do all in my power to help you and your son. You may see him every day at lunch, though only in my office. I know you'd prefer to take him out, but I am afraid that isn't feasible, at least not for now. And listen, please pray, as I also will, that he'll be able to keep our secret, because if he does not, I fear for both of us."

The less one has of time, the more skillfully one learns to use it. An hour a day with Teymour, sometimes an hour and fifteen minutes—these precious minutes every day were the equal of many hours in the ordinary lives of mothers and children. Truly, the joy of Tey's and Barbara's time together was heightened, sharpened and quickened by the time limitation. Barbara used some of the time to make Tey comfortable about the divorce; she assured him that both she and his father loved him very much. And she praised Esmat, who would soon be his stepmother, as good and kind. It hurt her to laud these people she hated, yet she knew she had to for her child's sake. And it did seem, happily, that Tey was not nearly as damaged by his family's upheaval as Barbara feared he would be.

Certainly Teymour suffered, or seemed to suffer, less than either Rocky or Dawn. Dawn...who would ever have believed that she, who was at first the "angel child" with her peaceful, happy disposition, and then the frightened recluse...could have become transformed, almost overnight, into a child of flamboyant self-assertion, a swaggering, warlike young person ready to protest and fight for her rights against any and all odds, a stubborn, if pitiful, little heroine?

Twenty minutes before noon, three days after Barbara had won her daughters' custody, Aga Alam, Dawn's principal, a man with a

goatee and fierce gaze, called her out of her classroom and instructed her to come with him.

"Where are we going, Aga?"

"You will see when we get there, Dawneh."

"No, I want to know now. I won't go unless..."

"You come with me immediately, and with proper feminine gra-
ciousness and..."

"Well, see, I will not come, Aga–because I know, I KNOW that
you are going to bring me to my father. And you are not supposed
to bring me to him." Dawn tilted her little chin defiantly and gab-
bled fast. "I won't let you bring me to my father, you're not supposed to bring me to my father, not supposed to let him see me,
because my mother gave you pishkesh. She didn't know I saw, and
you didn't know, but I did see. And I heard her, I heard you, and
you said, 'You can be sure I will protect Dawneh from her father.'
And now...She gave you a lot of pishkesh because you thanked her a
lot, and you said, 'I give you my word of honor, Sultaneh, that if
Dawneh's father ever comes here and tries to take her, or even to
speak with her, I will stop him and call you immediately.' And now
you want...I know, Aga, that you lied to my mother and are taking
me to my father, and I WON'T GO."

Aga Alam looked at Dawn in astonishment. He'd never expected
such a speech from the Dawneh he'd known in former years. He hit
her a stinging blow on the chest. Knowing he'd never have abused
her in such a fashion if he hadn't been certain her father would
approve, Dawn hit him back with lightning rapidity. Now Aga Alam
clutched Dawn's hair and dragged her, shrieking and howling,
through the long hallway and into his office where, as she'd suspect-
ed, Bahram was waiting.

As soon as Aga Alam put her down, and before Bahram could
reach her, she made a mad dash out of the office. And when Bahram
caught her in the hallway, she spat and kicked and smacked 'til he
overwhelmed her and held her fast, while roaring all the familiar epi-
thets at her. And she, beyond pride, beyond humiliation, with nothing more to lose now that everyone knew her degradation, returned
her father's curses, giving as good as she got.

Bahram put his hands around Dawn's throat and lifted her off her feet. As she struggled to free herself, his grip grew tighter, tighter, 'til she heard the sound of her own gagging. She also heard, dimly, other voices: teachers', children's, even Aga Alam's, pleading with Bahram to release her before he choked her to death. But she did not see Barbara's servant Gholam come to pick her up early for a dental appointment, and fortunately, neither did Bahram. Gholam was short, heavy, well into his sixties, respectful of his "superiors" and a coward at heart. Yet today, in a flash that both he and Dawn would remember, he knotted his plump fist and slammed it all over Bahram, swinging wildly, flailing, thrashing 'til he was forced to put Dawn down. And while Bahram ranted, Gholam placed himself behind Dawn as a shield and propelled her down the stairs and out the door.

Bahram, having again appeared in Judge Rabii's courtroom, was threatened by him with a long prison term "if you ever dare show your face anywhere that Dawneh and Roxanne are." Therefore, Bahram evolved methods of torturing Dawneh and Roxanne (and thus Barbara) without openly violating Rabii's order. Hence, some two weeks after the incident at Dawn's school, two policemen in uniform, followed by Khanoum Mansaur, vice-principal of Rocky's school, came into her classroom. The moment she saw them, Rocky knew that the policemen's presence had something to do with her and her father.

"Roxanne, dear, listen," Khanoum Mansaur bent over her, touching her shoulder and stroking her hair. "There's nothing to worry about, but...Let's you and I step outside a minute."

Rocky rose, and with head held high, she led, rather than followed, Khanoum Mansaur and the policemen out of the classroom. Quite a confident camouflage this young girl had developed to hide her deep vulnerability!

"What exactly do you want of me?" she inquired of the officers as soon as they were in the hallway. One of them, embarrassment on his face, handed her the arrest warrant. She did not cry; it was not in her nature to cry, but the shock-volts seemed to move through the whole of her body as she read Bahram's allegation that two days ago, she'd stolen thirty thousand tomans out of his home safe.

"Roxanne," Khanoum Mansaur's voice was quiet but urgent, "when was the last time you were in your father's home?"

"A month ago."

"Well then," Khanoum Mansaur said, relieved, "There is nothing to worry about. Since your father says the burglary...occurred only two days ago, and you haven't been in his home for a month, we really have nothing to worry about after all."

Nothing to worry about except that all the anger Rocky had felt at Bahram over the years, all of the fury she'd felt at his torturing of Dawn and Barbara and Shirley Kashani, especially Shirley, as well as of herself...All of it seemed to have congealed today, to have hardened and grown larger, and beyond her ability to control.

But Rocky, being herself, did not share her feelings with Khanoum Mansaur or anyone, including Barbara. Especially Barbara who, although she'd acted calm enough when she'd come to bail her out of the Women's Reformatory, and also during the five days afterward that preceded her trial, seemed to Rocky to be on the verge of a breakdown. From the moment they left the prison, therefore, Rocky behaved as though she were the mother and Barbara the young girl in trouble who needed to be cherished and protected. And even during the trial that lasted no more than an hour (Judge Aazhari, like Judge Rabii before him, excoriated Bahram for his "inhumanity", his "barbarousness toward your own daughter"), she sat patting Barbara's shoulder and holding her hand.

But Barbara knew how much Rocky's cool control cost her. She knew that both Rocky and Dawn had been at least as damaged when Bahram humiliated them and deprived them of their "face" in the eyes of their peers as they'd been by his private beatings and abuse. So long as people did not know that the beatings were happening, so long as the public face they were able to project was one of beloved daughter of a benevolent father, they could endure. Once the truth was out, though, their humiliation, their shame, was all but unbearable. Rocky began once more to have her dreams of horror. And Dawn resumed her miserable solitude.

Some three months after she'd gained Rocky's and Dawn's

custody, Barbara realized that, for their sakes, she had to go away from Iran. Bahram would never leave her daughters in peace so long as she was there to suffer at his being at war with them. Thus, she went to see Hoveyda and explained all the tragic details to him. She then begged him to "act as my representative" and to offer Dawn's and Rocky's total custody back to the Mosallai family, so long as they would allow them to live in Khanoum-June's home. And also, so long as they, themselves, would treat the girls with the same concern for their welfare and future as they did Tey. She was not asking for the impossible, not asking them to love her daughters as they did her son...Khanoum-June would love them...but only that they would be decent to them.

"And now comes the tough part, Amir Abbas. Since I'll be leaving Iran...I know it's asking a lot, maybe too much, but I'm going to ask anyway...I'm asking you to watch over my kids. To use your authority to make certain that the Mosallai men don't hurt them any more than they've been hurt already."

For a long time Hoveyda sat silent.

"I...I guess," Barbara finally concluded, "that it's asking too much, and...It's just that I don't know where to turn, don't know anyone else Bahram and Hajji Khadivar and Baba Bozorg could possibly pay any mind to. And if you won't help us..."

Hoveyda rose and went to sit beside Barbara, taking her hand. "I'm going to help you, Barbara, but not in the way you're asking...I'm going to help you, Dawn and Rocky to go to America."

She looked at him for several stunned minutes, not daring to believe it. "Amir Abbas, you're not just...Oh my God, you do mean it, YOU DO MEAN IT." Barbara locked him into a jubilant embrace. After a while she began crying as though she would never stop, and when she finally did stop, she and Hoveyda made their plans for the escape.

They were, basically, very simple plans. Hoveyda would supply passports, complete with identification photos, for Edward Broder, his wife Carole and his two blond daughters. The daughters were seventeen-year-old Mary Jo (Rocky, in a blond wig, would easily pass as two years older than her age) and nine-year-old Laurie

(Dawn would doubtless balk at the loss of two years, but Barbara would find a way to soothe her).

On August 1st, in five days, Barbara and her "family" would be boarding the 3:45 Pan-Am flight for Madrid. And from there, Houston, Texas was the place in America where Barbara and her daughters would put down their roots; she chose it for no more reason than that Betty Belkis, her former college roommate, lived there.

Immediately after Barbara left Hoveyda, she went home to Dawn and Rocky and told them, laughing and crying, as they would also be before she was done, that they were going to America. America, where girls were cherished as much as boys, women respected as highly as men (so Barbara told her daughters–and she well might have, after all the years in Iran, believed herself in what she said).

On the day she, Dawn and Rocky would leave for Madrid, Barbara and Tey had their last lunch together. She couldn't take her eyes off him as he ate. She kept remembering back to when he was born, when he was a couple of months old, a year old, two, five. Catching every image and fixing it forever in her mind. Tey on his third birthday, blowing out the candles on his cake. Tey in red and white striped swim trunks, running around the pool with Dawn. She pictured them chasing each other. He looked away for a moment, and then Dawn dove in and he looked around and panicked. He didn't know where she was. He'd sometimes said he hated her, but the look on his face when she emerged from the water was one of such happiness and pure love that Dawn, who sometimes said she hated him, was touched enough to kiss and hug him.

Barbara envisioned Tey chewing up the ends of a dozen pencils and breaking the points, while writing out the lessons assigned by his tutor before he'd even entered kindergarten. She saw Tey at bedtime cuddling with Barbara and reiterating that he loved her more than all of his stuffed animals put together.

Tey, today at nearly nine, was tall like his true father, slender but with large feet and hands that were tough paws, also like his father's. The baby was gone. This was Tey, expert swimmer, equestrian, roller skater, tough guy...with chocolate on his face. This was Yah Yah's son Tey—strong, healthy, full of life.

Barbara agreed with Hoveyda that Teymour must not be informed of the trip to America, agreed that even Rocky and Dawn's knowing was a dangerous thing. But how do you go away from your son for what may be years, if not a lifetime, without telling him good-bye and letting him know you love him? And how can he believe you love him when you also must tell him that you're splitting from him in order to save his sisters?

"Tey," Barbara said, holding both his hands, "I hate it, and I know that you will too..." She talked on and on, touching his shoulder, which was becoming sinewy, and his cheek, still little-boy soft and round. For how long, she wondered? Would those little-boy cheeks have changed to a man's by the time she'd see him next?

"One question, Mama," Tey said when Barbara told him to ask her anything he wanted, "why don't you love me as you do my sisters?"

Oh my heart, my darling, how, under these circumstances, will I ever be able to give you any comprehension at all of what you mean to me. If nothing should ever happen to you, no one ever hurt you—I'd gladly give up half my life if I could be assured of that, my little boy.

"Tey, Sweetheart, you must know how much Mama loves you."

But Tey got up from his seat and stood ramrod-straight in front of Barbara. He tried to stop the tears that rolled down his cheeks; all he said was that he guessed he needed to get back to his classroom. She tried to take him in her arms, but he pulled away from her. Then he went through the door, and the last thing she saw were his eyes looking at her...Oh, my Tey, with the great black eyes, was the last look you gave me one of love or hate? This was the question that would haunt Barbara all through the trip to America, and for the rest of her life.

BOOK TWO

Roxanne
and
Dawneh

CHAPTER XXI

Pot Pie and Pizza, Pizza, Pizza

Houston had, from the day of their arrival, an altogether different significance for Barbara than for her daughters. To her, it was the home she'd been hungering for. It was the place where she, Rocky and Dawn, their women's souls having been crushed and so nearly destroyed in Iran, could finally be warmed and fed and bolstered. Yet to Rocky, with her fear of sex and hatred of men, Houston was a city of utmost terror that made her long for the protection of a chador. Matured at fifteen with a gorgeous, lithe body and silken red hair that hung down to her hips, Rocky had been serenaded nightly by the resident musicians of the Hilton Inn where the family lived while house-hunting, and cars had stopped right in the middle of the road while the drivers called, "Hey, Beautiful!"

For Dawn, Houston was a melancholy, mean place of compassionless, cruel men, women...and especially children. On September 4th, the opening day, Barbara accompanied Dawn to Lee Junior High School with its green, lush campus and formal modernistic buildings. She escorted her to her sixth grade class, taught by Miss Cates, a gentle, friendly, pleasant-looking woman. Miss Cates received Dawn kindly, introduced her to her future companions and led her to her seat beside Marion, a heavy girl wearing jeans embroidered with sunrises.

On this first day nothing much happened. Dawn sat in her class, the others kept looking at her and she at them, and the lessons proceeded routinely. Miss Cates explained what they were going to learn that semester. Then the day was over, half an hour early, and the children rushed onto the campus. Dawn stood alone, leaning against a tree while she waited for Barbara. A little group of boys and girls, led by Marion, approached her suddenly.

"What are you anyway?" Marion demanded with energy.

"I...I am Dawneh."

"I didn't ask who you are, I asked what you are."

Dawn could understand English fairly well. Barbara had, of course, spoken it to her since she was little (although she'd generally answered in Persian), but such nuances as the difference between who and what were beyond her, and she said again, "I am Dawneh."

"Are you a Chicano?" Marion asked.

One of the others, a tall, thick boy named Ronnie said, "She can't be a Chicano, Marion, because she isn't dark enough. Her skin's as light as a regular person's; she's got an American skin, and even her eyes are kind of American. It's only her eyebrows that are dark like a Chicano's, or...She must be a gypsy girl. Are you a gypsy girl, Dawneh?"

Dawn, unable to understand the torrent of his jargon, and especially the significance of "Chicano" and "gypsy girl", stayed silent.

"Why don't you answer a question, Dawneh? I don't think you're deaf, but...Are you deaf, or what?" asked Ronnie, more in puzzlement than hostility.

"Naah, she's not deaf, just dumb," opined Marion.

Now, though not altogether understanding the English words, Dawn did get the gist of what was going on; and the rebel, the hellion who'd dared to do battle in her Persian school with both Aga Alam and Bahram, took over. Eyes flashing and voice shrieking the Persian curses she'd learned from her father, she struck Marion's nose with her fist, not hard enough to knock her down as she perceived it, yet Marion did fall. And Ronnie entered the fray, shaking Dawn and throwing her down so she ripped her new blouse. She got up and flung her arms around Ronnie, wanting to throw him onto the ground beside Marion, who wasn't trying to get up but was instead crying and shrieking that Dawn had tried to kill her.

Miss Cates, on her way out of the school, came running. "Children! Children! What's happening here?"

All the children echoed Marion, saying that Dawn had tried to kill her.

The only thing she said in answer was, "Look, look what they did to my new blouse."

Miss Cates turned her around. Her cool fingers fiddled with the blouse at Dawn's back. "It'll be easily fixed, dear, you'll see...

Dawneh, where are you going? You can't go, your mother'll be coming to pick you up any minute."

But Dawn was already gone. Off the campus and around the corner she fled.

Dawn's assertiveness secured for her an important place among the two outcast groups of her class, the group of three black children and the group of four Chicano children. But the twenty other students, all middle or upper-middle class WASPs, marked her as their victim. They nicknamed her Moosehead—Moosehead Mosallai—and outdid one another in doing her harm. Whenever she walked past other students, they pretended she'd tripped them and started fights. They threw down her coat from its peg. They stole her lunch. They soiled her homework papers. They mocked and jeered and contradicted her, whatever she said. Whoever made any mischief laid the blame on Dawn, and the entire class would swear to the truth of the lie.

Many of Houstons public and private schools during the early '70s, the years of Dawn's attendance, were rife with drugs. And some of Dawn's classmates were able to get their hands on all the drugs they needed or wanted for themselves, and plenty more besides. Therefore, they evolved a new and intriguing pattern for tormenting Dawn: "the planting of drugs on Moosehead Mosallai." Miss Cates, and later Dawn's other teachers, would often find, courtesy of varying informants, pot, hash and especially Quaaludes or Valium in her locker or hidden in her gym shoes. Of necessity, then, they would have to bring the matter to the principal, Mrs. Folger. A haughty, sour woman, she would gladly have expelled Dawn "the troublemaker," and even turned her over to the authorities for selling drugs. However, Dawn's basically empathetic teachers, knowing the truth although they could not, in fact, prove it, fought hard to stop her.

And how did Dawn respond to all the harassment leveled at her daily? By wishing to leave the school from the moment she arrived in the morning, to go home and hide and sleep, never to wake up. Yet acting always as defiant and warlike as she did on her first day.

Barbara wanted her to transfer to the progressive private Briar Hill School, and the principal and teachers there were very eager to have her come. But Dawn, after one visit, was unbending; she would "never, ever go to that place," no matter how Barbara begged and pleaded. And her mother, realizing her reason, could not force her. For these children, especially the girls in the jeans and sweaters they wore with such style, looked to Dawn to be more "American-perfect" than even the most confident and arrogant of the Lee girls; they made her feel even more stupid and "out of it" and vulnerable than she did at Lee.

Barbara, therefore, suggested a compromise to her; she'd not mention another word about Briar Hill so long as Dawn would agree to be tutored in English for two hours every day. And Dawn said "fine," to that bargain; she said "fine," but her acts did not coincide with that word. She refused to cooperate with her tutors, never carrying out their assignments and paying little attention to anything they told her.

Neither would she, no matter how Barbara cajoled, accompany her and Rocky on their Saturday trips around Houston. She had no desire to experience downtown, or the Galleria with its elegant shops and restaurants, or the movies or the children's zoo, or puppet shows...not in Houston, not in America.

What was her desire, then? To be left alone to watch television and eat her fill of ice cream, pot pie and pizza, pizza, pizza. And yes, certainly she knew she'd gained weight, forty pounds to be exact, in the weeks that seemed like months, and the months that seemed like years, and the two years that seemed like twenty since her first day at Lee. And nobody knew better than she how much she'd changed, and that she was, in fact, UGLY. That was the plain word, and she wouldn't skirt around the use of it. Ugly. U-G-L-Y.

And the reason she could say the word while Rocky and Barbara could not, was that she really didn't want to be pretty because, when you came down to it, pretty could hurt as much as ugly, maybe more. Take Rocky as an example...what good had her stunning figure and beautiful face done her in her school? She didn't complain, because that was not her way, but Dawn knew that she, too, was miserable. The fact was that Rocky, although she could speak and understand English almost as well as if she'd been born in America, had no more friends than her sister. This was in spite of, or maybe because of, all that beauty of hers.

Rocky's first day at the new, plush Northbrook High, though not as rough, was as bitter as Dawn's first day at her school. She came into her homeroom class feeling self-conscious in her tight blue jeans, which were like any American girl's, wearing the same bright red lipstick and turquoise eye-shadow that her peers (who didn't have her startling, satiny hair hanging to their hips) also displayed. She was greeted immediately by a chorus of whistles from a few of the boys. And though the teacher, Mr. Jamison, raised a hand to command silence and said, "Okay, fellows, that'll be enough of that," Rocky noted a hint of amusement in his eyes. And she (child of both her strict Iranian culture where "decent" girls could not wear makeup, tweeze their eyebrows or shave their legs 'til after marriage) blamed herself for what she perceived as the boys' and the teacher's contempt for her.

But she was too proud to show her dejection or feeling of defeat, so she walked to the seat Mr. Jamison assigned with head held high and an icy look on her face. And the boys, who'd expected she'd be grateful for their notice were, naturally, challenged to break through her facade. At lunchtime, therefore, several of them clustered around her in the cafeteria, and giggling together and poking one another, outdid themselves in telling jokes and teasing her. And when she left her table a couple of the boys followed her, and one even touched her hair; she ran out of the cafeteria to the sound of the boys' laughter.

Rocky was desperately lonely throughout her first year, since the boys ignored her after a while and she was not able to break into the tight little groups of girls who'd grown up together, and didn't easily welcome any strangers into their midst, least of all foreigners like Rocky. In her sophomore and junior years, though, her circumstances changed somewhat. Older boys—seniors, and even some in college—began courting her with such compliments as had to rouse some response in the awakening woman, the solitary young soul who yearned for approval. But she would not pet or French kiss, or even kiss, for that matter. The most a boy could expect from her was that she'd let him hold her hand. The boys, then, soon tired of her. And one day in her junior year, Allen Patterson, a football hero who had all the girls except Rocky at his feet, told her angrily, when she'd refused to let him kiss her, "Don't put on that holier-than-thou act with me, honey, because I know, and everyone does, that you're nothing but a lesbo."

Rocky stared at him uncomprehending. "A what?"

"A lesbian, baby. You're not fooling anyone with that act of yours."

And, as had been the case when she was a freshman, there was even less link, less contact between Rocky and the other girls than between her and the boys. Not one single girl asked her to go to one of the many parties happening nearly every weekend. Here she was, after having lived nearly three years in America, as alien to her American peers as she'd been on the day that she'd arrived from Iran. The girls she wanted so much as friends wanted nothing to do with her.

"I don't care about those girls who don't want me for a friend," Rocky told herself, "or about the boys either, for that matter," and stubbornly repeated: "I don't care about them." And after a while, because she did care so very much, her upper-class Persian snobbery that had only been pushed down during her pitiful fling at "making it in America" reasserted itself. And she thought to herself that it was, indeed, absurd that she, Roxanne Sultaneh, should be coveting acceptance by such manifestly lower-class young people as had no noble titles, and owned neither village nor mansion.

As for the parties from which they excluded her...At home in Tehran she could join her cousins and friends in their glamorous activities that these girls who rejected her and called her lesbian would not be able to imagine, because it all was too far out of their mundane ken. There were grand galas in Tehran or Shiraz or Isfahan, from imperial parties given at one of the Shah's palaces to the buffets, tennis parties, swimming parties and dances at one another's mansions or any of the fifty foreign missions accredited to

Mohammed Reza's court. Such a life of splendor Rocky could have if she returned to Iran.

And there were so many in Iran who loved her and whom she loved. Khanoum-June, Peri and all of Barbara's friends at Tehran University, as well as her own friends and cousins. And Teymour, her sweet brother. Now there was also a new brother, Habib, nearly two years old, whom Rocky didn't even know except from pictures. It's wrong, Rocky thought, for sister and brother who ought, by right, to be so close, to be strangers to one another.

Before Rocky, sick at the thought of what she had to do, could tell Barbara she'd decided to "go home again", at least for a long visit, Barbara said something to her that made the telling easier. "I haven't told Dawn this yet, Sweetheart, because she surely won't understand, while you..I am hoping that you will help me tell your sister that...I'm going to marry Charlie Bell, Rocky."

Rocky was shocked, although there was no reason why she should have been. She should have known from the look on her mother's face and the sound of her voice as she'd introduced her and Dawn to Charlie on their first date, that this would be the result. She shouldn't have beaten down her fear of him, as she'd done at the time and during all of the following months. She should have known that this handsome man in his fifties (she had to admit he was handsome), with his slender, tall figure, thick white hair and blue eyes, was a rival for her mother's love. She'd thought, though, that although Barbara wanted Charlie as a friend, she'd never marry him, or anybody, after all she'd been through with Bahram. And she could not imagine how her mother could have brought herself to believe in Charlie's promise to love and respect her as an equal for the rest of their lives. What man ever loved and respected his wife as an equal, that was what Rocky wanted to know. Barbara would become Charlie's servant, and wouldn't even be well-paid for it as she'd be if she decided to marry, say, someone of Bahram's wealth and importance. Who was Charlie Bell anyway, except a land-less, property-less person who had to work at a lowly job. How much money could a school principal, a "chalk-eater", be earning?

Charlie was a "plebeian" because during all the months of his courting of Barbara, he'd never given her a single diamond or even a necklace or gold bracelet. That was a lowering of Barbara's "face" though she didn't seem to know it; she said, whenever Rocky told this to her, that Charlie heightened her "face" by his love and respect, that were worth more to her than all of the jewels in Persia. Further, Charlie never would beat her, and whether Rocky realized it or not, there wasn't a diamond in the world big enough to compensate a woman for a husband's physical abuse.

Rocky agreed that nothing, nothing in the world was payment enough for the kind of abuse her father had inflicted on her mother. Her question to Barbara, though, was this: How could she know that Charlie Bell would not, after marriage, end up as a Bahram? Bahram had made her many fine promises, too, and look what they'd come down to. And if Barbara wanted to risk herself and her life a second time, maybe that was her business. Or it would be if she didn't have two daughters. It was them and their lives she was risking, though, as well as her own. Hadn't she and Dawn been through enough with their own rotten father? What made Barbara think now that they'd accept a stepfather? She, Rocky, would be all right because she was old enough to cope, and anyway was making other plans for herself. But what, for God's sake, would happen to poor Dawn?

Barbara and Charlie were married on June 27th, 1975 by a Justice of the Peace with Dawn and Rocky, and Janie and Sue, Charlie's seventeen and nineteen-year-old daughters, as the only witnesses. And Rocky was able, by then, to overcome some of her hostility toward Charlie and to feel happiness for Barbara. But her heart hurt for Dawn, who'd come to the wedding sick, and not only because Barbara was, as she perceived it, abandoning her by marrying Charlie. It was also because she, Rocky, was returning to Iran. Rocky–who was not only Dawn's sister but also her idol and friend, her best friend, her only friend in America–was leaving her. And sitting beside Dawn at the wedding feast, Rocky heard her whispering to herself, "I'm going to get my revenge on them, I'm going to get my revenge."

Dawn's "revenge" on her mother and sister took the form of

self-destruction. She ate more voraciously than ever and allowed her school grades to drop so low that her long-time enemy, Mrs. Folger, not only had her put back into seventh grade, but also declared she had a learning disability and insisted that she be placed in "a special school for children of that kind."

Now began a series of tests of Dawn's intelligence that necessarily grew into confrontations that Dawn and Barbara had to face with the psychologists, who were blind and deaf to Dawn's misery and ignorance of English. Hence, their test results legitimized Mrs. Folger's conclusion.

Then, just when the abilities of Barbara, and certainly of Dawn, to keep on questioning the authorities' conclusions was at its lowest ebb, Dr. Effat Attabei, whom Charlie located, appeared. A vibrant, empathetic woman of Iranian ancestry though born in America, she had long worked with disturbed young people. And she managed early on to win Dawn's trust. It was so good, so good to feel close enough to another person who is not your mother or sister, that you can lay your sorrow in her lap. So good to be able to tell her, with no worry over "face", the whole tale of your life, spewing out your pain and rage without shame.

During the months of her treatment with Dr. Attabei, Dawn came to know that under that ugly flab was a girl who, with her huge warm brown eyes, small straight nose and fair, velvety skin, was quite as beautiful in her way as Rocky was in hers. And Dr. Attabei's tests, different from those of the other psychologists' only in that they translated into Persian the English Dawn couldn't grasp, showed her, to be sure, as emotionally troubled, but also exceptionally bright. Thus Doctor Attabei recommended that Dawn transfer to St. Jerome's Catholic School, because the classes were small and the Dominican teacher-nuns were qualified by both their education and dedication to meet students' special needs.

Dawn's teacher for homeroom, as well as for Speech and English, was Sister Sharon Millstone. She was in her early thirties, small and on the stout side, with a neat, pretty face and dirty blond hair tied in, of all things for a nun, a ponytail. Her first act after assigning the students their places was to introduce Dawn to them as "a member of one of the world's oldest, richest cultures, from whom we all have much to learn," and to make her welcome in the eyes of her fellow students.

Sister Sharon, though, was speaking only for herself as an inhabitant of the brave, new, humanistic, liberal (as she saw it!) world opened to Catholics by "Good Pope John" as long ago as 1963. But her welcoming words to Dawn did not represent the views of the majority of her students. All too many of them and their parents had, despite Pope John, remained conservative and closed even to other Christians–and certainly to people like Dawn, out of a culture that worshipped a God of a different name and claimed Christ to be a mere man, albeit a good and worthy one. They let her know from her first day that she was headed for hell, since she was not a Catholic and there was no salvation outside the Catholic Church.

And Dawn's first Friday morning at St. Jerome's served to prove their argument. She sat in the church chapel with her teachers and fellow students, everyone serious, no smiling, no whispering, no moving in pews. A priest, looking to Dawn to be as grand and majestic as the Shah himself, at first knelt with his splendid golden back turned on the people. Then as the organ played, he turned and faced toward them, chanting some words that seemed to be an invitation to everyone to march to the altar and be given, by the priest's own hand, the grape juice that represented the blood of Christ, and the consecrated hosts that stood for His body.

Dawn, wanting to be part of this majestic ritual, rose from her pew and walked toward the altar for her turn to receive communion. She was prevented by, of all people, the kindly Sister Sharon, who muttered to her something about communion being the holiest of Catholic ceremonies and not something to be shared with non-Catholics.

And Dawn, knowing nothing about the tenets of Catholicism and the doctrinal significance of Holy Communion, perceived her exclusion to have been an insult personally directed at her. And being her immature self (how differently Rocky, even at the age Dawn was then, would have behaved), she craved revenge. So, on the following Friday, she went to the chapel before anyone else arrived and stole the juice and wafers. So long as there could be none for her, there wouldn't be any for anyone else. She was, of course, caught as she'd expected to be and, in her self-destructiveness, perhaps hoped that she would be. She was brought to the office of Sister Joshua David, the principal, who asked her WHAT DEVIL drove her to commit such an outrageous and unnatural act. She merely shrugged. And when Sister Joshua David warned that unless she "improved her ways," she'd be expelled, she said, "Well, maybe you'd like to throw me out now, Sister...I don't know if I'll ever 'improve my ways', and anyhow, this school's nothing all that special to me since I'm not even a Catholic and wouldn't want to be."

From the day that she thus declared herself to Sister Joshua David, Dawn set out to break every rule of the school. She refused to have her fingernails cut when Sister Sharon insisted it was the regulation and, in fact, polished them a bright red. She walked wavering like a drunk, instead of militarily straight, on her classroom line. She mocked her teachers, snapping her fingers and cracking her prohibited bubble gum in their faces. And she fought with the other students much as she'd done at Lee. And although the nuns initially, in Christian compassion, tolerated Dawn for as long as they were able, the day came when they saw no choice except to expel her.

CHAPTER XXII

The Low, Vile, Debauched Ways of America

The Iran to which Rocky returned in 1975 was a very different country from the one she had left only two years earlier. Mohammed Reza, obsessed with his grandiose fantasy of making Iran "the fifth industrial and military power of the world", bought "defense" equipment from Britain, France, Italy and the USSR, but mostly from the United States. Over one-third of U.S. foreign military purchases in the years 1974-1977 were made by the Shah.

Along with all this equipment came a large number of foreign technical advisers and instructors. And American military suppliers like Grumman, Lockheed and Westinghouse took over key positions in the economy.

Americans were also vital in the carrying out of Mohammed Reza's industrial strategy that included the development of steel, copper, hydroelectric and thermal power, an auto assembly industry, telecommunications, airlines, arms factories and textile factories.

And on the farms...The Shah and his Western advisers favored huge agribusiness and farm corporations that used modern mechanization in place of peasant labor. Thus, the peasants were either bought or driven off the land and into the urban slums.

As were also the nomads whose sheep markets were, on the advice of American businessmen, replaced by the Shah's underwriting of large farms of imported American cattle and poultry. These were fed by American grain, and the farms utilized American equipment of such sophistication as demanded American or other foreign technicians and workers. This, despite the fact that Iranians have always preferred lamb to chicken and beef. The tribal peoples joined the peasants in fleeing their pastures for the city slums that had neither jobs nor housing to offer them. Those who already lived in the slums, the mass of factory workers who'd once been comparatively well off, were now devastated further by the ever-rising inflation.

The factory workers and displaced peasants and nomads were, therefore, united in their resentment and detestation of Mohammed Reza and his foreign, especially American, allies. They perceived Americans, falsely, as owning the country (actually U.S. investments were never higher than $200 million dollars), and, realistically, as encouraging corruption and profiting from their miseries.

The people might not have known the sordid details of the corruption, i.e. immense quantities of monies passing from foreign companies to the royal family and others close to the Shah, in payment for contracts. They did know, though, that it was happening. And they knew too that, gallingly, "the low, vile, debauched ways of America" had been adopted wholesale, and were constantly being flaunted in their faces by upper-class Iranians, their sons—and especially, their daughters.

Rocky had her first intimation of the changed Iran the moment she left customs and entered the huge main Mehrabad International Airport, that was thronged with briefcase-carrying arms and corporate negotiators and salesmen from all over the world. And teeming, too, with countless armed soldiers; militiamen, paratroopers with their black berets and Imperial Guardsmen with the impressive red hats and white boots Rocky had only seen at parades before.

Life among the Iranian travelers, though, seemed to be going on as always. And Rocky felt herself caught up by the purely Persian smells and sights and sounds of Mehrabad. There were the pungent, intoxicating odors of herbs and spices biting the air. And she saw the alluring diversity of people, ranging from women in jeans, minis and the latest Paris fashions, to those in the most traditional of chadors, and men in everything from Saville Row suits to workmen's clothes to tribal fashions. Here were people going to, or coming from, America or France, or Germany, or even Shiraz, surrounded by friends and family—from babies to grandparents—plying them with gifts, laughing, crying, kissing, chanting:

"God keep you,

"God watch you,

"God return you to us,

"You are never alone,

"We pray for you,

"Our prayers go with you."

This was the warm, sweet prayer of farewell of the warm, sweet people of Rocky's country. And while she was relishing it and them, there came Teymour, nearly knocking several people down in his eagerness to get to her. His eyes sparkled at the sight of her, and he hugged her so hard that she nearly lost her breath; then he pulled her through the mammoth crowd to where her family stood waiting.

She kneeled and kissed her grandparents' and great grandparents' hands, then embraced her father and was embraced by him. Once these formalities were done, she could turn to her girl cousins, always among her favorite people; they charged her now, shoving each other, each one determined to have the first kiss.

"Hey, Rocky, hey!"

"Rocky, hey, Rocky!"

She was clutched, inundated, smothered, everyone pressing cheeks against hers.

At last the cousins fell back, giving Rocky a chance to catch her breath and to examine her family one by one. Baba Bozorg had grown very frail; he wore dark glasses because he was nearly blind, and was supported on one side by Bahram and on the other by Hajji Khadivar. Everyone else, though–parents, grandparents, aunts and uncles–seemed mostly the same...except for Rocky's cousins. The sight of them shocked her to her depth, because there seemed to be no connection between them and their former selves. No connection between them and the ideal of Persian girlhood to which she and they had been born and bred. Their nails were long, glossy and bright red, their makeup heavy, their eyebrows unmistakably tweezed and their clothes as provocative as any Rocky had seen in Houston.

Eighteen-year-old Sheherezade, her poetic, sensitive cousin with a long, slender body and calm, cool mien, had had her nose shortened and her long, black, beautiful hair cut and bleached blond. And tall, strong-boned, tomboy Fahri, now at age sixteen, wore a sexy mini-skirt that revealed her freshly shaved bare legs and sling-back high-heeled shoes. And both girls, along with Shikuh, were braless. A couple of months younger than Rocky, Shikuh, with her blue-black hair and long-lashed green eyes, was her most classically-beautiful cousin whom artists delighted to paint for her resemblance to ancient queens and princesses. Now she wore a tight summer sweater under which her breasts jiggled, and jeans that fit like skin on her body.

These were girl-women who did not seem to be, as Rocky felt herself, nervous in their womanhood. And she felt, illogical though it was, a pall of betrayal at their new look. Here she was, returned after a painful try at American "freedom" to what she expected would be Iran's warm womb with its sense of security, and there were Shikuh, Sheherezade and Fahri, all so familiar and soft and sweet around the edges when she'd left them, now looking as hard and as much to be feared as the American girls from whom she'd fled.

Rocky rode home to Shemiran with Baba Bozorg, Khanoum-June, Toobah and Mitrah, behind several convoy trucks full of sol-diers. The traffic, even to one like her, accustomed to the Houston rush-hour jam, was beyond belief. It took better than three hours on the North-South expressway to drive the thirty miles from Mehrabad to Shemiran, during which time people read books, magazines and newspapers, and children hawked cigarettes and Coca-Colas to the stalled drivers. Baba Bozorg cursed and spat watermelon seeds at the head of the chauffeur in the front seat. Toobah and Mitrah divided their time between a card game and caressing Rocky's hair and cheeks as she sat facing them on the jump seat. And Khanoum-June asked her many questions about Barbara and Dawn, "whom I'll always love as I do my other grand-daughters and great granddaughters."

All along the way, while helicopters roared overhead, they passed uncountable numbers of armed soldiers on foot and fre-quent sentry boxes. And Rocky, as anyone in her place would have done, felt in mortal fear and asked Baba Bozorg whether Iran was at war. He, though, smiled lugubriously and said, "No, not war; the soldiers and their arms are toys of Mohammed Reza."

Bahram's gray Mercedes was already parked in front of the mansion when Baba Bozorg's black Cadillac drove up. In the doorway was an unchanged Naila; she lifted up her plump hand and touched Rocky's cheek, and whispered that God had been kind to have brought her little one home. Rocky had such a feeling of nostalgia and soft, warming pleasure as she stood with Naila that all she wanted was to go together right away to her room and catch up on the years she'd been away. But Bahram had left a message that she was to come to his office immediately when she was home.

When Rocky entered her father's office she did not sit, as she was impelled, but instead waited for his permission. He waved her into a seat with a magisterial gesture, then settled back into the chair behind his desk, studying her for a long time. Cowed by the intensity of his gaze, she diverted her eyes and looked around the room. It was the way she remembered it, with its forest green wall with the vulgar, large, autographed portrait of Mohammed Reza, and the red chairs and sofa on which she and Shirley had sat, stunned, while Bahram had spewed his obscenities at them. The memories attacked like tapeworms in Rocky's stomach as her father turned an inquisitorial face toward her, and demanded to know whether she was "still a virgin." She thought to herself then that the roles had become scrambled during the years she'd been away; young girls were now permitted to look like whores, but had, all the same, to remain virgin.

Rocky had expected her father's question and intended, even wished to let him know that, despite her years in America, her virginity was as important to her as to him. But his look and tone made it clear he didn't even feel the need to ask the question because he'd already condemned her in his mind. And this forced Rocky to conclude that, having come home again, she was once again engaged in a fight for survival with her father, as she, Dawn and Barbara had always been. This question, asked by the man who'd taken Shirley's virginity, was only the first in his battle to grind her down, and unless she would emerge from it as a person of independence and courage...

"You asked about my virginity. Do you think I am a virgin, Father?"

Bahram's face filled with rage, and he screamed, "WHEN YOUR FATHER ASKS YOU A CIVIL QUESTION, YOU ANSWER IT IN A CIVIL MANNER."

"It was not a civil question," Rocky's voice almost broke, but didn't, "because the way that you asked it...I knew that what you meant was not 'Are you a virgin?' but rather, 'You aren't a virgin, are you, Roxanne?' If you'd asked decently..."

"If I'd asked decently, she says...The daughter of the whore who begged me to fuck her before we were even married dares ask me if I think she is a virgin, she dares."

"My mother is not a whore, Father, and I am willing to prove to you that I am a virgin; you can have a doctor examine me any time you wish."

And she told herself that she would never forgive the indignity if he did have her examined, yet said again, "You can have a doctor examine me any time that you wish."

To Rocky's amazement, her offer to prove her virginity, made with no sign of its cost to her pride, softened Bahram; he told her that she had "grown into a beauty," and said he had a surprise for her. He then sent for Esmat who came with two servants, carrying a whole new wardrobe. Daytime dresses, pants, shorts, skirts, blouses, sweaters, bikinis. And evening gowns of flamboyant red, green and purple, that were cut so low and fitted so tight around the buttocks that they embarrassed Rocky. They made her wonder what Barbara, who herself sometimes dressed too daringly for Rocky's taste, would say if she could see them.

She wondered, too, what had possessed her father, always so conservative where she and Dawn were concerned, to choose such clothes for her. The answer, as she would soon come to realize, was that Bahram would have been perceived by his peers as "old-fashioned" to the ways of the West if he hadn't dressed his daughter in the "latest mode."

She, though, unaware of this fact at the time, was touched not so much by the extravagance of the gift as by her father's insistence that she try everything on for him. And his looks of pleasure at each "appearance" she made caused her to think that maybe, just maybe, something had happened to change the cruel Bahram into the loving, caring father of her early fantasies.

She would, however, discover all too soon what Barbara had told her from her own experience: Rocky was in a position now to serve Bahram's needs. And as had once been the case with her mother, he was willing to indulge her and pay highly for what she would do for him. But if the time came when she couldn't or wouldn't meet his demands...

"When you and I go down to meet the family, Roxanne," Bahram said, "your male cousins will be there to greet you. Ali Reza, your fiancé, will be among them."

"My...What did you call Ali Reza, Father?"

"I called him what he is, your fiancé."

Rocky remembered then what she'd somehow cast out of her mind: Her father and uncle had betrothed her and Ali Reza when she was born and he was three.

"Your Uncle Cyrus, Roxanne," Bahram grinned, "is the wealthiest of all the Mosallais. And Ali Reza is his only child. The union will, therefore, be of great advantage to our branch of the family. And also to you, of course."

"You know, Father, that I haven't seen Ali Reza since I was very little," Rocky said.

"That is the reason," Bahram smiled benevolently, "that I've arranged for you to see him now."

"But I remember not liking him the one time that I saw him. And, well, suppose I don't like him any better now?"

"And if you don't, what then, Roxanne?"

"I can't imagine being married to a person I didn't love or even like, and besides," now the words came in a burst, "I haven't even finished high school, I've a whole year to go yet, and then there'll be college and...I just don't think this is the time for me to marry anyone."

Bahram careened across the room and came to stand in front of Rocky; he screamed out that her position as an Iranian daughter...First of all, she had no need to go to college or even to finish high school; she was already too fucking much inured to her

American mother's message, that women should be independent and that education was a step toward attaining that independence. Furthermore, she'd marry Ali Reza all right, whenever he and her Uncle Cyrus and Baba Bozorg ordered her to.

Rocky, already wishing she'd never come back, walked behind her father down the stairs and into the main salon where the family was gathered, now including Darius, eighteen, Nadir, nineteen, and Sadegh and Ali Reza, both a couple of months older than she. And her male cousins proved to be as frighteningly different from her remembrance of them as the girls were. In their clothes that were, in reality, their "disco outfits" (Rocky would come to know that her cousins spent literally all their nights, including Friday, in discos), they were as self-consciously sexual in what they perceived to be the American mode as were the girls. They wore pink, orange, purple or gold bodyshirts in imitation of their favorite rock stars. Ali Reza, sitting in their midst, was clad in tight white pants and a shirt open to nearly his navel in order to reveal as much as possible of his sun-bronzed chest. And this was the person her father had declared would bring security to Rocky's life.

After some hours of small talk on Ali Reza's part, mostly about rock stars he'd come to know personally, Rocky asked whether he was studying abroad or in Tehran.

Ali Reza brushed back his shiny, black hair. "Oh, I'm not studying anywhere."

"You mean that you aren't in college, or..."

"That is exactly what I mean."

"But...Could I ask why you aren't in college?"

"Because," his dark eyes flashed with humor, "college doesn't fit into my style."

"Well, then, what do you do?"

"If you mean what do I do for a living, the answer is nothing. Why should I work when my father...? Cousin, dear, need I inform you that my father's wealth...No, I can see I don't need to do that, because your father's already taken care of it."

Rocky flushed with anger, the blood visibly coursing under her skin. "Listen, Ali Reza, I don't care a damn about your father's money, and as for you, yourself..."

"But whether or not you care a damn doesn't really matter, does it, since your father does care. A very great deal. And you will, therefore..." He let his voice rise, holding the statement suspended.

"Will what?" Rocky asked as though she didn't know.

"Will marry me so your father can get his hands on my father's money."

Rocky stared at Ali Reza for some time before saying, "One thing, Ali Reza. I'm part American and...Don't be so sure I'll marry you just because my father wants it. You may find you won't need to be burdened with me after all, because I'll find a way..."

Ali Reza looked at her then with compassion and a new respect, and begged her forgiveness for having teased her. He said, too, that he realized, even from their short conversation, that she really did have no interest in his father's money, and also that she might well stand up to her father and refuse to marry him.

On her first night home, Ali Reza and Rocky's other cousins took her on a tour of some of the North Tehran nightclubs and discos, of which there were uncountable numbers. They began with the elegant, refined clubs: "The Blue Heaven", named for its ceiling that was an artificial sky spangled with stars; "The New Blooming", with carts beside each table that were always filled with fresh flowers; and "La Chansonnette", with a sumptuous Louis XIV decor and pretty young chanteuses from Paris.

But the cousins gave little attention to the clubs; the discos were what pulled them. First there was "The Cage", called that because one had to enter a cage to get to the dance floor where couples gyrated under dizzily flashing strobe lights, their knees, hips and rumps bumping. And on the stage outside, a black singer from Texas wearing a sequined satin dress and a feather boa screamed out, "You just got to turn on, honey, got to let it all hang out, got to let your body feel itself."

Then they moved on to "The Canary", with its revolving mirrored lights and phantasmagoric colors. And to the "Bump in the Night", where showy young upper-class Iranians danced "The Philadelphia Sly", "The Puerto Rican Hustle" and "The Detroit Shuffle", while a Mick Jagger look-alike, with stuffed jock strap, black leather pants and halter top, wailed out "Sometimes you got to get away some way, and now you're walking ten foot tall."

Every club or disco to which they went was thronged with Rocky's cousins' friends, streams of young men and women who wanted to meet "the American cousin". A number of the men asked Ali Reza's permission to dance with her. But Rocky, who'd left Iran at a time when unmarried girls, even at parties at one of the Shah's palaces or at a diplomatic ball, could dance only with cousins or sons of her parents' old friends, was amazed that she was permitted to dance with strangers, whether or not they needed her escort's permission. Hair blowing loose as she'd not permitted it to do since her first day at Northbrook High, she went from partner to partner, happy in this exhilarating world where she seemed to spin through the night on the edge of delicious danger (who knew what intent these strange young men might have toward her?) yet safe because she was with her cousins.

But her feeling of well-being changed in a hurry when it got to be three in the morning and North Tehran's air-conditioned, civilized and glamorous discos and clubs closed, and she and her cousins had to come out into the streets. There was an elderly beggar whining the traditional begging words in the traditional begging fashion. But when the cousins disregarded him, his cries and moans transformed to yelps and curses. In all of Rocky's former life in Iran, she'd never seen a beggar who did not, even in the face of negative reaction, remain humble toward his "betters".

And here were four women, squatting on their haunches, their chadors tight around themselves. One rose and screamed, "You rich children have no hearts, but only your satanic weaknesses for which you will pay one day."

And a man with sunken cheeks forming gray hollows in his face said, with an air of superior tiredness, "Your world of despotism will soon be destroyed by all good Muslims banding together. It can't stay yours much longer, you know."

But most terrifying of all to Rocky were the large numbers of children of fourteen, thirteen and twelve years old. They came in their rags, not to beg from the rich (they'd been schooled by their mosques and religious schools to hold them in too much contempt for that) but to make clear their condemnation of their "sinfulness". They did not, at the time, engage in acts of violence, but only spat in the paths of those like Rocky and her cousins.

Rocky's life, from her first day in Iran, was a matter of routine. Night-time was for drinking, doping (though she, unlike her cousins, smoked only occasionally) and discoing. Morning was for recovering from the night before, and afternoon for lunching, shopping and being made beautiful. Or, occasionally, for watching her aunts during one of their interminable card games at which nine or ten of them gambled for hundreds of thousands of dollars.

Rocky, having gone with Naila to visit her family in South Tehran as well as to her hereditary village out of Shiraz, and having come to know families whose children had died of hunger, felt shame at her aunts' excesses that might have supported whole villages for months. And she was ashamed, as well, of her own and her cousins' outrageous expenditures, of the non-stop abandon to their pleasures.

And whenever she thought, as she often did, about the lives of the poor in comparison to the rich, she also had to ask herself what validity her own life of wealth had, even on a selfish level. What good were the indulgences her father and Ali Reza lavished upon her so long as they could be withdrawn at their will? So long as Bahram could foist Ali Reza upon her? And so long as Ali Reza, despite being intrigued with and admiring of her for the present, could nevertheless regard her as he did, as his property? Taking pride in her as in any of his other possessions?

She had some answers to her questions when she thought about her aunts. Their Parisian wardrobes and trips abroad and gambling sessions and lovers (sometimes taken for pay) did not begin to compensate them for the lovelessness of their lives with their husbands. She knew that they were frustrated, driven, addicted to liquor and pills and "nervous breakdowns" that were, in reality, acute episodes in their living patterns of chronic depression.

And she knew, too, that unless she escaped Iran now, she'd end up as they had. Her father, though, would never give his permission for her to leave the country; she had to find another way...Ali Reza seemed to be that way.

On the night the thought occurred to her, Rocky drank with a purpose at the discos; enough to drown her inhibitions, yet not so much that she wouldn't be conscious of what she did. On the drive home, she snuggled close to Ali Reza, and when he kissed her good-night in the prescribed chaste fashion, she became all lips and tongue and arms and warm body and exultant expression. Ali Reza's breath was accelerated as he said, "You're a stranger tonight, Rocky, and...what's happened to make you so different than you've ever been before?"

Rocky whispered that she loved him very much, and "I hope you won't think me sinful for saying this, but...I keep dreaming about our making love. I know it's wrong, but...I want us to be married very soon and without all the preparations that'll put our marriage off, because if we're not..." She released a deep guttural breath that might have been taken for an orgasmic moan. "Needing you as I do...I know I've got to remain a virgin, but loving you, needing you...Oh, I wish we could be married tomorrow, really I do. In the meanwhile, please just hold me close and don't let me..."

She perceived as she rested in Ali Reza's arms that she'd wakened his passion for her beyond what it had been before, and also that he would resist it out of feelings of protectiveness. He assured her that he would guard her virginity 'til they married, and that he would see to it that the wedding would take place soon and without the time-consuming ceremonies. He'd always had his father under control, getting everything he wanted when he wanted it from him, so if he told his father he wanted to be married right away, he'd agree and would influence Baba Bozorg and Bahram to do the same. "And all that you'll need to do, my sweetheart, is set the date."

"How about in a month from now, Ali Reza? There's one thing though: I wouldn't want to be married without my sister here."

"Well, let's get her here. I'll send her a round-trip ticket."

"It's not that simple, Ali Reza. I doubt my mother would let her come. I had to fight her all the way when I decided to come home. And Dawn's so young and easily influenced. If I went to get her, though, my mother would have to let her come, like it or not." The words were out. Finally. "But, of course, I'd need a letter of permission from my father and..." she trilled laughter, "Would you believe, Ali Reza, that my father is convinced that if I ever got to my mother's I'd remain with her, and...That's so ridiculous since she's so poor. She lives in a house that's only got three bedrooms."

Ali Reza looked at Rocky with such empathy for the deprivations of her life with Barbara that Rocky warmed to her subject. "And would you believe that my allowance when I was with my mother was fifteen dollars a week? And I'll tell you something else. I didn't even have a car of my own, and..."

Ali Reza's head tilted up, his expression incredulous. What, not even a car of her own?

"My mother said," Rocky continued, "that if I wanted a car, I'd have to work to help pay for it."

In her mind Rocky giggled to herself, thinking of the complex psychic changes she'd undergone in the past few years. First she'd wanted to escape her life of luxury, because it included her father, for any other life, no matter how poor. Then, in America, as part of the middle-class which had never accepted her, she'd longed for the expensive life Iran could provide. Once arrived there, though, she'd realized that the price demanded for the money expended on her was not only her freedom and independence, but also her dignity, her personhood.

Rocky clung to Ali Reza, pressed herself against him and whispered against his chest that she loved him so much, so much and couldn't wait for their marriage. But he did understand, didn't he, how important it was for her to get Dawn? And he was the only one who could influence her father to let her go; she was depending on him to help her and her sister.

Three days later, on the plane, Rocky wrote to Ali Reza apologizing for having abused his trust. She wished, she wrote, to remain his friend. She knew, though, that Ali Reza's pride would never permit him to feel anything but the bitterest enmity toward a girl who'd outwitted him and so lowered his "face". And she hoped that he wouldn't take out on his future wife all the hate and hostility he'd wish to vent on her.

Desire vs. Revulsion

Despite her initial anticipation, Rocky's return to Houston was far from joyous. She'd fled from her life in Iran, but what, exactly, had she fled to? What had she ever found in Houston except rejection? Was there a place for her in either her mother's or her father's land? Would she always be an émigré in a strange city, looking with longing into the faces of strangers?

And then, three weeks after her arrival home, Rocky met Twon Vu. He was a pre-med student at the University of Texas, and worked during his offtime in the same Seven-Eleven store where she worked after school so she could help pay for the car she wanted.

Twon was twenty years old at the time, thin and tall and gentle-looking. And he had a warm smile that drew Rocky to him, as his reticence also did; he asked if she'd have tea with him as though requesting a favor.

On their first date, Twon told Rocky all about himself. The eldest of eight children, he had been born in South Vietnam. Although he and his brothers and sisters had followed Western ways, his father, Tung, believed as the ancients had, in the morality propounded by Confucius mixed with a kind of vague Buddhism that revered the spirits of his ancestors, the spirits of great men past, the spirits of sky and earth, of good and evil, and all in between.

But for all his own deep devotion to his religion, Twon's father was open-minded toward the West and never condemned his children for their ways. A highly educated person, he'd been a general in the Army of the Republic of South Vietnam. Twon's mother was of peasant descent, with no education, and little tolerance of Western ways. But Twon, his sisters and brothers showed her "the utmost respect"; his father insisted on it.

A sharp, quick ache for her mother and her aunts and all the wives of men like her father and his peers shot through Rocky as she said softly, "I guess your father would never beat your mother."

"My God, no," Twon laughed.

Rocky then asked how Twon's father felt about his daughters.

"He loves them very much, of course."

"Does he want them to go to college?"

"He wants all his children to go to college, but the girls...He's a Seven-Eleven manager, and he works day and night jobs so that he can help the girls meet their college expenses because he feels that we boys are in a better position than our sisters to help ourselves."

So that's the way it can be, Rocky thought. That's the way some women's husbands and some girls' fathers can feel about and behave toward them.

Mrs. Vu was a tiny woman, and very wrinkled although she could not have been much older than forty at the time of Rocky's meeting with her. She wore *au dai*, the national outfit, hers consisting of black bell-bottom pants and a high-necked, long-sleeved black gown. She appeared very demure and shy.

Mr. Vu was small, wiry and pasty-skinned, hardly the picture of an army general. But his eyes were gentle and very soft, the sort of eyes that caused Rocky to know the instant she looked into them that here was a man whom she, despite her suspicion and hatred of the species, could trust.

Later, after they'd married, Rocky would sometimes tease Twon by saying she'd only married him so she could have his father as her own.

"Well, that's all right," he'd answer, "since there's a lot of my father in me."

Rocky and Twon were married the day after her high school graduation by a notary public, in a small private chapel full of flowers provided by Mr. and Mrs. Vu. The only guests were Twon's parents, sisters and brothers and Barbara and Charlie, who gave the white-gowned bride away, and Dawn, who stood up with her. Afterward they went to the Vu home where Rocky's mother-in-law had prepared a Vietnamese feast.

Though Barbara had urged a honeymoon trip upon Rocky and Twon as part of her wedding present, they spent the first night of their marriage in Twon's room over the Vu's garage. It was clean and white and full of plants that, when the lamps were lit, sent a cool green light through the room. There were built-in bookcases on the walls, and brightly colored posters and prints hung, in museum fashion, on the other walls. There was a low double bed covered with an orange spread and heaped with brown and yellow throw cushions. Rocky felt more at home there than she ever had in either her mother's or father's houses.

Twon and Rocky sat on the bed talking about how each was the most important thing in the other's life, and how neither had been happy before they'd met. Then Twon undressed first himself, then Rocky. And as he kissed her eyes, her lips, her neck, her breasts, an immense warmth flowed from him to her. Why, then, couldn't she kiss him back? Why did she feel such a strange mixture of desire for the husband she loved and revulsion—inseparable, incompatible chemicals within her brewing to form a sickening potion, black and bitter in her mouth; a memory-producing drug that sharpened her perception of things past, of Shirley Kashani and Bahram.

And there were other memories that went further back than that; she'd not shared them even with Barbara for fear that her mother, who'd still lived in the mansion at the time the situations occurred, would blame herself for them. As, in fact, she did when her child wept them out for the sake of this book.

First of all, there'd been the days and nights when Rocky was very young, five, six, seven, when Barbara had been away from home. Bahram, drunk, had come to Rocky's room, sat her on his lap and touched her undeveloped breasts and vagina, saying that he wanted to see how she was growing and developing. Rocky had been even younger, four years old, when Barbara had been away over Friday and Bahram had been engaged with his gambling cronies. She'd been wakened in the night by the servant, Cyrus; he, as best as she can remember today, masturbated on her. She had run to Naila and asked to be bathed. When Naila realized what had happened, she'd told Bahram who, with his friends, had beaten Cyrus in Rocky's presence. So brutal was the beating that she'd been sure they would kill him. So, wanting them to stop, she'd wept and declared that "Cyrus didn't do anything, Father, so don't beat him, beat me instead, because I lied to Naila."

And from then on other male servants—who, because of Bahram's proclivities were preferred over females and thus had always been a majority in the Mosallai household—abused Rocky by fondling her. Having witnessed her protectiveness toward Cyrus, they felt certain that she would not reveal them either.

Oh, Twon, I never should have married you. For all you've given to me, you deserve so much more than I can give back. I feel so much love in my heart for you, yet I can't give it with my body. I can't love you as a wife should love a husband, Twon. And if I can't love you this way, then whom can I love?

Sensitive, generous Twon, though not knowing all that Rocky was experiencing, did sense her wish not to be overwhelmed. And so he controlled his own passion and let her know that he was satisfied to go slowly, letting her lead the way. And he held her tenderly through the night, making her feel protected by him and, at least temporarily, far away from her father and the other men who'd hurt her.

The months that Rocky had spent in Iran turned out to have been very important ones in Dawn's life, as well. When the St. Jerome's nuns rejected her, she'd been forced to return, at age fourteen-and-a-half, to the Lee Junior High she hated with a passion. And she was also obliged to resume treatment with Dr. Atabei that she pretended, for the sake of "face", she didn't want, but had actually been yearning for. Under Dr. Atabei's guidance, then, she explored her "defeats" at St. Jerome's and Lee. And she came to realize that although part of the reason for people's rejection of her was, indeed, her foreignness and their narrowness, another, probably larger part was her ridiculous pretense that she was tough and self-centered, and as contemptuous of them as they seemed to be of her. If she were to survive in Houston, or anywhere, she had to overcome the infantile stubbornness, thick-headedness and impulse to torment everyone at no matter what expense to herself, that had driven her from her early years because they seemed the only possible bastions against her father.

Once these truths penetrated her, Dawn, then as now a person of action, set out to change herself. She stopped challenging fellow-students and teachers; she did her homework regularly so her grades became satisfactory, and even superior in such subjects as music and drama. Most importantly, she went on a rigid diet, lost fifty pounds in four months and became, although characteristically she was the last to realize it, as beautiful as Dr. Atabei had promised she would be.

But her beauty served her no better in Houston than Rocky's had done her...The boys' silly passes offended her Islamic sensitivities, and the girls would not accept her into their circles.

She had, of course, longed for Rocky's coming and been ecstatic when she'd arrived, expecting that now she wouldn't be lonely anymore. Then Rocky had met and married Twon, and a part of Dawn, the good, generous, loving part, had been happy for her. In another part of her, though, she'd felt devoured by a less decent emotion. She had felt her stomach eating itself away with envy of Twon for having Rocky, and of her for having him, as well as the envy of Charlie and Barbara for having one another while she had nobody. So Dawn got mad when those feelings hit her; she couldn't stand them and couldn't stand herself. She had to get away from these two whom she loved most in the world, yet sometimes hated. She had, despite her father and her horrendous experiences with him, to return to Iran where she might, just possibly, find a place for herself.

Barbara begged, pleaded and threatened Dawn. And Rocky argued with her for hours, citing her own experiences and concluding, finally, that "You'll be a slave to our father and whatever husband he chooses for you." And Dawn countered with, "And here in Houston I'm nothing to anybody, so what's the difference?"

Eventually, and after consultation with Dr. Atabei, Barbara and Rocky concluded sadly that Dawn had to have the opportunity to find herself in Iran as she'd not been able to do in Houston.

CHAPTER XXIV

It Will Be My Sin

When Dawn arrived at Mehrabad Airport, neither aunts, uncles nor cousins were there to meet her, but dozens of people she didn't know, women and little girls in chadors and men in turbans who would turn out to be Mohammed's and Esmat's extended family, were. Also, Bahram himself...The first sight of her father caused Dawn to stand gazing at him in surprise and disbelief. Dashing, debonair Bahram was dressed this day in a black workman's suit and white religious turban.

Dawn, controlling her shock at his appearance, went forward to kiss and hug her father, to be kissed and hugged by him. But he drew back, keeping sufficient distance between them to forestall her embrace, and held out his right hand. She, not knowing what else to do, shook it desperately.

"You are supposed to kiss your father's hand, Dawn," Tey whispered urgently, "not shake it like you are his equal."

Accustomed to kissing her traditional grandparents' and great grandparents' hands, but never her westernized father's, Dawn nevertheless did as Tey instructed and received, finally, a smile and "Welcome home, daughter."

As had been the case with Rocky, Dawn was summoned to her father's office as soon as she arrived at the Shemiran mansion. It was much as she remembered it, except that the autographed picture of the Shah that used to be over Bahram's desk had been replaced by a white silk hanging embroidered in black and red with the Islamic command, "Turn then thy face in the direction of the sacred mosque; wherever ye are, turn your face in that direction."

As Dawn sat in her father's office, dusk fell and the chant Allah Akbar, Allah Akbar, Allah Akbar ("We believe in one supreme God") that is the Moslem call to prayer five times a day, came over the muezzin. And Bahram went to his shrine, prostrated himself on his sajadeh (prayer rug), bowed toward Mecca and bowed again.

He rose finally, and told Dawn that, as she could tell from his dress, he was a true man of Islam now; he had been converted when the Hidden Imam had come and summoned him to "become a warrior in God's Army."

Hearing him, Dawn marveled at the power of a religion which could tame Bahram. Only later did she come to realize that his transformation might well have been motivated by practical considerations. An opportunist and political sophisticate, he must have recognized, after months of riots and demonstrations, that the people's hatred for America, for the Persian ruling class and for the Shah—of which Rocky had been so terrified in 1975—had increased to the point where Iran was a country in crisis. He must have also realized that the religious leaders, more than any others, commanded the loyalty of the masses. It was, after all, 1977—the year that heralded "the people's revolution" and Khomeini's rise to total power.

Done talking about his religiosity, the first question Bahram asked Dawn was whether she, daughter of her "American whore mother with the hot blood", was a virgin. And when she, unlike Rocky who'd maintained her dignity despite her hurt, screamed her fury out at him, he beat her with his belt strap and ordered her to her room. This, on her first day home.

At a little after four o'clock the next morning, she woke to the sight of Esmat, fully dressed and in her house chador. She said that it was time for Dawn to "wake and wash," to cleanse herself in preparation for the first of the day's devotions that would take place at sunrise.

Dawn told Esmat that she hadn't prayed since she had left her Iranian school, that she was not, in fact, a Muslim in her heart and so believed that it would be hypocritical of her to pray now.

Esmat said that she hoped, for the sake of peace in the family, that Dawn would not defy her father's command.

Dawn's first impulse was to tell Esmat to tell her father that whether she prayed or not was her business, not his, but the recollection of yesterday's beating stopped her cold.

The Mosallai family observed the morning devotion as a group in the "modern", not traditional, fashion in which men and women prayed in separate rooms. Everyone was already in the family salon when Esmat and Dawn entered. Dawn, forgetting her Islamic indoctrination at her school into the ritual system that required praying women to kneel behind men, placed her sajadeh beside that of her half-brother Habib, who was by then four years old, in what she'd soon learn was the men's row. She was roughly ordered by Bahram to "get back where you belong, in the women's row." The women's row consisted of Esmat and herself, over whom even little Habib took precedence.

After devotions, Bahram beckoned Dawn and Tey to remain behind while Esmat led little Habib out of the salon. He screamed at Dawn that her American conceit, causing her to believe that she was so much men's equal that she could pray beside instead of behind them, had to be "driven out of you so that you may take your place as a properly deferential woman of Islam." He then turned to Tey and said, "I will leave it to you, Son, to teach your sister her lesson."

Tey, as soon as Bahram was out the door, began smacking and kicking at Dawn. She smacked and kicked back, but was so shocked at his attack that she was no match for him, and her body felt bruised all over when he was done with her.

"I'm sorry that I had to hurt you, Sister," Tey said, "but I must tell you that I am going to beat you every time you offend against Islam, because it will be my sin if I do not."

Dawn looked at Tey, in all of his assumed inviolability, and remembered back to the years they'd lived together. He'd been so gentle when he was younger, gentler than either she or Rocky had been, even though they were girls. There was a time after Barbara had left the home when, despite the small difference in their ages, he had run to Dawn with all his little worries and troubles; she could still remember his sweet, dispirited little voice:

"Sister, I lost all of my toy soldiers,"..."Sister, my ball fell into the pool and floated out into the middle,"..."I hurt my knee, and it's bleeding."

"When I left here, Tey," Dawn said, "you were my baby brother, and now you're my god."

Tey informed Dawn that, although he was not her god, he was their father's deputy, and so had power second only to Bahram's over her.

Three weeks after her confrontation with Tey, her father informed Dawn that the family, including her, would soon be making the pilgrimage to Mecca. And she, though disliking the idea, did not dare to voice her feeling.

CHAPTER XXV

Going To Mecca

Eight hundred million people—one fifth of all humanity—regard Mecca, Saudi Arabia, as their prime sanctuary, their holy of holies. And for more than thirteen centuries, Muslims, some two million annually in recent years, have heeded the command of Allah to Abraham, later revealed to the Prophet Mohammed, "And proclaim unto mankind a hajj." Islam is the dominant belief not only in Iran and the Arab Middle East but also in Africa and Asia. And there are, besides, numbers of Muslims to be reckoned with in every country of the world; forty million in the old USSR, for example, and sixteen million in China.

Mecca, unlike Jerusalem or Vatican City, is off limits to all but the faithful. Yet it must certainly be, during the height of the seventy-day pilgrimage season (which begins annually with the start of the tenth month of the Muslim lunar calendar), the most cosmopolitan metropolis in the world. Pilgrims who once took months or even years to make the journey, sometimes walking much of the way from Africa, say, or trekking from Indonesia, now arrive by chartered jet or boat in hours or days from every corner of the globe. Thus a walk down any street introduces one to an immense variety of faces—Caucasian, Black, Oriental and all the blends created by generations of intermarriage—and to every tongue that humans speak.

"Here we come, O Allah, here we come!

Here we come. No partner have you

Here we come! Praise indeed, and

Blessings are yours...the Kingdom too.

No partner have you."

This <u>tabiyah</u> (hymn of praise) marked the formal beginning of Dawn's and her family's two-week-long hajj to replicate the Prophet's own last pilgrimage. She wore a chador that left only her face and hands exposed, and Esmat was already clad in her hajj chador that provided only a tiny rectangle of embroidered lace around the eyes through which she could see, but not be seen. And Bahram, Tey, little Habib and Mohammed were in workmen's clothes. Dawn's family waited most of the night in the teeming Hajj section of the Mehrabad Airport so they could board their jet flight to Mecca's gateway, Jeddah, with the first rays of the sun. Here at Mehrabad Hajj, so different in its essence from the general cosmopolitan airport, were hundreds of pilgrims. Old and young. Educated and illiterate. People like Dawn's family, wealthy enough to make the hajj annually and to stay at the sumptuous Mecca Intercontinental Hotel which, except for the absence of bars and nightclubs, offers the same services as its sisters in Paris, Rome or New York. And there were those so poor as to have to camp out in the streets after having saved a lifetime for this most important of journeys. There were blind people guided by relatives or friends, cripples in wheelchairs, lame people with canes or walking sticks, pregnant women desiring their babies to be born in Mecca, and people with the look of death in their faces, yet rapt with the knowledge they'd die in Mecca.

And Dawn, despite her resentment at being here by Bahram's order, could not help but be at first beguiled by, and then caught up in, the mood of these people united in their love for their God. She could not help but become hypnotized into chanting along with them, "God, Thou art my companion on the journey, and Thou art The One Who remains with my people."

At nine o'clock Dawn's plane landed in Jeddah, with its Islamic flag proclaiming, "There is no God but God, and Mohammed is the messenger of God," underscored by the sword of righteousness. Here the Mosallais were met by Karim Sanjabi, a twenty-one-year-old student who would be their mutawalf (licensed guide). He escorted them through the huge airport terminal, a steampot of miasmas with its mass of humanity, pilgrims with no other available shelter camping out on the five acres of concrete floors. Finally, they reached their waiting air-conditioned Chevrolet, and were driven the forty-five miles from Jeddah to Mecca past the ship harbor and terminals. They drove along some streets that made Dawn feel like she'd intruded on a Biblical scene, and others that were broad, tree-lined boulevards of high-rise apartments, hotels and splendid shops and boutiques of such fashion giants as Christian Dior and Yves St. Laurent. And finally, they went to Pilgrim City on Mecca's outskirts.

Here, in their separate quarters, Dawn and her family cut their nails, shaved their underarms and pubic hair and perfumed themselves. Then Dawn put on her hajj chador while Bahram and Tey and Habib donned sandals and the traditional men's pilgrim garb, two pieces of seamless white cloth designed both to erase distinctions between rich and poor and to symbolize the pilgrims' search for spiritual purity.

The short drive from Pilgrim City to Central Mecca, although along a one-way six-lane highway, took hours because it was chaotic with people by the thousands moving by car, bus, truck, donkey, horse, camel and on foot. At last they were in Mecca proper with its sign, "Stop for Inspection, Prohibited for Non-Muslims". This caused Dawn, who would always recall bitterly her exclusion from Friday Communion at St. Jerome's School, to think to herself with a certain smugness, "I can, if I wish, sit right in the middle of the Catholics in their church, but they can't set foot inside my holy city." They drove through the Gate of Peace into the immense courtyard of Islam's holiest shrine, the Great Mosque, with its seven lofty minarets and marble and granite galleries gleaming in the white-hot desert sun. In the center of the courtyard the stark, cube-shaped Kaaba, the House of God draped in black silk, loomed fifty feet above the sea of humanity surrounding it.

It is told that Abraham built the Kaaba, dedicated to God's worship in the place where it stands today, in about 570 A.D., the time of the Prophet Mohammed's birth. Forty years later, Mohammed, after his revelation from the archangel Gabriel that there is but one God, cleansed it of its idols and rededicated it to God's worship. Since that time, the faithful, from whatever part of the world they are in, face toward the Kaaba five times daily in their prayers and live for the moment that they, themselves, may cast their eyes on it.

No wonder that pilgrims tell that the moment they first looked upon the Kaaba before circling it seven times in the ceremony of the Tawalf, was one of the deepest, most exhilarating moments of their lives. The wonder is, though, that Dawn, with no record of prayer or consciousness of the tradition, and here in the first place against her will, should have shared in their experience. So caught up did she become in the whirling scene of these thousands upon thousands of people shedding tears of joy to be finally looking upon, and then orbiting, the House of their Lord, so uplifted was she by the poetry of their prayer, ending with "In the name of God; God is most great," that she felt herself to be an integral part of the mass.

She wept as everyone did, perhaps for the sweetness of her new-found love for God, but more likely because she was so deeply moved by the ineffable power of membership, of finally belonging to something. On this day she was connected to all her thousands of brethren in faith, transformed in a way that was beyond the powers of people unseasoned by the Meccan experience to comprehend.

Dawn's ecstasy at the sight of the Kaaba persisted through the whole two weeks of her hajj. She was all joy as she carried out the complex rituals in the company of her family, to whom she'd begun to feel as close (whether or not they responded to her feeling) as she'd always dreamed of being. Together they were drinking sacred water from the Well of Zem Zem where Ishmael and Mohammed had also drunk. Legend tells that the infant Ishmael and Hagar, his mother, were on God's command to Abraham, left alone by him in a barren valley with only some dates to eat and a minimum of water that was soon gone. Hagar, desperate for Ishmael's sake, hunted everywhere for water and prayed to God to save her child; she never forgot, though, to reiterate her faith in His encompassing goodness. And she was rewarded, finally, by the appearance of an angel who led her to Zem Zem.

Dawn and the other pilgrims re-enacted Hagar's search for water in the ceremony of the sa'ay by making, as she had done, seven trips between the hills of Sofa and Marwah; these are now enclosed in a long gallery inside the mosque. They hurled stones on three separate days at the three pillars (symbolizing the devil) in the village of Mina just outside of Mecca; they commemorate the time when Allah ordered Abraham to sacrifice Ishmael, and father and son threw stones at Satan when he thrice tempted them to resist God's command.

Next, they celebrated the feast of Id-al-Adha, Festival of Sacrifice, in gratitude for Allah's sparing of Ishmael and substituting of a sheep to take his place. In this ceremony, Dawn's family, finally out of ihram (Hajj dress), donned their most festive clothes (at least Bahram, Tey and Habib did, while Dawn and Esmat remained in chador), and, along with huge numbers of other pilgrims, thronged Mina. There they laughed, joked and bargained with the Bedouin herdsmen for sheep for performance of their own family sacrifice. Most hajji paid butchers to wield the knives, but some, Bahram among them, performed the sacrifice themselves. The Koran commands that the sacrificed meat be distributed to the poor, but since there are so many pilgrims and, therefore, much more meat than can possibly be given away fresh, the vast quantity is frozen for later distribution.

For Dawn, as for all pilgrims, the high-point of the hajj was the wuqhf (the standing). From noon until sundown she stood in the scorching sun, praying and chanting, on the Plain of Arafat from whose Mount Mercy the Prophet had imparted his last revelation: "This day have I...completed my favor upon you and have chosen for you Islam as your religion."

Surely the wuqhf must be, to anyone who has been part of it or heard about it from one who has, or even seen photographs of it, one of the most impressive displays of faith to be witnessed in the world. And Dawn, during those long hours of exaltation and fellowship, experienced an intense sense that all Islamics were her sisters and brothers, an awareness greater than she had during the orbiting of the Kaaba. She was filled with such an abundance of universal love as made her future seem joyful. Surely, such love as this, while being its own reward, must also elicit love from others—say, her father and brother. And after her formal chantings and prayers continued for hours, she prayed informally for herself, petitioning Allah for a clear soul instead of one seething with anger and resentment of life, as hers had been before she'd come to Mecca. And she prayed that God would deliver her from her daytime fears and night terrors, and chaos and shame over not knowing who she was or where she really belonged. Prayed that she would be able to retain, for as long as she lived, her consciousness of His presence, and therefore, also, the sense of harmony with herself.

And Dawn prayed, too, that Allah would change the hearts and minds not only of her father and brother, but of all Islamic men about their women being their slaves, and that the day would come when they would realize them to be equals.

CHAPTER XXVI

A Good Girl of Islam

During Dawn's first weeks at home after the hajj, Allah seemed to have granted her prayers, albeit with limitations. First of all she did, indeed, feel His constant presence, and so overcame the depression under which she'd lived for so long. And, although her relationships with her father and brother were not what she'd prayed they'd be (Bahram hadn't ceased, certainly, to look upon her as his property, and both he and Teymour still felt her to be unequal), they were improved upon what they'd been before the hajj. Bahram appreciated her religious dedication that signified to him, although it was not, a rejection of her American mother and heritage. And he took pleasure in her beauty and charm. Once she'd truly absorbed the lesson that Esmat and the other women surrounding her didn't even realize they were teaching...the lesson that women cannot hope to gain their ends except by dissembling...she literally delighted her father by playing to the hilt the role of loving, "good" daughter who would never challenge, but only praise, flatter and cajole. All the same, he did not love her as he did her brothers, and made it clear he never would.

Teymour, though, did love Dawn (he had not, after all, forgotten the affinity between them as young children). But his love, like Bahram's continuing indulgence, was patronizing and demeaning because it was available to her only so long as she kept her spirit, with its zest for self-assertion, hidden from him. And although it hurt her very much, she, accustomed as she'd become throughout her young life to either fighting battles that were lost even before they were properly begun, or to making concessions, did keep it hidden.

But most of the time that Dawn didn't spend in school was lived not with her father and brother, but with her stepmother, in a fashion that was at least as traditional as the style that Toobah and Mitrah had imposed on Barbara before her marriage. Each morning before going to school, she assisted Esmat in her household duties. Together they interviewed Fatima, the cook, about food for the day and made up a marketing list for her. And although Esmat would examine the food herself for quality since Dawn would have gone to school, she waited for her return before querying Fatima on the prices paid, so Dawn could participate in the questioning.

As had been the case with Barbara in Toobah's home, Dawn never knew at Esmat's what relatives or friends might drop in at what hours, or how long they would stay. She would return from school at four o'clock to find ten women or forty sipping tea and gossiping in the company salon. More often than not she, as daughter of the house, would be required to entertain the women by performing the traditional songs and dances she'd learned before going to America. And on the afternoons when there were no guests, Esmat and Dawn made return calls on mostly the same people who called on them.

Always on Thursdays, or sometimes also on other rare afternoons when Esmat had no social obligations, she and Dawn, despite each having a private bath of her own, went to the public bath in South Tehran. One of the last of the old-time traditional baths, it was administered by an elderly lady who sat on a high stool at a table. Before taking women's money, she examined them carefully to be certain that they were Islamic and therefore "clean", and also that they were of the right class to be bathing at her establishment.

The bath consisted of two vast rooms built of brick, one containing a cold pool, the other a hot one, and with low-built ledges for clothes and other belongings.

Dawn and Esmat always sat with Esmat's mother, sisters and old friends who hadn't moved up, as she had, to North Tehran. They were received with quantities of fruits and cakes, to be eaten with tea or the cardamon-accented drink called sharbat over the long hours of gossip and joke-telling. The jokes were mostly about men whose women outwitted them, whether in seducing them into buying them extra-expensive jewelry or fooling them into believing they were virgins. And some jokes were, despite the women's religiosity, not only aimed at mullahs, but also quite lusty. One told about a beautiful young woman married to a sterile old man; he, unable to accept his condition, proclaimed her barren and sent her to a mullah for a charm to induce pregnancy. The mullah was young and handsome, and so when he asked the woman whether she would trust him and accept any charm he offered, she said that she would. And when he showed her his huge penis and asked whether that charm gave her umbrage, she said that it did not. Nine months later she had a son and her husband's "face" was saved.

Despite the tenor of some of these jokes, both Esmat's sisters and her friends looked upon her with awe because she'd married Bahram, and they outdid one another in their fawning upon Dawn. They told her that her beauty was "perfectly angelic," her skin "the freshest and most velvety" they'd ever seen, her lips "of a gentle ripeness," her manners "enchanting." And her figure, ah, her figure was "quite perfect, impeccable, the figure of a goddess."

At first Dawn found their unctuous acclaim humorous, then embarrassing, and finally, love-starved child that she was, necessary. For the sake of the women's adulation she'd have come to the public bath every day if it had been possible, even though she knew that they praised her out of ulterior motives. She, being a Mosallai daughter of marriageable age, would bring prestige and affluence to whichever upward-striving family of South Tehran might capture her as a daughter-in-law. And all of Esmat's relatives and friends who did not have sons, did have brothers, nephews or cousins to proffer as candidates for Dawn's hand.

But the women in Esmat's inner circle were not the only ones who competed for her and Dawn's attention. In Iran, except among the most Westernized of families, the women are actually the true, or at least, the preliminary suitors always on the prowl for likely girls for their kinsmen. Thus Esmat was constantly approached by bath attendants of women who had tipped them to tell about their menfolk who would be worthy husbands for Dawn.

Some of these men hadn't yet seen Dawn for themselves, and were depending on their kinswomen's evaluations of her. Others, though, had caught glimpses of her when she'd come to and gone from the bath, and had been "driven out of their senses" by the "unforgettable beauty" of her face and figure. They could not think of school or work or anything but Dawn. One, a future doctor, had abandoned his medical texts and did nothing all day but read poetry or compose his own poems in Dawn's honor. Another, a future attorney, had vowed that he would kill himself by jumping under a car unless he could have Dawneh Sultaneh.

When Dawn spoke on the phone with Barbara and Rocky, as she often did, she declared that "the American in me" was outraged at such customs of courtship and marriage which demeaned women by treating them as pieces of goods to be negotiated about, "and which make me feel as though I'm living in tribal days instead of the modern world." But in truth, once she coaxed out of Bahram the promise of not forcing a husband upon her she didn't want, she reveled in the tradition that enabled her to experience men and their families' fine words and flattery without paying what she felt was the exorbitant price demanded of her in America. She could flirt as she willed, without risking her priceless virginity.

Dawn's would-be husbands were mostly students and men in business and the professions, with a sprinkling of sultans, of whom there would have been more if her father had not earlier eliminated men who were not practicing Muslims. They ranged in age from twenty to fifty-three, although most were in their early or middle thirties. They and their "female suitors", i.e. their mothers and as many female relatives as cared to involve themselves, had come to the Mosallais, having seen Dawn in a variety of places, not just the South Tehran public baths. Mohammed Apbar, a music professor at Tehran University, had seen Dawn in a music shop. Faryar Amajani, a reporter on Etalaat, had seen her at a bookstore. Rabii Mo'infar, a doctor, had seen Dawn at the Caspian Sea. And Yar Kashani, a student in the Department of Sociology at Tehran University, son of a doctor and grandson of a noted mujtahid, had seen her in the Shah's Mosque.

Yar Kashani, Dawn's eleventh suitor, wooed her in the traditionalist style. Thus, before she'd ever laid eyes on Yar himself, Dawn received his "female suitors"—his mother Mahede, aunts Fahri and Fahti and sister Fatima, a year older than she—in the fashion of the traditional "good girl" of Islam. Her hair hung loose and she wore no makeup, so that any blemish she might have would be apparent to the suitors. She proved her knowledge of etiquette and capability as a hostess by pouring tea, passing cakes and other sweets and paring oranges and apples in a way that left just enough skin attached, to enable the daintily separated sections to lie like open flowers. And she entertained the suitors by dancing and singing the traditional songs and dances.

Esmat once told Dawn that some "female suitors" rubbed girls' hair between their fingers to test its texture, and others examined their teeth for whiteness and strength. Dawn warned that any suitor who'd stick a finger into her mouth could expect to have it bitten off. But Yar's "female suitors" were not the kind who rubbed girls' hair or examined their teeth. Young Fatima was gay, lively and very intelligent. And Yar's mother and aunts were elegant ladies who had traveled widely in Europe and America. They were, besides, filled to the brim with jokes and funny stories. But once the pleasantries were done, Dawn felt herself subjected by them (except for Fatima) to the most intense scrutiny; they were here, after all, not to discover a crooked tooth or a pimple on her face, but more important things. What were the customs in Dawn's home, and what were her own customs? What were her vanities, her temper, her tempo, her style? Was she an Iranian at heart, despite her half-American heritage and years spent in that country? And most important of all, how real was her conversion to Islam and how fundamental her present religious conviction?

Dawn answered their questions honestly and courteously, although with some inner indignation at the fact that there was no opportunity for her to probe them in return. She wanted to know how old Yar was, and how tall, since most of her would-be husbands had been shorter than she. And she wanted to know whether he was handsome, and as delightful to be with as his sister, mother and aunts, or as sedate and "old mannish" as many of his predecessors had been. But it was Dawn's place to satisfy the suitors, not to be satisfied by them, to answer questions, not ask them.

Two days after the "female suitors'" visit, however, Dawn

received a call from Fatima. She said that she believed it unfair for Yar to know everything about Dawn while she knew nothing about him, and she suggested a meeting, "so I can tell you about my brother before you meet him."

Dawn learned from Fatima that Yar was 21, the age she'd hoped he'd be, that he and Fatima bore a resemblance, though most people considered him the better-looking of the two (at least that's what Fatima told), and that he was both a poet and dedicated revolutionary.

From the day of their meeting, Dawn and Fatima were "best friends." Dawn, who'd not had a friend since she'd left Iran, adored Fatima because of her warmth and easy acceptance of her. And Fatima returned her feeling.

Finally, some two weeks after Dawn's meeting with Yar's "female suitors", Yar, his parents and grandparents came to call on her, her father and Esmat. First came his grandfather, Mujtahid Ali Vanani, in his seventies, turbaned and gray-bearded. Then there was his father, Dr. Hussein Kashani, a tall, slender, dignified-looking man. Behind the father and grandfather came Yar's grandmother, a bent, shriveled lady, and then his mother. Yar came behind the women.

After Dawn had served tea to Yar's parents and grandparents, the men retired to one corner of the room and the women to another, leaving her and Yar on a sofa in the room's center. Yar talked to Dawn of many things: of America, which he'd had no desire to visit 'til his meeting with her; of Fatima, about whom he was concerned, though he never answered Dawn's questions about the reasons; of his father, of whom he was extremely proud; and of the mujtahid, his grandfather, who seemed to be his idol.

And especially, Yar talked about "our loving, generous, beautiful people who have been degraded and trampled by Mohammed Reza's despotism." The Shah had to go, Yar concluded. And he added that he was among many who stood ready to give his life for that purpose. He hoped, he said, that Dawn would stand with him.

CHAPTER XXVII

The Flagellants

One of Yar's early steps to make a revolutionary of Dawn was to take her to the home of his grandfather, the mujtahid. He lived in Quom, which has always been known as "the Vatican of Iran". Located only ninety-six miles from Tehran, it was, even in the Shah's day, a symbol and a model of the Iran the mullahs yearned to preserve. Then, as now, all women and girl children wore chadors, and many were rug weavers. There were no places of entertainment and no public cinemas or even television aerials to mar the pristine sky.

Although a city of less than 300,000, Quom was home to the most important seminaries in the country, as well as to some of the most revered of the religious. The prime strategists of the revolution lived, taught and spoke out from Quom. Among them were Khomeini himself, who came when he was very young and remained 'til his expulsion to Iraq in 1963.

Dawn's visit to Quom occurred during Moharram, a month of mourning commemorating the martyrdom of Shiites' favorite saint, Hossein, on the plain at Karbala in Iraq in 680. It is a month of incredibly intense and open, high-pitched lamentation all over the country, and in no place more than in Quom.

On Dawn's first night in Quom she, Khanoum Sheherezade, Khanoum Kashani and Fatima, in black dresses, stockings, shoes and chadors, and Yar, his father and grandfather, also dressed in black from head to toe, went to a ta'ziyeh, a passion play depicting Hossein's martyrdom and death. It began at six o'clock with a procession. First came six black-dressed men riding black horses and blowing shaypurs, six-foot wooden horns with brass flares at their ends. Next, on foot, came the men of the dastehs (neighborhood religious brotherhoods) following their leaders, who carried black velvet banners and "The Great Standards", silver crossbars each holding five plume-shaped silver plaques dedicated to Mohammed, Ali, Hussein, Hassan and Mohammed's daughter Fatima.

The hundreds of men who followed the banner and standard bearers held chains, with which they scourged themselves while they chanted, "Ya Ali, ya Hossein, ya Hassan." They wept as they walked, and many watchers wept with them.

At nine o'clock, after the procession was done, Dawn and her party proceeded to the hosseiniyeh, the headquarters for the ta'ziyeh that, in this case, was the courtyard. It was perhaps the size of a football field, of the Mosque of Mohammed. On stage were a trumpeter, a dozen drummers and Mujtahid Kashani, who was narrator and interpreter of events. First came a blast from the trumpet, then a booming of the drums, then more trumpets and more drums. Now came a dozen black-clad flagellants chanting the names of Ali, Hossein and Hassan and beating themselves to the rhythm of the drums. Then came another blast from the trumpet as the mujtahid outlined the story. It began with "The Thirst", in recollection of the time when Hossein, his family and followers had no water in their camp on the desert. The Euphrates River, which Allah had decreed belonged to all, was nearby, but it was guarded by forces to the "villain caliph" who refused to share it with Hossein's people.

Now came the characters: Hossein, tall and handsome; his brother Hassan; and Zeinab, Hossein's wife, played by a man. Zeinab, two small children clinging to her chador and carrying a baby in her arms, paced the stage, crying, "My children thirst, my poor babies thirst."

And forward came Hossein and Hassan, their hands clasped. They joined Zienab in morning for their own children and all the children in the camp, and begged God to grant them water.

The drums struck again, the trumpet blasted and Part Two, "The Massacre", was played. Hossein, having temporarily left the camp in Hassan's charge, returned to the sight of simulated bloodied heads, hands, arms and legs thrown onto a blood-stained sheet on the floor of the stage. And Zeinab and Hassan were throwing dust onto their heads and crying out that "the forces of the wicked caliph have massacred our people and innocent children."

Now the mujtahid introduced two new characters: Yazid, the caliph's general with eyes, nose and lips lined in black, and a lion, "the good lion who loved Hossein because he was the animals' friend and protector."

A white horse wearing headplumes of green, the color of the House of the Prophet, was led up the ramp and onto the stage by a green-clad groom. And Hossein, vowing vengeance against the caliph and Yazid, mounted the horse and set off for the caliph's camp.

Having ridden across the stage and down the ramp, he arrived at the camp, where he was greeted by scores of Yazid's men waving their swords. Despite their number, though, he managed to bravely slash his way into their center where Yazid, sword drawn, stood waiting. The two men began a long swordplay. Hossein was the better swordsman, and would have been the victor had it not been for the distractions created by Yazid's men. They came at him from back and front. They didn't actually attack him, but gave the impression that they might, and so drew his attention from Yazid who was able, finally, to fatally wound him in the chest.

Now the good lion appeared. He knelt beside Hossein and touched his face solicitously. Then, from a pocket of his lion's costume, he pulled a bloodstained sheet, held it against Hossein's chest and waved it at the audience while crying, "See the blood of Hossein shed by the tyrants."

Bugles and trumpets rang out again to introduce the last scenes, which showed Hossein's death and Yazid's cutting off his head as a present for the caliph. Now there ensued intense weeping, wailing, moaning, scratching of faces and beating of heads in the audience. Dawn had witnessed ta'ziyehs before (there are as many versions of Hossein's agony and death as there are people presenting them), but she had never seen one that roused such wild expressions of grief.

The next day was the day of Tassua. That morning Dawn, Fatima, Khanoum Mahede and Khanoum Kashani, as part of a huge mass of women, stood watching a procession of men and boys, some as young as eight or nine, move through the streets. These, like the ones of yesterday, carried chains and wore black robes, tied today in a way that left their backs uncovered. And they slashed at their bare backs 'til the blood came. What troubled Dawn even more than the excruciating sight of the flowing blood were the men's expressions of elation, ecstasy, beatitude.

The Tassua procession, that had begun soon after noon, did not end 'til after midnight. At breakfast the next morning, Dawn felt nauseous. She wanted to ask Yar's grandmother's permission to remain away from that day's Ashura, which she intuited would be more shocking to her than the Tassua one had been. But she didn't dare ask, and so stood between Khanoum Kashani and Khanoum Mahede on Ashura morning looking out at the men with formerly black robes which had been replaced by white ones, and who now carried swords in place of their chains. They cut themselves with their swords, lashing not just at their backs, but also at their hands and faces; their excitement served as a sort of anesthesia. Many faint-ed from loss of blood or too intense ecstasy and were carried off on litters. And the procession leaders, seeming not to have noticed their collapsed colleagues, thrust through their own flesh with pins and fish-hooks.

During the three days after Ashura that Dawn spent in Yar's grandparents' home, she came to know Mujtahid Kashani. A man of largesse and humility, he invited her to "ask about our Islam, or about anything else you may wish, to which I, my daughter, may have an answer."

And Dawn, from the perspective of her time at St. Jerome's and her other slight exposure to Christianity asked, first of all, why weeping and wailing and suffering were such essential parts of Shiite observances. The mujtahid explained that perhaps no other people in the world lived such lives of quiet desperation as did the Iranian poor. When they wailed and wept and scourged themselves for Hossein's sake, they were enabled, also, to release their sorrow over their own oppression and suffering.

Dawn then asked what good temporary release of sorrow could do for a people who would only have, afterward, to return to their lives of misery. The mujtahid answered that her question had also been asked by the most profound of Islamic thinkers, including Khomeini himself. And their answer was, "Yes, the faithful should weep and scourge themselves in order to feel what Hossein did, to

SHARE his agony. And if they are thus helped also to resolve, even temporarily, their own depression, that is for the good. But what they may not do, is to selfishly use Hossein's agony merely to gain release from their own ills; they must use it, rather, as a means of coming to know that saint so that they may form themselves in his image. Who was Hossein, and for what did he die a martyr, are the questions they must ask of themselves.

"And the answers to those questions must be: Hossein was a soldier of God, and he died a martyr to God's cause. Now, you may ask, daughter, how all of this applies to you and me. And I would answer such a question with another one. What more wonderful privilege, Dawneh, can God grant during this evil time than for such as ourselves to die...as Hossein did in his time...martyrs in the revolution to overthrow the Satan Shah here in Iran? And, afterward, to overthrow all of the Satanic rulers of the world so God, Himself, may rule."

Dawn, as she perceived it, had only just begun to live and thus certainly did not want to die. And she was able to imagine many more wonderful privileges than dying that Allah could grant her. But out of her intense desire to please this holy man, she answered the question exactly as the mujtahid would have wished.

CHAPTER XXVIII

An Adventurer Without Faith

On January 8, 1978, Dawn, on a second visit to Quom with Fatima, was wakened early by Khanoum Kashani and told to come immediately to the family room. There she found Yar's family and many madrasa, seminary students who worked under the mujtahid, all looking angry and shocked. A few held copies of yesterday's Etalaat, containing an article that had obviously been released by the palace entitled, "Iran and Red and Black Colonization". It opened with a short discussion of the White Revolution and the opposition to it by the 'reds' (communists) and 'blacks' (clergy) and then proceeded to viciously attack Khomeini. It called him "the Indian ayatollah" (his grandfather had been born in India) who had, in his youth, written love poems (it was implied they were also pornographic) which he'd signed in Hindi, the literary and official language of Northern India. He was described as "an adventurer without faith...a man with a dubious past". Finally, the article declared that he was sponsored by the British in his fight against Mohammed Reza.

Mujtahid Kashani cried out that "this calumny of Mohammed Reza against our leader, our conscience and our soul, is the ultimate insult...Can the Shah, in his ignorance and arrogance, honestly believe that he can destroy him who is holy? Does he not know that he is accomplishing his own ruin and not our leader's?"

Dawn and everyone followed the mujtahid out into the street, where their numbers expanded by the hundreds, then thousands, with people chanting, "God is great and Khomeini is our leader." Suddenly, over a loudspeaker came a voice commanding the people to disperse. They stood firm, defying the order. The voice came again. The people remained as they were. The voice threatened reprisals. The people remained unmoving.

The voice thundered out, "This is our last warning to you." And in the next few minutes Dawn saw the Shah's soldiers with their rifles on the roofs of the houses around the square where they would be in position to cascade fire down on to the people's heads. And she saw other soldiers, setting up machine guns facing into the crowd. And then, suddenly and horribly, the war—a small war, but a war all the same—began with people falling dead or wounded in the head, neck, chest, stomach. Blood was everywhere. People ran, though not knowing where to go, crisscrossing and tripping over one another. Dawn saw a crippled woman fall out of her wheelchair, dead from a bullet that had entered her eye and blown out the back of her head. And Dawn witnessed a child of perhaps three or four with blood running from his right eye; his mother, dazed, carried him through the crowd while shouting over and over, "Why are they killing babies? What have babies ever done to them that they should kill them?" Then a mullah fell to the ground, his white turban stained with the blood from a fatal head wound.

By now some of the people, especially the madrasa students, driven by rage and hate, exploded into swirling groups that screamed, jeered, threatened and fought the soldiers with their bare hands, beating and punching 'til some of the soldiers were also bruised and bleeding. And the soldiers retaliated with clubs and heavy boots as well as guns. They were merciless, their cruelty perhaps beyond their own grasp. Dawn saw someone who looked like Khanoum Kashani but was not, lying on her back on the ground, her chador torn off, eyes shrieking, face contorted, body writhing, while one soldier kicked at her and another beat her with his club.

Then she saw Mujtahid Kashani fall to the ground. He, Yar and Yar's father had been trying to make their way toward fallen friends when he was shot in the head.

Dawn spent the days after the Quom bloodbath with Yar, his family and, indeed, the whole of grieving Quom. At the funeral for the "beloved martyrs of God", she, with the immense procession of other mourners, walked slowly, slowly behind the pallbearers of the sixty dead, their bodies washed and dressed in white burial shrouds, to the cemetery. Because all of the dead were Sars Allah, Warriors of God, many in the procession scourged themselves, as had happened at Tassua and Ashura, with whips, chains and swords. They chanted,

"Ya Allah, Ya Hossein, Ya Hassan," and then the names of their own martyrs. Dawn chanted with them, sorrowing for the mujtahid, her true martyr, as she'd not been able to do for the symbolic ones.

A ritual that goes back in Iran to the very dawning of Shiism, one so sacred and revered that the shahs, historically and throughout Mohammed Reza's own reign, have feared to combat it, is "the commemoration for the dead" that occurs on the fortieth day after a death. Family, friends, neighbors, entire neighborhoods and villages gather in the home of the deceased for a "ceremony of recall and lamentation". Going on round-the-clock as often as not, it is a time when people's pain and grief, and the ecstasy that comes with their catharsis, reach their outermost limits. And if the death was a violent one, as were those of the mujtahid and the other Quom martyrs–reminiscent, as these deaths were, of Hossein's martyrdom at Kerbala–then the wrath and hatred of the mourners comes out as well. Their need for retaliation and revenge can be, indeed, must be given full vent along with the agony and lamentation.

Forty days after the events at Quom, then, people gathered in the mosques and main squares of many towns and cities to commemorate the victims. And in Tabriz, home of the constitutional revolution, violence broke out: Crowds marched through the streets shouting, "Death to the Shah," and attacking banks, shops and cinemas, symbols of dependence on the West and on infidels (banks because of the high percentage of their foreign capital, cinemas because they showed mostly foreign and sexy films). But significantly and to their credit, the Tabriz revolutionaries, although ravaging buildings, did not hurt people, while the Shah's Army killed hundreds and wounded thousands.

Forty days after the Tabriz massacre, during another commemoration, the Army opened fire on demonstrators in Isfahan. More people died. Another forty days passed, and crowds mourned in dozens of cities and towns for those who'd fallen in Isfahan.

Now the religious qualities of the demonstrations changed, broadened. Workers flocked to the movement as did students of all affiliations, members of the National Front Party, now led by Mossadegh's nephew, and Tudeh. They were joined by the Marxist

Fedayeen-e-Qualq, a guerrilla group formed after the regime's suppression of the 1963 riots, on the then-popular model of Che Guevara. With ties to the Palestine Liberation Movement, the Fedayeen had carried out a number of assassinations of American military men and advisers and made several attempts on the life of the Shah.

Women students out of all these groups also came in huge numbers. Many of them, either out of genuine religiosity or in defiance of the Shah's "westoxicated" regime, wore either the chador or the uniform of the Fedayeen-e-Qualq women that consisted of large scarves covering hair and forehead, knee-length smocks and loose trousers.

Although women students played a vital role in the demonstrations, the traditionalist bazaari women were even more numerous. They came out, usually in separate ranks, to participate in the processions. In later months they even gave up their separateness and marched, sometimes with babies in their arms, in front of united processions, challenging the consciousness of policemen and soldiers.

Mohammed Reza, who had begun the year boasting, "Nobody can overthrow me since I have the support of 700,000 troops, all the workers and most of the people," made a few moves toward appeasement of the people which he named "democratization." But, as had always been his way, what he gave with one hand, he took away with the other.

After the Tabriz massacre, he dismissed the provincial governor-general of Aberbijan and a few other officers. Yet shortly after their heralded deposal, he ordered that the demonstrators for the Tabriz martyrs in Isfahan be surrounded and fired upon. More people were dead, more violence perpetrated. Knowing it was time for the dangling of another carrot, the Shah dismissed the head of Savak; this while Savakan atrocities continued even more intensely than in earlier years. Such games Mohammed Reza played in the very midst and almost 'til the end of the revolution. First, he made such a show of his strength and ruthless ability to shed the people's blood as would touch the wellsprings of their terror, and make them as obsequious as they'd always been. But each time he found that his acts, far from turning "his" people into their former abject states, were, instead, rousing them to meet his terror with their own. And each time he was stunned anew at this, and knew he had no choice but to offer them some atonement. Nor could he understand that their demands now were for full freedom and justice, not his favors.

After Isfahan came Meshed. And after Meshed, Mashad. In the end it happened in nearly every city and town. Every forty days another explosion of fury by the people, followed by the violence of police and soldiers of Mohammed Reza. Then in August came the fire-bombing of the Rex movie theater, an old wooden structure in a poor section of Abadan, in which 377 people, by the government's own count, were burned, suffocated or trampled to death. The arsonists had doused the walls with gasoline and then set off incendiary devices with no word of warning. No escape was possible since the theater's doors were locked.

The government maintained that the fire had been set by fundamentalist Shiites who believed the movies to be showing "corrupting Western (sexually oriented) films." And, indeed, many such fires had been set in Abadan and throughout the country by such groups. But they'd occurred only during off-hours and no person had ever been killed or injured. And the film at the Rex at the time of the fire was not such an offensive import of the time as, say, *The Diary of a Mad Housewife*, but was rather an Iranian-made movie called *The Reindeer* that portrayed the struggles of a poor peasant against dishonest officials.

Further, there was no question but that the local authorities contributed to the immensity of the death toll from the fire. Witnesses reported that nearly half an hour elapsed before the first firefighters arrived at the burning theater. Once they got there, they discovered that none of the hydrants were working. The mobile water tanks they brought to the scene ran dry before the fire could be brought under control. The screams of the dying filled the air, as would-be rescuers stood by helplessly. It would be charged later by witnesses that the police, whose station was located only a block from the Rex, made no attempt to free the trapped.

And whether or not there was truth to the rumor (it is hard to imagine that the Shah would be so self-destructive), millions of Iranians, Dawn included, believed implicitly that Savak, on order of Mohammed Reza, had set the fire, locked the doors and caused the policemen and firemen to bungle relief efforts. Now the people's anger and hatred would not be contained. Thousands had hardly finished weeping beside the fresh graves of their "martyrs" before "avenging" the murders by smashing shop windows and battling with police, who called for the always-ready military with their tanks and troops.

After the tragedy, dozens of pictures and films of the Abadan fire circulated all over Iran. Men, women and children, relatives of the dead, wailed and wept for their losses. Among them was a girl of perhaps six with huge, tragic eyes staring out of her chador saying, on cue from an aunt on whose lap she sat, "Yes, my mother, father and grandfather were killed in the fire, and now I am an orphan and pray God to let me join the ones I love who I know are in heaven." And there was a frail old lady sitting on the dirt floor of her hut and crying out in a voice that hardly sounded human, "The evil, ungodly Shah even took the lives of my unborn grandchildren...in that fire I lost eight sons and four daughters, two of them pregnant." She angled her head to the ground and entreated, "Please, please God, take me, too, because what reason do I have for living anymore?"

And Dawn, identifying with all the grieving people of Abadan from the vantage point of her sorrow over the mujtahid, wrote this to Barbara and Rocky: "Now, Mother and Sister, I too must join the revolution; I too must fight the enemies of the people."

CHAPTER XXIX

Yesterday a Muslim, Today a Revolutionary

At the time Dawn's letter arrived in Houston, Rocky was seven months pregnant and happier than ever before. She was deeper, calmer, more at peace and very proud of her pregnancy, what her father-in-law declared as "being honored by life, my daughter."

She generally visualized her child as a girl of four or five. In her daydream she picked her up at kindergarten and they walked home together; at home, often with Tuan's help and sometimes his father's as well (how treasured Rocky's daughter was by the men in her life), they were engaged in family projects. In fact, they were, in Rocky's imagination, building an elaborate doll house together, complete with carpets, curtains and antique American furniture, when Barbara came with Dawn's letter. Trying to make light of it for her mother's sake, Rocky quipped, "That's our Dawn for you. Yesterday a Muslim, and today a revolutionary."

"A Muslim revolutionary," Barbara's voice rose, "and that's what terrifies me. Those Islamic revolutionaries with their 'All for God, including the sacrifice of my life...and oh God, Rocky, Dawn with her need to challenge and to show her courage at no matter what cost...Can't you see her in one of their demonstrations think- ing, 'Look at me, everybody, I'm not afraid of the Shah's guns...I'M NOT AFRAID OF ANYTHING!'"

Rocky tried to cheer her mother by declaring that, really, she was underestimating Dawn's maturity and strength. Look how she'd managed to turn herself around during the few short months before she'd left for Iran. It had seemed like a miracle, but it was all due to Dawn's hard work. She wasn't going to throw her life away after all she'd put into salvaging it. She'd be bound to "run from those fanatics" if she had a place to run to. Rocky said that she would phone her cousins in Iran and ask them to "help free Dawn."

Barbara said that even if Rocky's cousins could persuade Dawn to leave her revolutionary companions, her father, "as another man of Islam, is going to do his best to stop her."

"I don't see him as 'another man of Islam', risking his own damn neck," Rocky said.

"The fact that he doesn't risk his own neck doesn't mean that he won't risk his daughter's, Rocky."

"The hell with him then, Mama. I'll call Sheherezade; she'll get her father, he'll get...The uncles will rescue Dawn, and..."

Rocky, herself, did not believe in the happy talk she spewed at Barbara; in her heart she shared her mother's fear for her sister. And in her panic she had a sudden idea, crazy maybe, but worth trying all the same, because when you're desperate, doing anything is better than doing nothing. So quickly, before her nerve could fail, she placed a telephone call to Bahram. Today she can't remember what inspired words she used to play on her father's vanity so successfully that he was persuaded that, after everything, she longed for his presence at her baby's birth. "Yes, yes, daughter," he affirmed, "I will be there to help bring my first grandson into the world."

Rocky grimaced and held back the impulse to ask, "What'll you do if my child's a girl–call her by the name you did Dawn and me?" Instead, she thanked him with all the humility he could desire. Then, feeling the sweat gathering under her armpits and on the palms of her hands, she said, "If you would do me the further favor, Father, of bringing Dawn..."

"Well, I really accomplished something with this call, Mama," Rocky said after she'd hung up. "I'm going to have as houseguests my father and Esmat, but not Dawn."

Rocky and Barbara talked then about whether or not to call off Bahram's visit, and decided they wouldn't. Their hope was that, once on their territory and not his, Rocky might be in a better position to bring pressure on him to let Dawn go.

Bahram arrived in Houston on August 14th, the hottest day of the year, yet Rocky shivered as she awaited his plane. Why, she asked herself as she waited, had she asked him to come? Had she really thought that if he came, she could influence him on Dawn's behalf?

When had anyone, least of all his daughter, ever influenced Bahram Mosallai about anything?

So, if not for Dawn's sake, why had Rocky asked Bahram to come? What sick, crazy thing inside her had led her to do that? Had the quiet and calm of her life, the warmth and affection by which she was surrounded, palled so that she had, deliberately, to seek out her father's cruelty? And she had no right to impose Bahram on Twon, for whom, since he was neither rich nor a Muslim, Bahram already felt intense enmity. How would Bahram behave toward him when they were actually thrown together? She promised herself that at the first sign of Bahram's hostility toward her husband, she'd tell her father to leave her home.

At the time of Bahram's arrival in Houston, Rocky and Twon had been in their two-bedroom furnished sublet apartment for a little less than a month. It had been depressingly drab when they'd first seen it, but they'd done wonders with paint and wallpaper and hand-made curtains and brightly-colored posters on the walls. They'd been so proud and pleased with themselves after everything was done. Now, though, Rocky was seeing the place through her father's eyes as desolate, a far cry from the mansion she would have lived in if she'd married Ali Reza. And the thought made her feel traitorous to Twon.

At the airport, Bahram in beard and turban and Esmat in her chador made Rocky feel self-conscious; she saw, or believed she saw, people tittering and laughing when she bent to kiss her father's hand. She got them, as quickly as possible, out of the airport and into her car.

At home, Rocky led her father and stepmother to the guest bedroom she'd worked hard to make attractive, with such amenities as Barbara's heirloom white chenille spread and Mrs. Vu's treasured Chinese vases for holding the welcoming flower bouquets. Bahram looked around the room with contempt. "It seems to me, daughter," he said, "that in the short time you've been away from Iran, you've forgotten our people's commitment to the fact that 'a guest is a gift from God'."

"I don't understand why you say that," Rocky said.

"Because if you had not forgotten, you would not have put a guest, especially one who is your own father and has come such a distance at your summons, into a...hovel." He spat on the rag rug Rocky had made herself, much as Baba Bozorg had been wont to spit on the Persian carpets of his mansions when he was angry at his children and grandchildren.

Rocky explained that she and Twon were struggling financially, that Twon was still in school and that "when he becomes a doctor, Father, we'll be able to accommodate you and other guests as we would wish to, as 'gifts from God'."

Bahram said, "The meaning of 'treating a guest as a gift from God' is this: Your guest is ENTITLED to the best that your household has to offer. Is this room the best one in your house? Or is your and your husband's own bedroom the best?"

Rocky had initially intended, while making the arrangements for her father's coming, to give up her and Twon's bedroom to Esmat and him. After her last visit to the doctor, though, she'd been told to spend long hours in bed. Twon had then persuaded her that nobody, Bahram included, would want, under the circumstances, to put her out of her own room. So she explained the situation to Bahram, saying, "I hope you'll find my reason acceptable, father."

A sly smile lighted Bahram's face. "Do you, yourself, find it acceptable, Roxanne?"

Twon came in while Bahram and Esmat were resting (in his and Rocky's bedroom), and Rocky was setting a lunch of their favorite foods on the table.

The door opened, and Bahram and Esmat emerged.

"How do you do, Father and Esmat, and welcome to our home," Twon smiled.

Bahram stared sullenly, first at Twon, then at Rocky and then at the food on the table.

"I don't understand," he pointed to the table, "exactly what this is, Roxanne."

"It's lunch, Father. I'm sure you're both very hungry, and..."

He mocked her: "Oh, she's sure we're both very hungry. My good daughter of Islam is sure we're both hungry and is, therefore, ready to serve us lunch. Did you hear Roxanne, Esmat? 'It's lunch, Father. I'm sure you're all hungry, Father. Come and eat, Father.' That's what you're telling me, isn't it, daughter? And I'm telling you, that this is the month of Ramazan, Ramazan, Roxanne!"

<u>Ramazan</u> (the Arabs say Ramadan) is the ninth month of the lunar calendar, in which faithful Muslims do not eat during daylight and drink only as much water as will leave them still thirsty. Rocky could have replied that, during all the years she'd known him, far from carrying out the commandments of Ramazan or any other Islamic holiday, even including Moharram, Bahram had mocked them as "the celebrations of raghead-o-maniacs." But Rocky held her tongue and waited for him to grow calm enough so she could inquire as to what hours he wished to eat.

"Well, I should think we can have dinner at nine or nine-thirty at night and breakfast at four-thirty in the morning, or maybe three-thirty."

Twon, taking Rocky's hand, told Bahram that he didn't wish to be impolite or seem inhospitable, but nevertheless had to inform him that they had no servants and that he both attended school and held a full-time job, "so that all the work of the house falls on Rocky. And our doctor is worried about her, and has given her strict orders about when to eat and sleep. So, you must understand that much as she, both of us, would wish to meet your needs, it...just won't be possible, sir. I'm sure that you, as Rocky's father, are as concerned with her and your coming grandchild's well-being as I am, and..." He left off, then added, "If I sound self-righteous or like I am lecturing, I ask you to forgive me."

"And what would you, Twon, suggest we do then?"

As strong as his respect was for parents and grandparents, Twon nevertheless felt compelled to act for Rocky's sake. He stammered out that "we might be able to find you a furnished apartment that'll be close enough so that..."

Now Rocky saw Bahram's eyes glaze over with the feral, gauzy look that always preceded the worst of his tempers. "YOU GOD-DAMNED ORIENTAL SCUM! Ordering your wife's father out of your home. Your wife's father! It's a shame and a sin, but what do you, heathen piece of Chink shit, know about sin and shame, and...No! Let me talk! Your family's not worthy to clean my family's toilets...you bastard of Vietnam. And you would order me out of this hovel you've got my daughter in? You would dare?"

Twon trembled. He'd never before faced a man—and that man Rocky's father, no less—who appeared to have gone so mad with rage.

"All right, Mr. Mosallai, because you're Rocky's father I'm going to try to forget the names you called me and deal with the facts. First of all, I never ordered you out of my house—that's also Rocky's—or said, or even implied that you weren't welcome here. What I did say, sir, was that Rocky, being pregnant, can't be giving you breakfast at three-thirty in the morning and dinner at nine-thirty at night." He threw out his hands. "If you and your religion could make allowances–because the daughter whom you expect to serve you, needs to be served herself..."

"You bastard Chink, how can you ever understand the purity of a religion like Islam? Islam doesn't make allowances for a pregnant daughter." He snorted. "I can tell you that my wife's pregnancy didn't stop her from carrying out her womanly duties."

Now Bahram was quiet, and he and Twon stood facing each other, bodies tremulous, faces hard with anger. And Rocky, remembering her promise to herself to put her father out of her home and her life if he abused Twon, tried to pluck up her courage and summon the words for doing it. But a part of her held her back, kept saying that she couldn't treat her father so.

And Twon, realizing Rocky's inner conflict, gained control of himself and apologized "humbly" to Bahram. He did not say what he was apologizing for, nor did Bahram, in his vanity, need any reason. He felt that he had rightly caused his daughter's "poor worm of a husband," as he would later describe Twon to Dawn, to "cringe and grovel." That was his perception of Twon's generous act of love for Rocky.

"And I have an idea, sir," Twon said softly, "that could resolve our problem. If you will do Rocky and me the honor of considering this apartment your home, we will stay with my parents. Thus, you will be enabled to carry out to the letter your religious obligations which, I assure you, I did not mean to underestimate."

Now, Rocky could at least sleep peacefully and have a nourishing breakfast at a proper time. By nine o'clock in the morning, though, she had to be at the apartment to take her father and Esmat shopping. She tried to prevail on them to shop every two or three days instead of daily, but that was not their custom and they would have none of it. And since Islam proclaims that every animal has a right to a drink of water and receive prayer before being slaughtered, Rocky had to drive miles out of town to find live chickens her father might later kill in the proscribed fashion. Further, Bahram was a night person; he slept long hours during the day and spent the nights talking to...at...Rocky, and sometimes also Twon, about Islam; he was determined to convert them.

Rocky, though constantly exhausted and often ill during the nights of her father's harangues, managed to tolerate them in return for opportunities to plead with him on Dawn's account. Always, though, he listened to her arguments only so that he could use them against her. Certainly, Dawn was young and easily led, he would not deny it, but what a wonderful path she'd been led onto. How full was her life on earth, and how infinitely fuller it would be in heaven if she were to die a revolutionary heroine.

In the midst of one of these discussions about Dawn, at two o'clock in the morning of September 23, Rocky's birth pains began unexpectedly. She knew that she had to get to the hospital immediately, and had to drive herself. Twon was working nights that week, but had told her he would be near a phone all night. She gave her father his number and asked him to call him and Barbara right away.

The birth was a brutal one, the pain unlike anything Rocky could have imagined as the baby crashed its way out, seeming to rip her open as the doctors and nurses shouted, "Push, push" at her. But in the holocaust of pain there was nothing left to push with, and Rocky felt herself sinking. And then in the overhead mirror she saw a tiny head rise from the bloodiness, and heard a bleat and a scream. And all the pain disappeared and a rush of gratitude went through her. Her and Twon's baby. Their Tyanne.

But where was Twon? Why wasn't he here to share this

moment? And where was Barbara? Rocky had cried and called for her mother during the worst of her suffering. Later, she would learn that her father hadn't called either her husband or her mother, and that they'd only learned what had happened after they'd called the apartment. "I have to tell you, Mother," Rocky heard Twon whisper to Barbara, "that this is a thing I'll never forgive."

On the fourth day after Tyanne's birth, a euphoric Rocky went to the home of her parents-in-law, flower-bedecked in her and her baby's honor. She'd no sooner gotten into bed, Tyanne in her arms, when Bahram and Esmat arrived. This was the first time she'd seen them since before her baby's birth, and she held beautiful Tyanne up for their inspection. Esmat put a finger into her tiny palm, and as had been the case with everyone who did that, her tiny fingers curled around Esmat's long one. How strong she was!

"Esmat!" Bahram said reprovingly, and Esmat quickly withdrew herself from Tyanne.

Rocky lay stewing at her father's rejection of her child, but stayed silent.

"Hold that baby up to me a minute," Bahram commanded, and Rocky did. He kept looking at her for a long time, then said, "Well, one thing's for sure, you can tell she's got Chink blood in her."

"Vietnamese blood, Father."

"What did you say, Roxanne?"

"I said that, yes, you can tell that my baby's got Vietnamese blood in her. And also Persian and American blood."

"And you, Roxanne, sound proud of it."

"I'm very proud, Father."

Bahram's eyes narrowed. "Do you know what her Vietnamese and American blood makes her to me? Shit to be stuck up your American mother's and Chink husband's asses."

Rocky stayed quiet for a long time, then said quite calmly, "You haven't mentioned her sex, Father. Don't you also hold the fact that she's a girl against her...and me?"

"Shit to be stuck up your American mother's and Chink husband's asses," Bahram repeated.

Suddenly, Rocky heard a sound escape from her gut, not a laugh or a sob, but some alien primeval sound that chilled her as well as everyone in the room, including her father. She grunted, and hissed words that had always been part of her father's vocabulary, never hers. Abandoning herself totally to the combat that, if it had occurred earlier, might have saved her years of anguish. Expressing, finally, everything she'd held down since Shirley Kashani's rape, or even years earlier. Assailing her father through broken, choking breaths of air, calling him "a rapist, killer, destroyer," and ordering him out of her family's life. Declaring that she knew that, if he had the opportunity, he'd do to Tyanne "what you did to my mother and sister and me. You say another word about her, you look at her once more the way you did before...A look like that at an innocent baby because she's a girl, and the result of my and my husband's love.

"Listen, you, who always threatened to disown me, now I'm dis-owning you. You're not my father anymore. You've only got one daughter now, and you, bastard, are willing to see her die for your own rotten conceit. What'll you be if your daughter dies a revolu-tionary martyr? The father of a martyr, right? That'll put you at the top of the heap, won't it? Your Islamic cohorts'll bow down to you then. What's the worth of a daughter's life when you compare it to your own goddamn vanity?

"I could kill you for everything you've done to my mother and sister and me, and would do to my daughter, as well, if you got the chance. And especially, for what you're still doing to the only daugh-ter you have left, I could put the butcher knife with which you slaughter your chickens through your ribs."

CHAPTER XXX

The Garden of Religion We Shall Water With Our Blood

The Abadan fire that had turned so many like Dawn into revolutionaries also persuaded the Shah, finally, that his reign was in crisis and he had to make some more significant "atonement" to "his" people.

His concessions to the secular opposition, therefore, included the lifting of press censorship, permitting freer debate in the Majlis, allowing open activities of all political parties except for Tudeh and permitting peaceful political demonstrations.

To appease the religious, he appointed a prime minister, Jafar Sharif-Ememi, who was known for his devotion to Islam. And he set up "a ministry for religious affairs" that abolished nightclubs, gambling casinos and cinemas showing Western films.

He also released clerics from prison. And the question Dawn, Yar, Fatima and the mass of people asked was: Was the Shah mad when he released those clerics, with their horror stories not only of what had happened to them in prison and to others who could not speak for themselves because they were dead?

One who emerged was the Ayatollah Teleghani, the same Teleghani who, in 1963, had led the student demonstration against the Shah's bloodbath at the University of Tehran. He wouldn't be able to lead any further demonstrations because he was not only more dead than alive by the time he left prison, but also had no eyelids. First, his torturers had forced him to watch as they raped his daughter and then, when he closed his eyes against the sight, they destroyed his eyelids with their cigarettes.

And Ayatollah Saidi died on the "frying pan".

And Ayatollah Azarshari died when the Savak agents threw him into a pot of boiling oil.

Could Mohammed Reza possibly have imagined that the

released clerics would remain silent about the atrocities? And did he think that the people would not want vengeance for such inhumanity to people, whether clerics or not?

Another "atonement" to both secular and clerics was the Shah's issuance of a code, dealing with royal family corruption, that was both too little and too late. Too little, because it never named the princes and princesses as "corrupt", but merely called upon them to close their offices and businesses. It was, therefore, not an apology or even an acknowledgment of the shocking ways in which they'd pillaged the people. It was too late because the plundering had been going on since 1972, when the family had first begun depositing vast sums of money in Switzerland, or using it for buying property in Europe and America.

Further, the code made no mention of royal moral corruption that began with Mohammed Reza himself. He, through his Pahlavi Foundation, owned five gambling casinos on the Persian Gulf and "a pleasure resort" on the Island of Kusch, staffed with prostitutes who were rumored to have been chosen by Madam Claude of Paris.

And for such reasons as these—as well as many others that involved Princess Ashraf, her son the "bad prince" Sharam and other favored royal relatives—the people wouldn't accept any account of Mohammed Reza's "atonements". All that would satisfy them would be the yielding of his throne and departure from the country.

For the first six months after the mujtahid's death, Dawn's participation in the revolution was "second-hand". She heard tapes, saw pictures and slides and was informed by Yar of what was taking place in the country. On September 4, though, she joined in her first anti-Shah demonstration in Tehran...That was the day on which the people abandoned their stones and rocks and, instead, threw flowers at the soldiers and chanted, "SOLDIERS AND BROTHERS, DON'T SHOOT!"

And many of the soldiers who were, after all, of the people themselves, looked out at the crowd that might have contained their brother, sister, best friend, lover, parent. And some cried at the horrors they'd been about to commit against their own. Others, less emotional, nevertheless had plenty of reason for anger against the Shah. Everything was for the officers—huge salaries, houses with staffs of servants—and nothing for them. And such arrogance as the officers showed toward the conscripts! Such abuse the conscripts were compelled to take from them! And it was those officers who degraded them at every opportunity, who'd ordered them to shoot at the people.

Well, they'd rather shoot at the officers than the people, rather shoot at the Shah. They, too, laid down their guns.

On September 7th Dawn, Fatima and Yar joined the masses and once again took to the streets, flowers in hand. This time they importuned the soldiers to join in their demonstration. Many did join, and some even donned the martyr's shrouds the people took off themselves.

Now, finally, Mohammed Reza felt impelled to accept the counsel of his military advisers that he'd formerly rejected. On September 8th, in the early morning hours, he declared martial law. Few people heard the declaration on Tehran Radio, and so on that day, nearly a million people, including Dawn and her group, massed on Jaleb Square for another peaceful demonstration. This time, though, the army attacked and killed more than 2,000 people.

The people named the 8th of September "Black Friday".

"Black Friday" occurred in the midst of the Camp David conference in America. The day after the massacre, Egypt's President Sadat, always Mohammed Reza's friend and ally, called to express his support of the monarch. And President Carter, perhaps at Sadat's request, also telephoned the Shah. Although expressing regret over the bloodshed, he reiterated, as he would continue to do until nearly the end of the revolution, his backing for Mohammed Reza.

And Tehran Radio announced Carter's "support for the Shah" immediately following the report of the massacre. This gave rise to the rumor, widely believed all over Iran, that America had ordered the Jaleb Square massacre. And that it was not the Iranian soldiers who had shot at the people, but American soldiers and Israeli commandos trained in America.

After "Black Friday", the people's rage and hatred for America became even more intense than it had formerly been. Vulnerable Dawn was thrust headlong between a collision of her two worlds, filling her with emotional conflicts. What was she doing among people who, as such bitter enemies of America, were also her and her mother's enemies?

But her next thought was that Americans were not her people, and that America was not her country. What had America ever done for her, except to reject her and heap scorn upon her for her nationality and religion? I'm Muslim and I'm Iranian, she told herself, and all of my love and loyalty, therefore, belong to Islam and my country of Iran. Yet, could all her loyalty belong to Iran and none to America, she who'd been raised by Barbara with the lovely American children's stories and tender American lullabies? She, whose American mother had come close to losing her own life in order to save her and her sister from their Iranian father? These were the questions that Dawn would continue to ask herself through all the months of revolution. And she would answer them first one way, then another. But she would, all the same, remain as ardent and unshakable as anyone in her group, or among the people, in her belief that to help overthrow Mohammed Reza was her assignment from Allah, and that its accomplishment would be a fulfillment of her divine duty.

Soon after the "Black Friday" massacre, Khomeini, from Paris where he'd been granted refuge after the Shah had him exiled from Iraq, issued his first call for jihad (holy war); he bade the people to "shed your blood to protect Islam and overthrow the tyrant and his parasites." And in Tehran, Quom, Isfahan and every other city, men, women and children rioted daily. They put the torch to shops, department stores, government buildings and airlines, except for Air France, which was garlanded with flowers in gratitude for their admission of Khomeini.

Next, Khomeini called for massive strikes, and they occurred and lasted until the end of the revolution: in public transit, railroads, postal and air transport services, textile factories, radio and television stations, newspapers, branches of civil service, universities, high schools and even primary schools. And oil income plummeted as production dropped to a fifth of its normal output, and cost Iran at least sixty million dollars a day.

No wonder an elated Khomeini could send the people this message: "Great people of Iran! The history of Iran, even world history, has never witnessed a movement like yours; it has never experienced a universal uprising like yours, noble people!

"Today, primary school children seven or eight years old stand ready to sacrifice and shed their blood for the sake of Islam and the nation; when has anything like that been seen? Our lionhearted women snatch up their infants and go to confront the machine guns and tanks of the regime; where in history have such valiant and heroic acts been recorded? Today, the thunderous cry of 'Death to the Shah!' arises from the hearts of the primary school child and the infirm old man alike..."

CHAPTER XXXI

Civilians With Guns

Now, finally, the Shah had to realize that his throne could only be saved—if not for him, then for his son—by the grace of the opposition. Therefore, he appealed to a former colleague of Mossadegh to assume the prime ministership and set up a regency council. Shahpur Bahktiar agreed on condition that Mohammed Reza leave the country on "a vacation of undetermined length."

On January 16, 1979, Mohammed Reza, weeping and with a packet of Iranian soil in his pocket, took the controls of his silver and blue 707 and, with Farah, flew to Egypt and exile. All over Tehran and throughout Iran, people thronged the streets, shouting, hugging one another and passing around trays of sweets that local shopkeepers provided. They carried mullahs on their shoulders and displayed banknotes with Mohammed Reza's portrait cut out. And newspapers proclaimed "THE SHAH IS GONE!" with the boldest headlines Iran had ever seen.

The image of Khomeini's homecoming seemed to Dawn, at the time, to be a divine moment that touched her as she'd never been touched before. She wondered to herself whether there ever could have been more people packed on the streets of any other city? And had there ever been so many millions of people bound together by their ecstasy at being in the presence, finally, of him who might, for all anyone knew, be the Hidden Imam himself?

For several weeks Khomeini remained in Tehran before going to live in his daughter's home in Quom. During this time, Dawn, Yar and Fatima, among many thousands of people, stayed day and night outside the South Tehran schoolhouse where he was quartered, awaiting any glimpse of him. And they went wild with excitement every time he came out on his balcony.

Khomeini gave bread and cheese to poor people, and Dawn, watching, envied them. Their poverty gave them access to the leader that she, as a member of her class, could never hope to achieve.

On February 5, Khomeini appointed Mehdi Bozargan as the "real" prime minister, making Bahktiar's government illegal. And America, in still another misreading of Iran, used its now puny influence to urge the military to "stay neutral" in the clashing of the forces of "Khomeini's Bozargan" and "the Shah's Bahktiar." This, in spite of the fact that troops and junior officers had defected right and left, and that the General Staff knew that the Army was in no position to deny Khomeini's appointee.

Khomeini lashed out at Bahktiar not only as "the Shah's tool", but even worse, "the tool of America".

On February 8, Dawn joined the million marchers in Tehran who were shouting "Long live Khomeini and Prime Minister Bozargan," and "Death to America and Bahktiar." And on February 9, Dawn and Fatima watched on television the "last battle" of the revolution. Units of the Imperial Guards known as "the Shah's Immortals", the only ones still loyal to Mohammed Reza, surrounded the barracks of the homafars (pro-Khomeini air force cadets and technicians) and opened fire. And the homafars, joined by a vast mass of armed civilians, fought back, the battle raging all night.

On the morning of February 10, more armed civilian revolutionaries poured into the streets and swore that they'd die before permitting the Guards' reinforcements to reach the base of the air force rebels. And when Imperial Guard helicopters came overhead, the civilian revolutionaries blazed away at them with automatic rifles, including American M-16's and Soviet A.K. 47's.

The Imperial Guards' stunning defeat by the people spelled the end of Bahktiar, who resigned on February 11 and later fled to Paris after months of hiding. And that night the revolutionaries blew up the Guards' barracks and raided their armories, taking possession of hundreds of thousands of weapons.

Now the revolution (as the days between Khomeini's return and the routing of the Imperial Guard came to be called) took a new tack. Power passed from the Army to the people who'd seized the weapons, to civilians with guns. And they organized themselves into komitehs in Tehran (of which Yar early on became a leader), and throughout the country.

The komitehs were, basically, extensions of several pre-revolutionary groups, among them the Fedayeen and Mojahadeen. But the largest number had been neighborhood committees organized around their mosques in 1978 to mobilize residents, arrange strikes and demonstrations and distribute scarce items like kerosene. And they had been among the most dedicated and disciplined groups of the revolution.

The post-revolutionary komitehs, though, were less motivated toward cooperation (they'd fought and won their battle and were now "THE CHOSEN"), less disciplined and, with all their arms, infinitely more powerful. Also, they'd taken in recruits of fifteen, fourteen, even thirteen years old, because some of the boys had come away from the storming of the armories with huge caches of arms the komitehs coveted.

From their inception, the komitehs perceived themselves as local security forces. On the positive side, they policed their districts and guarded government buildings and palaces. But they also, of their own volition and all too often with no reason except one that was dictated by their intuition or prejudices, confiscated property, made arrests and hauled people off to jail.

Working hand in hand with the komitehs were the revolutionary courts. These convened in secret; there were no defense lawyers or juries, and charges were as vague as "sowing corruption on earth," "crimes against humanity," "crimes against the people," "crimes against the revolution," and "violating the people's honor." Sentences were always death by execution, and most executions took place immediately after sentencing.

The courts, even more than the komitehs, had Khomeini's backing; he declared that those who campaigned for open trials and proper court procedures were "reflections of the Western sickness among us, or else they'd see that those on trial are criminals, and criminals should not be tried; they should be killed...The revolutionary courts are expressions of the people's will. If they don't execute the criminals, then the people will go on a rampage and do it themselves."To which Judge Khalkalli, chief of the revolutionary courts who was known as "Judge Blood", added that his courts were "totally in keeping with our Islamic principles of justice."

CHAPTER XXXII

Unveiled Infidels

To idealistic Dawn, both Khomeini's declaration and Khalkalli's statement that equated the revolutionary courts' procedures with Islamic principles, were incomprehensible. To her, Islam meant love, not hate; good, not evil. Wasn't it for the sake of eliminating the Shah's evil and turning the country to goodness that the people had faced the tanks? Wasn't it in order to drive out Savak, with its burning and killing and torturing, that the people had faced death? Why, then, were they now, through their own revolutionary courts, killing people as Savak had done and boasting about it as even Savak had not dared to do?

You couldn't pick up a newspaper or turn on the television without seeing pictures of the sentenced men (later there'd be women as well), with their weary, sagging faces and eyes full of terror. And reporters and commentators would describe in detail what the condemned men said, and how they behaved in the face of their impending death. And all of this coverage was a mere prelude to the most eagerly-awaited features of all: grisly photographs of the corpses.

Dawn was, of course, saddened and infuriated by all this. Yar, himself part of the bloodthirsty mass, immensely resented Dawn's indignation at the court procedures and executions, an indignation Yar saw as too similar to that of the Western world.

One night, a little after ten, Yar, accompanied by eight other young men and three women with whom Dawn was not acquainted, came to get her at her house. She asked where they were going, and Yar said it was a surprise, but that he and his friends were going to give her the experience of her life. She asked who these friends were, and he said they were co-members of his komiteh.

Dawn and the others piled into cars and drove across the city to South Tehran to a schoolhouse much like the one in which Khomeini had been lodged. Yar knocked at the door and a man with a beard, wearing a religious turban, opened it. Without speaking a word, he led the party up three flights of stairs to a dimly-lit room in which sat five men and one woman. Dawn and her group took seats beside them.

Soon, three men in judges' robes entered and sat down at a table in front of the room. Now Dawn knew herself to be in a revolutionary court. But how could this be, since the court's sessions were supposed to be secret?

Yar, reading her expression, answered her question before she voiced it. "I," he said, "was able to secure permission for our attendance here; it was hard to accomplish, of course, but," he grinned, "isn't everything that is worthwhile hard to accomplish?"

"Why did you bring me here?" Dawn asked with as much control as she could muster.

"Because you're half-American."

"What's that got to do with anything?"

"What it has got to do...It's my aim to make a true Iranian of you, and to help you overcome your ridiculous American squeamishness."

Before Dawn could say anything to Yar, four prisoners—beaten, vacant, beyond hope—were dragged in by their chains and brought one by one before the judges. They were all charged with "the crime of having sown corruption on earth", and each was given two minutes in which to answer the accusation. One man—eyes wide-set, moist and animal-like in mute appeal—drew Dawn forward, sobbing uncontrollably as he begged for mercy. "Please, please don't kill me. I'm a good person. Whatever I did wrong, I was forced to do. I've always been one of you in my heart. I love the people. I love Khomeini. Give me a chance."

Another man, big and heavy-set, went berserk; his entire body convulsed as he lay moaning on the floor.

A third, a former general, urinated in his pants when his sentence was pronounced.

Dawn sat through all of this like a trapped animal, not moving a limb. And after a half-hour, which was as long as all the "trials" took, Yar helped her up and led her to the schoolhouse roof. There, sobbing to herself, she had to stand by and watch the "guilty" men shot, and see Yar and his friends thrill with excitement at the sight of the killings. And finally, in numbed horror, she had to watch while Yar and the others, shouting and screaming as though they had gone insane, surged forward to dip their hands in the dead men's blood, first sprinkling it on themselves and then rubbing it over their hands and faces. The looks of exaltation were like none Dawn had ever seen before; the harsh, discordant jumble of their talk and laughter was like no sound she had ever heard before.

"My God, my God," she kept repeating to herself, "THEY'RE ANIMALS, ANIMALS! AND YAR IS ONE OF THEM!"

Actually, this was not the first time Dawn had witnessed such a "ceremony". During the months of the revolution, she'd often seen people dipping their hands into the blood of their dead martyrs. At first she'd been as horrified at those sights as she was at this one tonight. Yet she had forced herself to give some credence to Yar's explanation that the act, being motivated by love, respect and people's desire to merge for the last time with their martyrs, was not as gruesome as she perceived it.

Tonight, though, was a different matter, even more perverse; there wasn't, after all, the rationale, for whatever it was worth, of "we are doing this because we cherish our dead."

Yar called Dawn to come and join the crowd; she'd see that what they were doing was fun. Fun, he called it. And hearing him, watching him, Dawn felt that she must be having a nightmare. It seemed utterly beyond understanding that any cultured person like Yar, or any civilized person, could behave with such appalling bestiality.

Yar once more called Dawn to "come and join the circle." She ran instead to the door but found it locked. As she pounded and screamed for somebody to come and let her out, two girls left the group and came to her. She believes today that they weren't angry and didn't intend to hurt her, but only to bring her into their circle. This, however, might not have been the case at all; maybe, having felt Dawn's disgust at them and their companions, they'd reacted with their own anger and decided to teach her a lesson. Maybe, though, it had been merely a power play that had caused them to place their bloodied hands on her cheek.

Dawn shrieked at the girls to get away from her, and so stimulated them to more frenzied action; they rubbed their bloodied hands all over her face, including in her eyes and ears. She scratched and kicked at them 'till they were finally forced to let her go.

And all the time that this went on, Yar did not raise a finger to help Dawn; he stood among his friends, laughing with them at her. And Dawn would always remember their laugh. In that laugh she was, yet again, the outsider. She had always been a Muslim among Christians, a Persian among Americans, an American among Persians, a woman among men...And she knew that from now on, her hurt at feeling rejected by whatever group she was with would bring back the picture of those people laughing, and Yar laughing with them.

On that night all of Dawn's love and trust of Yar changed into hatred and fear. She did not express her feelings in words, but they must have shown on her face. And Yar, reading them and knowing his friends did too, salvaged his macho pride; he clutched Dawn's hair and yanked her head back, hitting her face over and over again with his fist. Then he smashed her a blow across the chest that sent her reeling against the wall. He picked her up and hit her in the face again, then threw her down and kicked her in the chest and stomach.

When he was done with her, she lay on the floor moaning, blood running from her nose and mouth.

For a week after Yar's attack on Dawn, Naila nursed her as faithfully as she'd once done with her mother. Khanoum-June and Fatima were also constantly with Dawn, and Peri visited as often as she was able.

Dawn wondered to herself, and finally asked Peri, how she could have been so wrong about Yar. She asked how she could have loved him and believed in him for so long, and thus not have recognized him as "her father's spiritual son."

Peri explained that Dawn had, after all, never known Yar as his normal, everyday self. From the time of their meeting he'd been Yar the revolutionary, not Yar the traditional Islamic man. And as Yar the revolutionary, willing to make any sacrifice to attain his goal of overthrowing Mohammed Reza, he'd been full of courage, generosity and love. Dawn had quite naturally loved and wanted to marry him, believing he'd be as caring a husband as he was a revolutionary.

And Yar, realizing Dawn's dedication to him and his cause, had looked at her not merely as female, but as his fellow revolutionary, regarding her with the same pride and satisfaction with which he'd looked at himself and his male comrades. It could have been said that the revolutionary in Yar had overcome the ego demands of Yar, the Islamic fundamentalist. It could have been said that the vast majority of revolutionary men had been the same way...during the time of the revolution. Now that the revolution was done, though...

Yar did not call Dawn during the time she was ill. And when he did finally call, she, encouraged by Peri, Fatima and Naila, was able to tell him she never wanted to see him again. He called her "a whore like your American mother," and threatened to teach her "a lesson you'll never forget." Pretending a confidence she didn't feel, Dawn said that "Your lesson will affect me no more than my father's lessons did."

Two weeks after Dawn felt herself physically recovered (she'd not recover emotionally for a long time), she went with Fatima to lunch at the Intercontinental Hotel. Both girls, dressing up for the first time in many months, were excited. They did themselves up in high heels and attractive sport suits, and wore eyeshadow, rouge and kohl. They looked gorgeous and knew it.

Since the day was lovely, they decided to walk a while before hailing a cab. They hadn't gone more than a few blocks when they were stopped by four dirty, skinny kids of perhaps thirteen to fifteen, dressed grotesquely in green U.S. Army fatigue jackets made for men twice their weight and height. They described themselves as "komiteh men", though showing no identification, and pointed the barrels of their guns into Dawn's and Fatima's faces while their leader, with his somber zealot's eye, questioned them.

"Married or single?"

Fatima said, "Engaged," speaking for Dawn as well as herself.

"And do your fiancés know that you are out only with one another?"

"They do," Fatima answered.

"And suppose," the leader cleared his throat, "I were to ask you for the telephone numbers of your fiancés, and that I were to call and ask them the question I asked of you, what would their answer be?"

Dawn's body shivered and would not be still, then grew hot as she thought of what Yar's answer might be, under their circumstances. Yet she collected herself sufficiently to say, "Their answer would be that we are telling the truth."

"They must be Jews then. Or Americans. Or Bahais."

Fatima said, "They are not; they are men of Islam and revolutionary brothers."

"And you," the leader sneered, "are you going to tell me next and expect me to believe, unveiled Infidels, that you are revolutionary sisters and women of Islam?"

"We are telling you that," Fatima said, "because it is the God's honest truth."

Now the leader went on waving his gun and yelling that Dawn and Fatima, "walking around the streets to show off your faces, your necks, your bodies," were prostitutes, not revolutionary sisters; even the mere words "revolutionary sisters" became defiled in their mouths. Thus he would now be compelled to take them to his komiteh's headquarters, and there give them papers to sign, on which would be written, "I AM A PROSTITUTE." And then he would see to it that they were taken to the Women's Prison where they belonged.

So Fatima, as a last resort, asked him whether he knew about Mujtahid Kashani, the Quom martyr.

"And what would the likes of you know about Mujtahid Kashani?" the leader reviled.

"He was my grandfather."

The leader looked directly into Fatima's eyes. "I'm warning you that...PROVE IT, UNVEILED INFIDEL!"

"My brother Yar, Yar Kashani, who's Dawneh's fiancé...I'll give you his number; he'll explain to you that Mujtahid Kashani is...was... my grandfather. And that I am...that Dawneh and I are not...not prostitutes, but revolutionary sisters."

The leader's eyes brightened. "I know all about Yar Kashani; I admire Yar Kashani. If you really are his sister and that is really his fiancé...I will call and invite him to our headquarters and let him help us decide what your punishment must be, whether jail or..." He let his voice trail menacingly off.

When Yar came into the cramped, littered komiteh headquarters, where more boys like those who had arrested Dawn and Fatima and a few dirty, unshaven older men sat around tables, he looked only once at his sister and fiancé, glaring, then went to join the men and boys. He did not, at first, even mention Dawn and Fatima, but talked instead about Khomeini and his ideology and the "New Iran" that men like those of this komiteh were helping to build. After a while he also talked about women. Women! he scowled. In truth, even the best of them, meaning those who'd stood behind the men during the months of the demonstrations (he never made mention of those who'd themselves led the demonstrations), were simple creatures who'd lost all realization of who and what they were. They'd come to believe, by virtue of the small part they'd played in the revolution, that they'd become the equals of men.

"And now they have, once again, to be taught their rightful place, have once again to be told that they are women, not men. As for these two," he pointed a finger at Dawn and Fatima, "I promise you that by the time I'm done with them, they'll be true examples of what proper Islamic womanhood ought to be about. Believe me, they'll never again commit the crime of going out without chador, because I, as the guardian of their morality, will tell them every single day that 'You women had better know this, and know it beyond doubt...YOU'LL EITHER WRAP YOUR HEADS, OR HAVE THEM WRAPPED.'"

Yar and the komiteh men and boys clapped each other on the shoulders then, and laughed heartily together over Yar's witticism at Fatima's and Dawn's expense.

CHAPTER XXXIII

In the Dawn of Freedom, We Have No Freedom

Dawn and Fatima's experience was only the beginning, however; the beginning of a time when the nightmare of all that women would be compelled to endure in Khomeini's Iran had not yet broken out into public vision. The komiteh men who'd arrested them and labeled them prostitutes had done it on their own. They'd not yet been granted Khomeini's blessing for making such arrests and putting such labels on women, for no more reason than that they did not wear chador.

On March 8, though, some two weeks after Dawn's and Fatima's arrest, Khomeini declared in a radio address that all women working in the ministries "should not go into them naked," meaning that they should wear chador. And all who heard him knew that his command that ministry-women wear the veil would soon be extended to all women.

That afternoon a number of teachers at Dawn's and Fatima's high school called meetings of their students to "talk about the matter of the chador and what we, as women who have just been through hell and fire to achieve freedom and democracy, are going to do about this denial of our human right to dress as we, ourselves, wish."

Dawn's group was chaired by her favorite teacher, Khanoum Barshani—always very vibrant and full of energy, and especially so today. She asked Dawn to tell about her and Fatima's arrest. Dawn, shaking a little, did so. Her schoolmates looked at her, shocked, and someone asked what would have happened to her if Yar hadn't been known to the komiteh men.

Dawn shook her head, not knowing what to say. Khanoum Barshani said that Dawn would, at least, have had a police record for prostitution; she could also have been sent to prison indefinitely. She then went on to "other important matters that must not be buried under the business of the chador." Khomeini had, she said, abolished the "Family Protection Act". That meant that girls could, as had been the way before the passage of the Act, be married (or sold into marriage) at eleven years old. And it meant that men could, once again, divorce their wives by going before a mullah three times. Finally, it meant that women no longer had the right to divorce, no matter how their husbands might abuse them.

"Khomeini has also outlawed co-educational schools," Khanoum Barshani continued, "calling them 'centers of prostitution'. Finally, he told us that the laws of Islam declare that we women may not become judges. And I say to you that that law is the Ayatollah's, not Allah's. He maintains that we women are 'too softhearted' to be judges. What he means by that is that we would not order the executions that are happening today, and that we would see to it that justice would be given to women as well as men.

"We want the rights that we earned by fighting in the revolution," Khanoum Barshani continued, "and they should have been ours by right of our humanity even if we hadn't fought and died in order to be free." And by rights, she meant the right to choose for themselves what they would wear; the equal right to educational opportunities; the guarantee of all legal rights and liberties; and the guarantee of personal and political security. "And," she added, "a new Family Protection Law that will go beyond the old one to ensure total justice for women.

"I tell you, girls, that we must say to Khomeini that, having already fought one revolution to overthrow the Shah, we now stand ready to fight another for achievement of our rights. Mohammed Reza's tanks and guns did not stop us, and neither...if he chooses to use them against us...will Khomeini's.

"And we must tell him, too, that the eyes of the world will be on us...and him...in this new revolution, if that is what our fight for equality must become."

She said, too, that tomorrow was May 8th, International Women's Day, "the one day on which women around the world unite in mind, heart and in the realization that we are one. It does not matter whether we are East or West; we are women together."

The last time Iranian women were allowed to celebrate International Women's Day, Khanoum Barshani said, was fifty years earlier. Reza Shah and Mohammed Reza had forbidden them after that.

Khanoum Barshani then informed the group that tomorrow there would be a women's demonstration at the Ministry of Justice, and that she intended to cut school in order to be there. And one girl, giggling, said, "I wonder what'll happen if we students also cut school in order to be at the demonstration." And a group of others, including Dawn, answered that the same thing would happen as had happened when they'd all cut school to march against Mohammed Reza: nothing. And Khanoum Barshani, smiling, said that since Khanoum Mardoni, the principal, would herself be at the demonstration, she'd hardly be in a position to raise questions with students who would do as she did.

Now the girls set about making demonstration signs. Everyone had suggestions: "Respect us as women, in or out of chador." "Our fight is not with the chador alone." "We go to the Ministry of Justice to demand justice." And, finally, the sign and chant of the total women's movement, "In the dawn of freedom, we have no freedom."

Popular Iranian women's organizations, necessarily underground, were hardly existent before and during the revolution. There had been one small group here, another there, but all of them had been isolated from one another. And then, a small number of women, maybe no more than nine or ten who were newly returned from exile abroad, determined to use "International Women's Day" as a medium for stimulating a true women's movement. They called friends, who called their friends and managed to interest a couple of hundred women which, to them, seemed phenomenal at the time. Then came Khomeini's declaration for the chador, following directly on the heels of his other enunciations against women's rights. And suddenly, women still imbued with revolutionary passion came out by the tens of thousands to protest. There was no formal organization, but only the kind of spontaneous gathering of women—in ministries, factories, shops, hospitals, businesses, colleges, high schools, wherever women worked or studied—that had happened in Dawn's school. And housewives of all ages, some in chador, joined their "sisters". "Sisters" was what they called one another, just as they'd done during the months of the revolution.

There were even some men, human-rights activists who also called the women "sisters", that supported their cause. During the days of the demonstrations, these men would clasp hands and form rings around the women as protection against the armed thugs determined to destroy them.

Early in the morning of March 9, Dawn, her classmates and Khanoum Barshani joined the other students and teachers in the school courtyard before beginning their march. Fatima left her own class in order to march with Dawn. And as they clasped hands while chanting "Azadeh, Azadeh, Freedom," Dawn thought to herself that if she had to die in this demonstration with someone, she would rather it be with Fatima than anyone else in the world, except for Barbara or Rocky. And she laughed, or anyway, tried to laugh at the morbid thought...If she'd come through the whole of the revolution unscathed, why was she now obsessed with the feeling that she might die while demonstrating?

She had her answer after the first few minutes she and the others hit the street, with their signs and chants and men protectors who, being few in number, were dispersed by the masses of enemy men. Some of these enemies entered the crowd of girls out of Dawn's school and ran them down, and beat them up. Dawn saw one man knock down a child of maybe thirteen with an overhead punch. She squatted on the street trying to cover her face, while the man went on punching her until blotches of blood spread over her face.

Another girl skidded down onto the street, and three large men jumped at her, beating her head with chains and clubs.

Dawn's class did not make it to the Hall of Justice demonstration. Too many enemies prevented them. And when, on the following morning, they returned to school to receive their marching orders for that day, they were told that four of their schoolmates had been stabbed yesterday. Three were dead, and one was in the hospital in critical condition. And that information filled Dawn and her class-mates with agony, certainly, but also made them stronger and more resolute.

Dawn, Fatima and their fellow students marched with their principal and teachers on March 10 and 11, and again on March 12, the day of the "great march" from Tehran University to Freedom Square; 20,000 women came out that day to show their force and were, in fact, recognized by Khomeini. He told "the beloved and respected ladies...(who) must have a share in determining their destinies" that he never had, or would, order them to wear chador against their will. That, really, all he hoped was that they would "dress modestly" as befitted their "noble Islamic status." He further declared that it always had been, and was now, illegal for men—whether or not they were members of komitehs—to "harass" (he called beatings and killings "harassments") women demonstrators.

The women, believing in Khomeini's words, came out on March 13 in even greater numbers than before. And, as during the revolution, mothers carried infants in their arms, some of them chanting, "We march for our daughters' freedom. Their freedom is what we would willingly die for." But the enemy men were also there in huge numbers; the fact was that they'd been transported to the scene of the demonstration in official government buses, despite Khomeini's declaration of the day before. And accompanied by a few chador-clad women, they carried out a massacre of women and girls.

On that terrible day Dawn saw Fatima slip and fall to the ground. And she saw two men leap on her while a chador-clad woman poured what must have been acid into her face. And she heard her cry out, "I can't see anything, I'M BLIND, OH MY GOD, DAWNEH, HELP ME!"

Dawn, dizzy with fear for Fatima, tried desperately to go to where she had seen her fall. But there wasn't any way to reach her, because the crowd pushed too hard in the other direction.

A long time later, after the street cleared, Dawn was still looking for Fatima, but couldn't find her. She arrived home late at night to find Yar and her father waiting for her. Yar told her that Fatima was dead, "having been trampled under the feet of her fellow demonstrators." And then he said that she'd "received no more than she deserved" for her defiance of Khomeini.

Dawn turned away from Yar and ran to her room. She locked the door, expecting that Yar or her father or both of them would bang it down in order to continue torturing her. But they did not.

For a couple of weeks Dawn lay in her bed, altogether enveloped by the cold, black fury that had taken possession of her at the moment that she'd seen Fatima fall. "I will get them for what they did to Fatima," she whispered over and over to herself. "I will get them." And the ones who represented "them" to her ranged from Khomeini to his thugs, and from Yar to her father. "I will get them. I will get them."

When Bahram, happening to be in her room one day while she raved, asked her who "they" were, she told him.

"You crazy...what the hell are you talking about, you're going to get Khomeini and Yar and me...Exactly how do you think you're going to accomplish anything like that, you lunatic?" Bahram exclaimed.

"Well, I don't know yet how I'm going to get Khomeini, or even Yar, but you, Father..." Dawn's madness gave her strength, and she grinned into Bahram's face as she said, "I know exactly how to get you, a good Muslim who drinks your bottle of brandy every night while begging God to forgive you and take the sin out of your drink. Maybe God will forgive you, but Khomeini won't. And the brandy's not the worst of what I have to tell the revolutionary government about my good Islamic father. You and Mohammed...OTHER MEN HAVE BEEN EXECUTED FOR HAVING SEX WITH ONE ANOTHER!"

Bahram put his hand around Dawn's throat and lifted her off the bed, then held her against the wall like a person being lynched. "This is it," she thought to herself, "This time he's going to kill me for sure." Then, as suddenly as he'd attacked her, Bahram released Dawn; he threw her away from him, and his eyes narrowed into slits as he attempted to study her, to figure her out. And he said, finally: "I could kill you...No Iranian court would hold a father guilty who'd kill such an undutiful, wayward, rebellious daughter as you.

Instead, though... I'm going to send you away as soon as we can arrange your passage. Go back to goddamn America and your fucking mother; let her deal with your craziness. Go be crazy in America, go be crazy in your mother's home, not mine!"

CHAPTER XXXIX

The Last Man

Dawn's homecoming was no happier than Rocky's had been; she, too, felt that she had no more place in America than she did in Iran. But while Rocky had Twon to help her through the time of re-adjustment, Dawn's first relationship in America was with a man who, like Yar, could have been her father's son.

Dawn and Jamal Shafiari met at ELAN'S, one of Houston's most elegant and expensive private clubs. A combination disco and five-star restaurant, it catered mainly to upper-class Middle Easterners. Nightly, the younger royals of Saudi Arabia, with their epidemic of wealth, would wine and dine large parties of which Jamal was always an integral part.

Jamal, like Yar, was very attractive in a tall, dark, sexy way. But he was Yar's exact opposite in temperament and personality. Where Yar had been all seriousness and commitment to his cause, Jamal was full of frivolity and play. The time of youth was, he maintained, for enjoyment, for pleasure, and that meant singing and dancing and partying all night. He reveled in turning strangers into friends (and followers), and would do so at Elan's or wherever he and Dawn were. "Drinks for everyone," he'd call out, and it wouldn't be long before he'd be surrounded. Then he'd announce: "My love and I are going to THE ARABIAN FLOWER, and everyone who wants is wel-come to come along." And whole carloads of people—Arabians, Persians, Americans and others who happened to be there—would be off to THE ARABIAN FLOWER or some other disco or club, where Jamal would foot the bill. He was the king of those nights, and Dawn was the queen.

After some weeks of being together day and night, Jamal and Dawn, to Barbara's and Rocky's consternation, became engaged. What kind of life, her mother and sister asked, could Dawn hope to have as the wife of an Arabian playboy? Jamal was in Houston to improve his English so that he might study engineering in America, but he hardly ever cracked a book, and instead paid "this brainy American dog" to do his homework assignments. His motto was: *If it gives you pleasure, do it. If it doesn't, don't.* And books and homework definitely didn't give him pleasure.

When Barbara asked him what would happen when "it", whatever "it" was, stopped giving pleasure—would he then discard it, or what?—he would smile craftily and say, "There are some things...and people...that never stop giving pleasure. My beloved Dawneh is one of them."

And how could Barbara ever have hoped to combat that with Dawn? Dawn, in love, said in answer to her mother's challenges, "I'm happy for maybe the first time in my life, Mama, and you're spoiling it by preaching at me."

Both before and for a while after their engagement, Jamal behaved with Dawn as her father had done her mother in their courting days. He seemed to be living his whole life for her. Then one night, Dawn went alone to Jamal's apartment with him. He took her in his arms to the couch and held her as he had during so many other times. He gave her a look of love, with what she perceived to be no thought of sex. He stroked her as she always enjoyed being stroked by him, murmured that he loved her and whispered, "Go to sleep in my arms; you can trust me, Dawneh."

Then, while she was half asleep, he began caressing her body with a different kind of passion, running his hands down her sides, down her thighs, her breasts...She felt herself breathing heavily, breathing in rhythm with Jamal...She put her arms around him and began to caress him, his sides, his chest. He undressed first himself, then her. His naked body was wrapped around hers now, and she clutched at him, clinging until she felt him inside her. She'd never before experienced such pain mixed with such pleasure, and she gave vent to her feelings with sharp little cries.

After Jamal pulled out, he dressed himself while Dawn lay naked on the sofa. She knew she ought to get dressed too, but she didn't have the strength. OH GOD, GOD! SHE WASN'T A VIRGIN ANYMORE! She felt her heart hammering against her chest; it was thumping steadily, clearly audible in the frightening stillness of the room. She waited for Jamal to say something, anything, but he did not. And so she told him, "I'm so ashamed to have behaved...The fact that I did it out of love for you...That doesn't really matter, does it, since I...? Oh, Jamal, will you, can you forgive me?"

Could HE forgive HER for his having taken her treasured virginity? The Dawn who'd faced death rather than accept Khomeini's denial of her rights as a person, the Dawn who'd ordered Yar out of her life once she came to know him as a traditionalist man of Islam, now groveled before Jamal. Obsessed by the memory, the echo of all she'd heard from babyhood of what was bound to happen to "girls like her", she had no choice but to grovel...If Jamal didn't marry her—and why should he marry a non-virgin?—no man, except perhaps for one who was lower than she, would have anything to do with her. And even more terribly, she'd go to hell when she died.

Jamal turned on a lamp, wiped Dawn's blood with her slip and said, "I'm going to keep this, Dawneh, to prove to my mother that you were a virgin for me "

"Does this mean... that you want to marry me, even though...?"

In a tone devoid of love or compassion, Jamal said, "Unlike most men under these circumstances...Yes, Dawn, I do still want to marry you."

She told him then how grateful and ashamed and sorry she was. She took his hand, but he drew it away and said, "I wish you'd stop talking about your shame and sorrow, and just tell me the truth about whether you were so aggressive with me because you've made love with other men and were just a technical virgin."

After Dawn's "disgrace", Jamal took her as a mistress, holding her with the promise he'd marry her one day. From the time of the establishment of that relationship she was, to him, "even lower than what my mother had been to my father." At Elan's, where they continued to go nightly, Jamal would have one drink with Dawn, dance with her once and, leaving her at their table, caution her to "be good, behave yourself and DON'T FLIRT." He, himself, then went to seek other dance partners. And Dawn, humiliated, would watch him dance through the night with glamorous, sexy American girls who'd been at the royal Arabian party tables. Sitting alone, she naturally attracted a great deal of attention from men. She did her best to turn them away, but even though she easily rid herself of some, others stayed around, urging, coaxing and putting pressure on her.

And Jamal blamed her for the men's persistence; he said that her "come-hither attitude toward every damn man around" was to be expected from "damaged goods". A girl who'd "thrown her virginity away" was inherently evil and "headed for a life of total whoredom", unless a man would be concerned enough "to beat the evil out of her."

Periodically, then, Dawn returned to her mother's home beaten, first with a black eye, then a bloody nose, later a split lip and a front tooth missing. And always, on those agonizing occasions, Barbara talked herself to exhaustion in vain attempts to persuade Dawn to put Jamal out of her life, to persuade her that the loss of her virginity was not the mortal sin she believed it.

"Sweetheart, how can I possibly make you realize that God loves you because you're honest and good and kind, and is really not concerned with whether or not you're a virgin?"

"Mama," Dawn always answered, "maybe your Christian God isn't concerned, but MY MUSLIM GOD IS!"

Always, then, Barbara would repeat to Dawn all that Aysha had taught her about true Islam's attitude toward women, as opposed to that of fundamentalist Islam.

But she knew in her heart that Dawn could not bring herself to believe that this "American Barbara" understood her religion as her Persian grandmothers, great grandmothers and teachers did not. And all of them had told her the same thing. Even Khanoum-June, out of her love for Dawn, had said that she had, no matter what, to guard her virginity, because if she did not...

After Dawn had been with Jamal for two years and showed no sign of being able to separate from him, Barbara, feeling at the end of her rope and not knowing where else to turn, phoned Peri one day in Tehran. And Peri gave her an idea that was so right, and yet so simple, that she wondered why she hadn't thought of it herself. Since Dawn could not accept her mother as one who was informed about the Koran, why not put her in touch with someone whose knowledge she could not reject?

And luckily, Peri knew just the person—Mujtahid Takezadeh had been a close associate of Mossadegh; he'd escaped Tehran soon after Mossadegh had been arrested, and joined his two sons who were professors at the University of Texas in Houston. He was deeply religious, yet not a fanatic; Dawn would surely be impressed with him.

Dawn, frightened yet hopeful, sat in Mujtahid Takezadeh's den with its exquisite Persian rug, and bookcases crammed from floor to ceiling. He was in his late eighties, and had a delicate oval face that reminded her of Mujtahid Kashani. He was also very warm, which enabled her to be altogether open with him. And when she was done telling her story, he said, "The prophet of Allah himself has told that God remains forgiving and compassionate even toward prostitutes...As for you, my daughter, no, Mohammed the Prophet said nothing about the loss of a girl's virginity being such a crime that it must be punished by eternal damnation. Nothing!!" And to Dawn's amazement, he repeated all that she'd been unable to believe when she'd heard it from Barbara, about the immense differences, as regarded women, between true and fundamentalist Islam.

Dawn was inspired then to repeat to the mujtahid a conversion she and Rocky often had about her and Jamal's future..."If you can't order that woman-hating patriarch out of your life for your and my and our mother's sake," Rocky had declared, "then do it for my daughter's sake. Do it for the sake of your own still unborn daughters. Say to Jamal and mean it: "IF YOU WERE THE LAST MAN IN THE WORLD, I WOULDN'T MARRY YOU AND MAKE YOU THE FATHER OF MY PRECIOUS DAUGHTERS."

And now that the mujtahid had restored her self-confidence and strength, Dawn spoke...in those exact words.

Barbara remains happily married to Charlie, who has now retired from the school system. She is a survivor of cancer surgery in 1991, during which time her husband and daughters were close by. Although she had been told by specialists that she would never speak again, miraculously this was not the case.

Barbara is working today with women's organizations seeking, albeit without much success, to help other American women who lose their children to fugitive, foreign fathers.

Roxanne, though with some trepidation, gave Twon this manuscript to read. It has accomplished much of what she'd hoped it would when Barbara told me her story. Twon was immensely moved by his realization of all that Rocky had experienced in growing up, and he is, if possible, even more sensitive to what she needs from him. And finally, after all the struggles, he is a physician in Houston.

Tyanne, at seventeen, is entering college where she will major in pre-med and expects to become a doctor. Her brother Anthony, sixteen, will enter college next year and also has ambitions to become a physician. Two other children, Michael and Matthew—ages five and three—are, like their older siblings, warm, friendly and outgoing.

Dawneh is married to her cousin, David Shapouri. He, like Dawn, has an Iranian father and an American mother, and was raised in the United States. They have three children: Kevin (six), Christopher (five) and Tiffany (two). The boys seem to have inherited their mother's flair for the dramatic, having acted in several TV commercials and dramas.

Dawneh, for all her former adventurous life, has settled down to be an involved and devoted mother.

Baba Bozorg died in February 1983 after a ten-month bout with cancer. During the early years of Khomeini's reign, many of his villages (that had not formerly been yielded to Mohammed Reza's "White Revolution") were seized by his peasants. And even the few villages the peasants left to him were eventually taken over by the state.

He was, however, more fortunate with his industrial enterprises, that comprised the bulk of his colossal fortune at the conclusion of the Revolution. None of these were expropriated, as were those of other colleagues who had not contributed as generously to clerical causes as he (under Bahram's guidance) had done. And the fact is that, upon his death, Baba Bozorg's heirs were not much worse off than they would have been if the revolution had never happened.

Khanoum-June still lives in the Shiraz mansion. Since she has always conformed to the strict Islamic code out of personal dedication, her life, unlike that of many women of her caste and class, remains basically unchanged. There is no one left to write letters from her to Barbara and her daughters, since Fifi and Fufu died— Fifi in 1981, and Fufu less than a year later. Khanoum-June and Barbara still keep in touch by phone, though, and Barbara says of her, "The saying that, as people grow older, whatever they are like they become more so, is certainly true of Khanoum-June. She comes through when we talk as even sweeter than she was, if that is possible."

Bahram is Baba Bozorg's prime heir, and so is wealthier than he's ever been. He continues to live in the Tehran mansion with Teymour, Habib, Esmat and Mohammed. Barbara is convinced that Bahram goes on with his life of indulgence, despite the government's prohibition against homosexuality and alcohol.

Teymour is, according to Barbara, "the complete creation of Bahram. I love him because he is my son, but must admit, in all honesty, that I can't like him. When he visited here a few years ago, it seemed his only desire was to rip off his sisters and myself. Sadly, I could not wait to see my only son depart from me, and want never to see him again, although I think often of the sweet baby he used to be and wonder how it might have been if his true father had been alive to raise him."

Farah spent some time at the Menninger Clinic in Kansas. And although she'll never stop grieving for Mehrdad, she is herself again. She and Soraya fled Iran in 1981 and lived in Paris, which was, in the 1980's, as much a refuge for displaced Iranians as it was for White Russians in the 1920's. She is, as her letters to Barbara tell, "as happy here as I can be any place, I guess..."

Peri was an early victim of Khomeini's rhetoric about the "Westernized intellectual" being "the source of all our miseries". In 1984, the year of Iran's "thorough Islamization of the educational systems", she, along with many other university administrators and faculty, was purged. Since then, knowing herself to be under constant surveillance, she has refused all contact with Maryam, Behdjat, or other friends. And they, while condemning themselves for lack of courage, have accepted her ban. She lives, therefore, as a virtual recluse.

Finally, in Barbara's words, "My most persistent fantasy is to somehow, some way, help Peri."

Sara Harris